GERMAN VERBS

WILLIAM ROWLINSON

D1115323

Oxford   New York

OXFORD UNIVERSITY PRESS

1994

Oxford University Press, Walton Street, Oxford OX2 6DP

Oxford New York Toronto
Delhi Bombay Calcutta Madras Karachi
Kuala Lumpur Singapore Hong Kong Tokyo
Nairobi Dar es Salaam Cape Town
Melbourne Auckland Madrid
and associated companies in
Berlin Ibadan

Oxford is a trade mark of Oxford University Press

© Oxford University Press 1994

First published 1993 in Oxford Minireference
Paperback issued 1994

British Library Cataloguing in Publication Data
Data available

Library of Congress Cataloging in Publication Data
Data available
ISBN 0–19–280019–1

1 3 5 7 9 10 8 6 4 2

Printed in Great Britain by
Clays Ltd
Bungay, Suffolk

CONTENTS

For more extended information on verb use see
German Grammar, also available.

HOW TO USE THIS BOOK

This book contains, in alphabetical order

- all German strong and mixed verbs in use
- all German weak verbs in common use today

  some 6000 verbs in all.

Each verb is listed with its principal meanings, the case it takes, and the prepositions that follow it and their cases. If the verb has a prefix, you are told whether this is separable or inseparable. You are also told whether the verb forms its past compound tenses with **haben** or **sein**, and whether it is weak, strong, or mixed: in the last two cases you are given its vowel and consonant changes. You are then given the pattern verb that it follows, and referred to one of 41 patterns, where the conjugation of all active tenses is set out in full.

There is also an introductory section giving complete details of the formation of German verbs, and an identification list for irregular parts of strong and mixed verbs.

1 Look up the infinitive of the verb about which you need information in the verb directory. (If you are not sure what the infinitive of the verb is, look up the part of the verb you do know in the identification list on p. 338.)

The directory lists alphabetically all strong and mixed (= irregular) verbs in current use and all commonly used weak (= regular) verbs. It also lists reflexive verbs separately where these differ substantially in meaning from the simple verb, or where the reflexive verb has a different prepositional construction or a dative reflexive pronoun, or where the simple verb is not in common use.

2 You will find in the directory entry:

- where the verb has a prefix, a symbol within the infinitive showing whether the prefix is separable (|) or inseparable (')
- the preposition or prepositions (if any) that the verb takes before a following noun or pronoun
- the case or cases used with such prepositions
- the commonest meaning or meanings of the verb (and prepositions)
- the case in which the object of the verb stands, if it has an object
- the auxiliary (or auxiliaries) with which the past compound tenses are formed
- whether the verb is weak, strong, or mixed
- if it is strong or mixed, the vowel and consonant changes it makes in the **du** and **er** forms of the present (if any), in the past, and in the past participle

- the pattern verb on which conjugation of this verb is based
- the number of that verb in the pattern tables

3 If the directory has not yet given you all the information you need about the verb you are looking up, turn to the pattern verb given.

4 The pattern verb shows:

- the present and past infinitives, the present and past participles, and the imperative
- all active tenses of the verb in full
- any special peculiarities of the pattern verb
- verbs similarly conjugated that have slight changes from the pattern verb

5 If the pattern verb to which you are referred is preceded in the directory by an asterisk, the verb you are looking up will show a slight deviation from the pattern. It will be listed at the foot of the second page of the pattern verb, and full details of its deviation from the pattern will be given there.

If you need a passive tense of the verb, turn to the pattern for passive tenses on p. xiv.

Abbreviations and symbols used in the directory are listed on p.3.

VERB FORMATION

Verb types

There are three types of verbs in German: weak, strong, and mixed. The three types differ from each other only in the present and simple past tenses (the latter is also known as the imperfect or preterite tense), and in their past-participle form.

Weak verbs

Most verbs are weak. They follow the pattern of **machen,** *to make* (21). The final **-e** of the **ich** form of the present is almost always dropped in speech.

Strong verbs

Strong verbs change their stem vowel and sometimes the consonant that follows it. They make these changes throughout the past tense, often in the past participle, and sometimes in the **du** and **er** forms of the present. The past participle of a strong verb ends in **-en** or **-n**. Strong verbs in the present have the same endings as weak verbs do.

Mixed verbs

This is a small group of verbs that make vowel changes as strong verbs do, but have weak-verb endings in the past tense and the past participle.

● All verbs in all tenses have six forms, according to their subject, **ich**, **du**, or **er** (these are sometimes called the first, second, and third persons of the verb), and according to whether the subject is singular (**ich**, **du**, **er**) or plural (**wir**, **ihr**, **sie**).

● All singular nouns and all singular subject-pronouns other than **ich**, **du**, and **Sie** are followed by the **er** form of the verb. This includes the pronouns **sie** (= *she*), **es** (*it*), and **man** (*one*). Plural nouns and pronouns and the pronoun **Sie** (the polite form of '*you*', which may be either singular or plural in meaning) are followed by the **sie** (= *they*) form of the verb.

● The various endings are added to the stem of the verb. This is the infinitive minus **-en** (if the infinitive ends in **-en**) or minus **-n** (if it doesn't).

Minor irregularities

Verbs whose stem ends in an **-s** sound (**-s**, **-ß**, **-x**, **-z**) add **-t** rather than **-st** in the **du** form of the present; strong verbs in this group add **-est** in the **du** form of the past. The pattern such verbs are referred to, if they are weak, is **heizen** (14).

Verbs whose stem ends in **-d** or in **-t** add **-est** and **-et** endings instead of **-st** and **-t** endings. Strong verbs, however, add only **-st** in the **du** form of the past; strong verbs that have a vowel change in the **du** and **er** form of the present and whose stem ends in -t add -st in the **du** form and nothing in the **er** form of the present. The pattern that weak verbs in -d and -t are referred to is **reden** (24).

Weak verbs whose stem ends in a consonant followed by **m** or **n** add -est and -et endings instead of -st and -t endings, if they would be impossible to pronounce otherwise. The pattern such verbs are referred to is **atmen** (2).

Weak verbs whose stem ends in -el or -er may drop the **e** in the **ich** form of the present: **ich wand(e)re**. The pattern such verbs are referred to is **angeln** (1).

Verbs ending -ieren and -eien have no **ge-** in their past participle. The pattern such verbs are referred to is **informieren** (15). Verbs with an inseparable prefix have no **ge-** either: see p. xviii

Modal verbs substitute their infinitive for their past participle when they are used with another infinitive: **ich habe gehen wollen**. See p. xxi.

Strong verbs whose past stem ends in -s or -ß add -t, not -st, in the **du** form of the past: **blasen, du bliest.**

Some strong verbs simply add an umlaut to their vowel in the **du** and **er** forms of the present tense, rather than changing it completely: **fahren, er fährt**. For the imperative of these verbs see p. xvi.

Compound tenses

These are formed regularly for all verbs, as follows:

Compound past tenses (*perfect, pluperfect*)

These are formed for most German verbs with a tense of **haben** plus the past participle, in exact parallel to English compound past tenses: **ich habe gemacht,** *I have made;* **ich hatte gemacht,** *I had made.*

However, past compound tenses are formed with **sein** instead of **haben** in the following cases: verbs of motion without a direct object, verbs indicating change of state, verbs meaning 'to happen', **bleiben** (*to remain*), **werden** (*to become*), and **sein** itself.

With some verbs either **haben** or **sein** may be used, according to whether the verb is transitive (i.e. has a direct object) or intransitive (i.e. has no direct object); additionally, with a very few intransitive verbs usage varies and either **haben** or **sein** may be used. In all cases the auxiliary verb (or verbs) that each verb takes is given individually in the verb directory.

The past participle is placed at the end of the clause. When a compound past tense is used in subordinate order, the part of **haben, sein,** or **werden** comes last in the clause after the past participle.

Compound future tenses (*future, future perfect, conditional, conditional perfect*)

These are formed with a tense of **werden** plus the present or past infinitive, in exact parallel to

English compound future tenses: **ich werde machen,** *I shall make;* **ich werde gemacht haben,** *I shall have made.*

The infinitive is placed at the end of the clause. When a compound future tense is used in subordinate order, the part of **werden** comes last in the clause after the infinitive.

The pluperfect subjunctive (**ich hätte gemacht, ich wäre gegangen,** etc.) may be substituted for the conditional perfect (**ich würde gemacht haben, ich würde gegangen sein**).

The subjunctive

The subjunctive in German casts doubt. Its main use is in reported matter, usually in order to disclaim personal responsibility for what is being said.

Present subjunctive

Identical with the present tense except in the **du, er,** and **ihr** forms:

du ...est, er ...e, ihr ...et

Past subjunctive

Identical with the past tense in weak verbs. Strong verbs modify the vowel of their past tense, if it is **a, o,** or **u**, and add the same endings as the present subjunctive: **fahren, er führe.** The **e** of the **du** and **ihr** forms of the past subjunctive of strong verbs may be dropped in spoken German: **du gingst, ihr wärt.**

Mixed verbs form the past subjunctive as if they were weak verbs.

Perfect subjunctive

The present subjunctive of **haben** or **sein** plus the past participle.

Pluperfect subjunctive

The past subjunctive of **haben** or **sein** plus the past participle.

Future subjunctive

Rarely needed. It is formed with the present subjunctive of **werden** plus the infinitive: **er werde gehen**.

Subjunctive for conditional

The past subjunctive of **werden** (**ich würde**, etc.) plus the infinitive is used to form the conditional tense; in the case of **sein, haben,** the modals and some of the commoner strong verbs a past subjunctive is often used instead of a conditional:

ich würde sein or **ich wäre,** *I would be*

The passive

A passive tense is formed by using the equivalent active tense of **werden** plus the past participle of the verb. All tense formations correspond exactly to the English ones, with **werden** the equivalent of *to be*. Note that the past participle of **werden** used in passive tenses is **worden,** not **geworden.**

When the passive conveys a state rather than an action **sein** is used instead of **werden:**

> **sie war gut dafür geeignet,** *she was well suited to it.*

The full pattern for a verb in the passive with **werden** is given overleaf.

PASSIVE FORMS OF THE VERB

loben, *to praise*

Pattern for all verbs in the passive.

passive infinitive	gelobt werden	*to be praised*
past infinitive, passive	gelobt worden sein	*to have been praised*
present participle	gelobt werdend	*being praised*
past participle	gelobt worden	*been praised*
imperative[1]	sei (du) gelobt!	*be praised*
	seien wir gelobt!	*let us be praised*
	seid (ihr) gelobt!	*be praised*
	seien Sie gelobt!	*be praised*

present
ich werde gelobt
  I am praised
du wirst gelobt
er wird gelobt
wir werden gelobt
ihr werdet gelobt
sie werden gelobt

perfect
ich bin gelobt worden
  I have been praised
du bist gelobt worden
er ist gelobt worden
wir sind gelobt worden
ihr seid gelobt worden
sie sind gelobt worden

past (imperfect)
ich wurde gelobt
  I was praised
du wurdest gelobt
er wurde gelobt
wir wurden gelobt
ihr wurdet gelobt
sie wurden gelobt

future
ich werde gelobt werden
  I shall be praised
du wirst gelobt werden
er wird gelobt werden
wir werden gelobt werden
ihr werdet gelobt werden
sie werden gelobt werden

[1] The imperative may be constructed with **werden** (**werde gelobt!** etc.), but the forms given, using **sein**, are more common.

pluperfect
ich war gelobt worden
  I had been praised
du warst gelobt worden
er war gelobt worden
wir waren gelobt worden
ihr wart gelobt worden
sie waren gelobt worden

conditional
ich würde gelobt werden
  I should be praised
du würdest gelobt werden
er würde gelobt werden
wir würden gelobt werden
ihr würdet gelobt werden
sie würden gelobt werden

future perfect
ich werde gelobt worden sein
  I shall have been praised
du wirst gelobt worden sein
er wird gelobt worden sein
wir werden gelobt worden sein
ihr werdet gelobt worden sein
sie werden gelobt worden sein

conditional perfect
ich würde gelobt worden sein
  I should have been praised
du würdest gelobt worden sein
er würde gelobt worden sein
wir würden gelobt worden sein
ihr würdet gelobt worden sein
sie würden gelobt worden sein

present subjunctive
ich werde gelobt
  I may (might) be praised

du werdest gelobt
er werde gelobt
wir werden gelobt
ihr werdet gelobt
sie werden gelobt

perfect subjunctive
ich sei gelobt worden
  *I may (might) have been
  praised*
du sei(e)st gelobt worden
er sei gelobt worden
wir seien gelobt worden
ihr seiet gelobt worden
sie seien gelobt worden

past (imperfect) subjunctive
ich würde gelobt
  I may (might) be praised

du würdest gelobt
er würde gelobt
wir würden gelobt
ihr würdet gelobt
sie würden gelobt

pluperfect subjunctive
ich wäre gelobt worden
  *I may (might) have been
  praised*
du wär(e)st gelobt worden
er wäre gelobt worden
wir wären gelobt worden
ihr wär(e)t gelobt worden
sie wären gelobt worden

Present participle

This is formed for all verbs by adding **-d** to the infinitive:

machen: present participle **machend**

The present participle can only be used as an adjective in German:

das wartende Auto, *the waiting car*

Imperative

The imperative forms are based on the equivalent present-tense forms, with the subject following. The subject is usually dropped with the **du** and **ihr** forms:

mache (du)!
machen wir!
macht (ihr)!
machen Sie!

The **du** form of the imperative ends in **-e**, but this is often omitted, especially in speech.

● Strong verbs with a complete vowel-change (not just an added umlaut) in the **du** and **er** forms of the present also make this change in the **du** form of the imperative. The final **-e** is never used with these verbs:

geben: du gibst; gib! but
fahren: du fährst; fahr(e)!

● The forms **wollen wir machen, wir wollen machen,** and **laß(t) uns machen** are frequent alternatives to **machen wir.** In notices an infinitive is often used for the imperative: **nicht hinauslehnen!,** *don't lean out.*

● Third-person commands are expressed by the present of **sollen** or by the imperative of **lassen**:

er soll das machen / laß ihn das machen, *let him do it*

The subjunctive is found in some set third-person commands: **Gott sei Dank!,** *thank God;* **es lebe die Republik!,** *long live the Republic!*

Compound verbs: separable and inseparable prefixes

Compound verbs follow the pattern of simple verbs; they are formed by adding a prefix to the simple verb. This prefix may be either separable (**auf-, an-, zu-,** etc.), or inseparable (**er-, be-, ver-,** etc.), or sometimes separable, sometimes inseparable according to the meaning of the verb (**um-, unter-, durch-,** etc.) The directory indicates whether a prefix is separable or inseparable.

Separable prefixes

● A separable prefix is found attached to its verb in the infinitive:

ich muß aufstehen, *I have to get up*

● Once the verb is used in any of its tenses, however, the prefix separates from it and moves to the end of its clause:

ich stehe früh auf, wenn ich in die Schule muß, *I get up early when I have to go to school*

If the verb itself is at the end of the clause (as is the case in subordinate order) the prefix and verb join up again:

ich weiß nicht, ob ich heute aufstehe, *I don't know whether I'll get up today*

● If the infinitive is used with **zu**, the **zu** is inserted between prefix and verb:

ich versuche aufzustehen, *I'll try to get up*

● In the past participle the **ge-** appears between prefix and verb:

ich bin zu früh aufgestanden, *I got up too early*

Inseparable prefixes

The only difference between a verb with an inseparable prefix and a simple verb is that the former has no **ge-** in its past participle: **bedienen: ich habe bedient**.

Double prefixes

A separable prefix followed by an inseparable one separates, but the verb has no **ge-** in its past participle:

er bereitet das Mittagessen zu, *he's preparing lunch*

er hat das Mittagessen zubereitet, *he's prepared lunch*

The separable prefixes **hin-** and **her-** imply respectively motion away from and motion towards the speaker, and as well as being added to simple verbs they may also be added to compound verbs, producing a double separable prefix. This behaves like a single separable prefix:

er kommt herauf; er ist heraufgekommen

Reflexive verbs

Reflexive verbs have the same subject and object. In English the object is either one of the *-self* words (*he scratches himself*) or *each other* (*they dislike each other*). Verbs with the latter type of object are sometimes called reciprocal verbs in English. In German the reflexive pronouns are **mich, dich, sich** (singular) and **uns, euch, sich** (plural). The reflexive form of **Sie** (polite *you*) is **sich** (note the small **s**).

● With a reciprocal verb, **uns, euch,** and **sich** are used, but if there is ambiguity, **einander,** *each other,* is substituted for the reflexive pronoun. **Einander** is invariable.

sie bedienen sich, *they're serving themselves*
sie bedienen einander, *they're serving each other*

● A small number of reflexive verbs take a direct object that is not their reflexive pronoun; in this case the reflexive is in the dative:

das kann ich mir denken, *I can imagine that*

The dative reflexive only differs from the accusative in its **mir** and **dir** forms.

● Reflexive verbs are listed separately in the verb directory if they have a completely different meaning from the simple verb, if the reflexive pronoun is dative, if the simple verb is no longer in use, or if a special prepositional construction follows the reflexive form of the verb.

Modal verbs and lassen

The modal verbs are **dürfen**, *be allowed to, may;* **können**, *can, be able to;* **mögen**, *like, may, want;* **müssen**, *must, have to;* **sollen**, *be supposed to;* and **wollen**, *want to, will.*

Lassen + an infinitive means *to get something done* or *to have something done:*

ich lasse mir die Haare schneiden, *I'm going to have my hair cut*

sie ließ uns holen, *she sent for us (had us fetched)*

In this meaning **lassen** behaves like a modal verb.

● The modals and **lassen** are followed by a dependent infinitive without **zu**. All other verbs take an infinitive with **zu**. The modals can also be used without a dependent infinitive:

du mußt nicht, *you don't have to*

ganz wie du willst, *just as you like*

● The modals and **lassen** have two past participles. Their normal one is used when they stand alone; a second one, identical with their infinitive, is used when they have a dependent infinitive:

> **das habe ich nicht gewollt,** *that's not what I intended*
>
> **das habe ich schon lange machen wollen,** *I've wanted to do that for a long time*

● In subordinate order the compound tenses of the modals involve two infinitives and a part of **haben** coming together at the end of a clause. In this case the part of **haben** comes before, not after the infinitives:

> **schade, daß er nicht hat kommen können,** *a pity he hasn't been able to come*

The same applies to the position of **werden** in the future and conditional tenses of modals in subordinate order. The construction is usually avoided in spoken German.

● Modals, as in English, may be followed by a passive infinitive, formed by the past participle plus **werden**:

> **es muß getan werden,** *it must be done*

Dative verbs

A number of verbs whose English equivalents take a direct object take a dative object in German. The commonest of these are

begegnen, *to meet*	**gehorchen,** *to obey*
danken, *to thank*	**gratulieren,** *to congratulate*
dienen, *to serve*	**helfen,** *to help*
drohen, *to threaten*	**stehen,** *to suit*
folgen, *to follow*	**trauen,** *to trust*
gefallen, *to please*	

es hat mir sehr gefallen, *it pleased me a lot*
sie ist mir begegnet, *she ran into me*

Begegnen and **folgen** are verbs of motion: since they do not have a direct object they form their compound tenses with **sein**.

● In addition to the above verbs, many separable verbs whose prefixes are prepositions taking the dative also have dative objects:

sie rief mir nach, *she called after me*

● The verbs **erlauben,** *to allow,* **glauben,** *to believe,* and **befehlen,** *to order* have an accusative if the object is a thing

das glaube ich, *I believe that*

but a dative if the object is a person

ich glaube ihr nicht, *I don't believe her*

● All dative verbs are shown as such in the directory.

Impersonal verbs

As in English, a number of verbs in German have an impersonal *it* (**es**) as subject. Many of these are weather verbs:

es regnet, *it's raining*
es schneit, *it's snowing*

Others have a personal object, either accusative or dative. Some of these correspond to an English impersonal

es ist mir recht, *it's all right by me*

some do not

es tut mir leid, *I'm sorry*

● Among the commonest verbs of this kind are:

es fehlt mir an (+ D), *I lack*	**es ärgert mich,** *I'm annoyed*
es geht mir (gut, etc.), *I'm (well,* etc.)	**es ist mir, als ob,** *I feel as if*
es gelingt mir, *I succeed*	**es ist mir (kalt,** etc.), *I'm (cold,* etc.)
es tut mir leid, *I'm sorry*	**es ist mir recht,** *it's all right by me*
es freut mich, *I'm glad*	**es scheint mir,** *it seems to me*

With the verbs in the second column above the **es** disappears if anything else is placed first in the sentence:

mir ist furchtbar warm hier, *I find it dreadfully hot here*

● There is a different use of **es** as subject which corresponds to the English impersonal *there*:

es bleibt jetzt sehr wenig Zeit, *there's very little time left now*

In this construction the **es** simply functions as a substitute for the real subject, which is held back until after the verb and so assumes greater importance. If the real subject is plural, so is the verb

> **es stehen viele Autos auf dem Parkplatz,** *there are many cars in the car-park*

and if an adverb appears before the verb in this construction, the **es** simply disappears

> **heute stehen viele Autos auf dem Parkplatz,** *there are many cars in the car-park today* (compare: **heute regnet es**)

With this construction in the passive no real subject need be expressed at all:

> **es wird hier gebaut/hier wird gebaut,** *construction work is taking place here*

● Where existence rather than position is to be expressed **es gibt** is used instead of **es ist, es steht, es liegt,** etc. to mean *there is, there are*. The **es** cannot be dropped in this case. The verb is always singular and is followed by an accusative:

> **es ist kein einziger Teller im Schrank,** *there isn't a single plate in the cupboard*
>
> **von heute an gibt es einen neuen Fahrplan,** *starting today there is a new timetable*

VERB DIRECTORY

The directory shows in alphabetical order:

- all strong and mixed verbs in current use
- all common weak verbs

You are given:

- the infinitive of the verb, with an indication of whether any prefixes are separable or inseparable
- the preposition(s), if any, that follow it, with the cases they take
- the commonest meaning or meanings of the verb (and its prepositions)
- the case of any object or complement to the verb
- the auxiliary verb used to form the compound past tenses
- an indication of whether the verb is weak, strong, or mixed
- if strong or mixed, the vowel and consonant changes in the present and past tenses and the past participle
- the model verb on whose pattern the verb is conjugated
- the number of the model verb in the verb tables

An asterisk before a model verb means that the verb you are looking up follows this model but with some slight deviation. You will find full details of this in the verb tables, at the foot of the second page of the model verb.

Bracketed material within a verb's constructions corresponds to bracketed material within the verb's meanings.

All active tenses are given in the verb tables. For the passive tenses, see pp. xiv–xv.

Reflexive forms of verbs are only given in this list where they have special meanings or special constructions, or where the reflexive pronoun is in the dative (which is then shown in brackets after it), or where the non-reflexive form of the verb is not in common use. A reflexive verb is conjugated exactly like its non-reflexive form.

The directory does not include obsolete, regional, slang, or technical verbs.

ABBREVIATIONS USED IN THE DIRECTORY

A	accusative
D	dative
G	genitive
h	auxiliary: **haben**
impers.	impersonal use
inf.	infinitive
insep.	inseparable
intrans.	intransitive (has no direct object)
m	mixed conjugation
N	nominative
past part.	past participle
s	auxiliary: **sein**
sb	somebody
st	strong conjugation
sth	something
trans.	transitive (has a direct object)
w	weak conjugation

| is used within a verb to indicate that it has a separable prefix and to show the point at which it separates.

' is used within a verb after an inseparable prefix.

ab|ändern *change* A h w	angeln	1
abandonnieren *abandon* A h w	informieren	15
ab|arbeiten *work off* A h w	reden	24
sich ab|arbeiten *slave away* h w	reden	24
ab|bauen *dismantle* A h w	machen	21
ab|beißen *bite off* A h st [i, i]	beißen	3
ab|be'rufen aus + D/**von** + D *recall*		
from A h st [ie, u]	rufen	25
ab|be'stellen *cancel* A h w	machen	21
ab|be'zahlen *pay off* A h w	machen	21
ab|biegen *turn off* s st [o, o]	kriechen	19
ab|bilden *copy* A h w	reden	24
ab|binden *untie* A h st [a, u]	binden	4
ab|blättern *flake off* s w	angeln	1
ab|blenden *fade; dim* A h w	reden	24
ab|blühen *fade* h/s w	machen	21
ab|brechen *break off* A h (**sein** when		
intrans.) st [i, a, o]	sprechen	33
ab|brennen *burn down* A h (**sein**		
when intrans.) m [a, a]	brennen	5
ab|bringen von + D *make give up sth*		
A h m [ach, ach]	*brennen	5
ab|bröckeln *crumble away* s w	angeln	1
ab|buchen von + D *debit to* A h w	machen	21
ab|bürsten von + D *brush off* A h w	reden	24
ab|checken *check (off/through)*		
A h w	machen	21
ab|dampfen *steam away* s w	machen	21
ab|dämpfen *muffle* A h w	machen	21
ab|danken *abdicate* h w	machen	21
ab|decken *uncover* A h w	machen	21
ab|decken mit + D *cover up with*		
A h w	machen	21
ab|dichten *seal (up)* A h w	reden	24
ab|drängen von + D *push away from*		
A h w	machen	21
ab|drehen *turn off* A h (**sein** when		
intrans.) w	machen	21

ab|drucken *print* A h w	machen	21
ab|drücken auf + A *shoot at* A h w	machen	21
sich ab|drücken in + D *make marks in* h w	machen	21
ab|dunkeln *darken* A h w	angeln	1
sich ab|duschen *take a shower* h w	machen	21
ab|ebben *recede* s w	machen	21
ab|er'kennen (D) *disallow (sb)* A h m [a, a]	brennen	5
ab|fahren *leave* s st [ä, u, a]	tragen	38
ab|fahren *wear out* A h st [ä, u, a]	tragen	38
ab|fallen *fall off* s st [ä, iel, a]	*schlafen	27
ab|fallen gegenüber + D *be inferior to* s st [ä, iel, a]	*schlafen	27
ab|fallen von + D *desert* s st [ä, iel, a]	*schlafen	27
ab|fangen *intercept* A h st [ä, i, a]	*hängen	12
ab|fassen *draw up* A h w	heizen	14
ab|fertigen *dispatch* A h w	machen	21
ab|finden mit + D *compensate with* A h st [a, u]	binden	4
sich ab|finden mit + D *come to terms with* h st [a, u]	binden	4
ab|fliegen *take off* s st [o, o]	kriechen	19
ab|fliegen aus + D *fly out of* A h st [o, o]	kriechen	19
ab|fließen *flow away* s st [o, o]	schießen	26
ab|fordern (D) *demand (of sb)* A h w	angeln	1
ab|fragen (D) *test (sb) on* A h w	machen	21
ab|führen von + D *take away from* A h w	machen	21
ab|füllen *fill* A h w	machen	21
ab|geben bei + D *hand over to* A h st [i, a, e]	geben	9
sich ab|geben mit + D *spend time on* h st [i, a, e]	geben	9
ab|gehen von + D *leave* s st [ing, ang]	*hängen	12

ab|ge'winnen (D) *win (from sb)* A h st [a, o]	sprechen	33
ab|ge'wöhnen (D) *make (sb) give up* A h w	machen	21
ab|graben *dig out* A h st [ä, u, a]	tragen	38
ab|grenzen gegen + A/**von** + D *separate from* A h w	heizen	14
ab|haken *tick off (on list)* A h w	machen	21
ab|halten von + D *keep off (sb/sth)* A h st [ä, ie, a]	*schlafen	27
ab|handeln (D) *beat (sb) down by* A h w	angeln	1
ab|hängen *take down; hang up (phone)* A h w	machen	21
ab|hängen von + D *be dependent on* h st [i, a]	hängen	12
ab|härten *harden* A h w	reden	24
ab|hauen *chop off;* (with **sein**) *clear off* A h w	machen	21
ab|heben *lift off;* (with **sein**) *take off* A h st [o, o]	kriechen	19
ab|heben auf + A *stress* h st [o, o]	kriechen	19
sich ab|heben von + D *contrast with* h st [o, o]	kriechen	19
sich ab|hetzen *rush around* h w	heizen	14
ab|holen *pick up; collect* A h w	machen	21
ab|holzen *fell; clear* A h w	heizen	14
ab|hören *listen to; 'bug'* A h w	machen	21
ab|jagen (D) *get . . . away (from sb)* A h w	machen	21
ab|kapseln *encapsulate* A h w	angeln	1
ab|kassieren (A/**bei** + D) *take money owing (from)* h w	informieren	15
ab|kaufen (D) *buy (from sb)* A h w	machen	21
ab|kehren *turn away; brush off* A h w	machen	21
sich ab|kehren von + D *turn away from* h w	machen	21

ab|klingen *grow fainter* s st [a, u]	klingen	16
ab|knicken *snap off* A h w	machen	21
ab|knöpfen *unbutton* A h w	machen	21
ab|kommandieren zu + D *detail to* A h w	informieren	15
ab|kommen von + D *stray from* s st [am, o]	kommen	17
ab|kratzen *scratch off* A h w	heizen	14
ab|kühlen *cool down* A h (usually **sein** when intrans.) w	machen	21
ab|kürzen um + A *shorten by* A h w	heizen	14
ab|kürzen mit + D *abbreviate to* A h w	heizen	14
ab|laden *unload* A h st [ä, u, a]	*tragen	38
ab|lagern *deposit* A h w	angeln	1
ab|lassen (aus + D) *let out (of)* A h st [ä, ie, a]	*schlafen	27
ab|lassen (D) *let (sb) have* A h st [ä, ie, a]	*schlafen	27
ab|lassen von + D *give up* h st [ä, ie, a]	*schlafen	27
ab|laufen (von + D/**an** + D) *flow away (from/off); run/wear down* s st [äu, ie, au]	laufen	20
ab|legen *lay (down); take off* A h w	machen	21
ab|lehnen *reject* A h w	machen	21
ab|leiten von + D/**aus** + D *derive from* A h w	reden	24
ab|lenken von + D *deflect from* A h w	machen	21
ab|lesen *read (aloud); groom* A h st [ie, a, e]	*sehen	29
ab|leugnen *deny* A h w	atmen	2
ab|lichten *photocopy* A h w	reden	24
ab|liefern bei + D *deliver to* A h w	angeln	1
ab|locken (D) *coax . . . out of (sb)* A h w	machen	21
ab|lösen von + D *remove from* A h w	heizen	14

sich ab|lösen *become detached; take turns* h w	heizen	14
ab|machen *agree* A h w	machen	21
ab|magern *become thin* s w	angeln	1
ab|marschieren *march off* s w	informieren	15
ab|melden *cancel* A h w	reden	24
sich ab|melden (bei + D) *report that one is leaving (to)* h w	reden	24
ab|montieren *dismantle* A h w	informieren	15
sich ab|mühen mit + D *struggle with; toil for* h w	machen	21
ab|nehmen *take down;* (D) *take . . . off (sb)* A h st [imm, a, omm]	*sprechen	33
ab|nutzen/ab|nützen *wear out* A h w	heizen	14
abonnieren *have a subscription to* A h w	informieren	15
ab|packen *pack(age)* A h w	machen	21
ab|pflücken *pick* A h w	machen	21
sich ab|plagen (mit + D) *slave away (at sth/for sb)* h w	machen	21
ab|prallen an + D/**von** + D *rebound off* s w	machen	21
sich ab|quälen mit + D *struggle with* h w	machen	21
ab|raten von + D *advise against* D h st [ä, ie, a]	*schlafen	27
ab|räumen *clear (away)* A h w	machen	21
ab|reagieren (an + D) *work . . . off (on)* A h w	informieren	15
ab|rechnen *cash up; deduct* A h w	atmen	2
ab|rechnen mit + D *call . . . to account* h w	atmen	2
ab|reisen nach + D *leave for* s w	heizen	14
ab|reißen *tear off/down; break off* A h (**sein** when intrans.) st [i, i]	beißen	3
ab|reiten *ride off* s s [itt, itt]	streiten	37
ab|richten *train* A h w	reden	24

ab|rollen *unwind* A h (**sein** when intrans.) w	machen	21
ab|rücken von + D *move away from* A h (**sein** when intrans.) w	machen	21
ab|rufen *summon* A h st [ie, u]	rufen	25
ab|runden (**auf** + A) *round off (to)* A h w	reden	24
ab|rüsten *disarm* A h w	reden	24
ab|rutschen von + D *slip off* s w	machen	21
ab|sagen *cancel;* (D) *put (sb) off* A h w	machen	21
ab|sägen *saw off* A h w	machen	21
ab|schaffen *abolish* A h w	machen	21
ab|schälen von + D *peel off* A h w	machen	21
ab|schalten *switch off* A h w	reden	24
ab|schätzen *size up* A h w	heizen	14
ab|scheuern von + D *scrub off* A h w	angeln	1
ab|schicken *send (off)* A h w	machen	21
ab|schieben *push away; shift* A h st [o, o]	kriechen	19
ab|schießen *fire off; shoot down* A h st [o, o]	schießen	26
ab|schirmen von + D/**gegen** + A *shield from* A h w	machen	21
ab|schlagen (D) *refuse (sb); chop off* A h st [ä, u, a]	tragen	38
ab|schleppen *tow away* A h w	machen	21
ab|schließen *lock up; conclude;* (**mit** + D) *be bordered (with)* A h st [o, o]	schießen	26
ab|schmecken *season* A h w	machen	21
sich ab|schminken *remove one's make-up* h w	machen	21
ab|schnallen *unfasten* A h w	machen	21
ab|schneiden von + D *cut off/down from* A h st [itt, itt]	*streiten	37
ab|schöpfen *skim off* A h w	machen	21
ab|schrauben *unscrew* A h w	machen	21

ab|schrecken *deter* A h w	machen	21
ab|schreiben *copy out* A h st [ie, ie]	schreiben	28
ab|schütteln *shake down/off* A h w	angeln	1
ab|schwächen *moderate* A h w	machen	21
ab|schweifen *digress* s w	machen	21
ab|schwören *renounce* D h st [o, o]	*kriechen	19
ab|sehen *predict* A h st [ie, a, e]	sehen	29
ab|sehen von + D *ignore; refrain from* h st [ie, a, e]	sehen	29
ab|senden *dispatch* A h w/m [a, a]	reden/senden	24/31
ab|setzen *take off; put down; dismiss* A h w	heizen	14
ab|sichern *make safe; substantiate* A h w	angeln	1
ab|sinken *sink; decline* s st [a, u]	klingen	16
ab|sitzen *sit out; serve* A h st [aß, ess]	*fressen	8
ab|sondern *isolate* A h w	angeln	1
ab|spalten *split off* A h w (past part. sometimes **abgespalten**)	*reden	24
ab|speisen mit + D *fob off with* A h w	heizen	14
ab|sperren *close/cut off* A h w	machen	21
ab|spielen *play through* A h w	machen	21
sich ab|spielen *take place* h w	machen	21
ab|sprechen (D) *deprive (sb) of* A h st [i, a, o]	sprechen	33
ab|spreizen *splay out* A h w	heizen	14
ab|springen *jump off/down* s st [a, u]	klingen	16
ab|spulen *unwind* A h w	machen	21
ab|spülen *rinse* A h w	machen	21
ab|stammen von + D *be descended from* s w	machen	21
ab|stauben *dust* A h w	machen	21
ab|stechen gegen + A *stand out against* h st [i, a, o]	sprechen	33
ab|stehen *stick out* h st [and, and]	stehen	34
ab|steigen von + D *get off* s st [ie, ie]	schreiben	28

ab|stellen *turn off; park; move away*		
A h w	machen	21
ab|stempeln *frank* A h w	angeln	1
ab|sterben *go numb; die out* s st		
[i, a, o]	sprechen	33
ab|stimmen (über + A) *vote (on)* h w	machen	21
ab|stimmen mit + D *agree with* h w	machen	21
ab|stimmen auf + A *match to*		
A h w	machen	21
ab|stoßen *push away; reject* A h st		
[ö, ie, o]	stoßen	36
ab|streichen *cross/wipe off* A h st		
[i, i]	gleichen	10
ab|streifen *pull off; remove* A h w	machen	21
ab|streiten *deny* A h st [itt, itt]	streiten	37
ab|stürzen *crash* s w	heizen	14
sich ab|stützen an + D/**mit** + D		
support oneself on/with h w	heizen	14
ab|suchen (nach + D) *comb (for)*		
A h w	machen	21
ab|tasten (auf + A) *frisk (for)* A h w	reden	24
ab|töten *deaden* A h w	reden	24
ab|tragen *wear out; take down* A h st		
[ä, u, a]	tragen	38
ab|treiben *carry away; abort* A h st		
[ie, ie]	schreiben	28
ab|trennen *detach* A h w	machen	21
ab|treten *exit; step down* s st	*geben	9
[itt, a, e]		
ab|trocknen *dry* A h w	atmen	2
ab|tropfen *drain; drip-dry* s w	machen	21
ab|tun *dismiss* A h st [at, a]	tun	39
ab|ver'langen (D) *demand (from sb)*		
A h w	machen	21
ab|wägen *weigh up* A h st [o, o]/w	kriechen/	
	machen	19/21
ab|wälzen auf + A *shift (blame etc.)*		
on to A h w	heizen	14

ab|wandern (aus + D/**in** + A) *emigrate (from/to)* s w	angeln	1
ab|warten *wait (and see); wait for* A h w	reden	24
ab|waschen *wash (up)* A h st [ä, u, a]	tragen	38
sich ab|wechseln *alternate* h w	angeln	1
ab|wehren *repulse; avert* A h w	machen	21
ab|weichen (von + D) *deviate (from)* s st [i, i]	gleichen	10
ab|weisen *reject* A h st [ie, ie]	*schreiben	28
ab|wenden (von + D) *turn away (from); avert* (always weak in this meaning) A h w/m [a, a]	reden/senden	24/31
ab|werfen *shed* A h st [i, a, o]	sprechen	33
ab|werten *devalue; belittle* A h w	reden	24
ab|wickeln *unwind; deal with* A h w	angeln	1
ab|wischen (von + D) *wipe away (from)* A h w	machen	21
ab|zahlen *pay off* A h w	machen	21
ab|zählen *count out* A h w	machen	21
ab|zeichnen *initial* A h w	atmen	2
sich ab|zeichnen *stand out; loom* h w	atmen	2
ab|ziehen *pull off; peel; run off* A h st [og, og]	*kriechen	19
ab|zweigen (with sein) *branch off;* (with **haben**) *set aside* A w	machen	21
achten auf + A *look after* h w	reden	24
acht|geben auf + A *pay attention to* h st [i, a, e]	geben	9
ächzen *groan* A h w	heizen	14
addieren *add (up)* A h w	informieren	15
adeln *ennoble* A h w	angeln	1
adoptieren *adopt* A h w	informieren	15
ähneln *resemble* D h w	angeln	1
ahnen *have a presentiment of; suspect* A h w	machen	21

akkreditieren (bei + D) *accredit (to)* A h w	informieren	15
aktivieren *mobilize; step up* A h w	informieren	15
alarmieren *call out; alarm* A h w	informieren	15
sich alliieren mit + D *ally oneself to/with* h w	informieren	15
altern *age; mature* h w	angeln	1
amerikanisieren *Americanize* A h w	informieren	15
amnestieren *amnesty* A h w	informieren	15
amputieren *amputate* A h w	informieren	15
amtieren (als) *hold office (of/as)* h w	informieren	15
sich amüsieren (mit + D) *have fun/a good time (with)* h w	informieren	15
sich amüsieren über + A *laugh at* h w	informieren	15
analysieren *analyse* A h w	informieren	15
an|bahnen *initiate* A h w	machen	21
sich an|bahnen *be developing* h w	machen	21
an|bauen (an + A) *build on (to)* A h w	machen	21
an|beißen *bite into; take a bite of* A h st [i, i]	beißen	3
an|betteln (um + A) *beg (for)* A h w	angeln	1
an|bieten (D) *offer (to sb)* A h st [o, o]	*kriechen	19
an|binden (an + A/D) *tie up (to)* A h st [a, u]	binden	4
an|blicken *look at* A h w	machen	21
an|brechen *open; break (into)* A h (**sein** when intrans.) st [i, a, o]	sprechen	33
an|bringen (an + D) *put up; fix (on to)* A h m [ach, ach]	*brennen	5
an|brüllen *roar at* A h w	machen	21
ändern (an + D) *change (in/about)* A h w	angeln	1
an|deuten (D) *hint (to sb)* A h w	reden	24
an|dichten (D) *impute (to sb)* A h w	reden	24

an|drängen (gegen + A) *surge (against)* s w	machen	21
an|drehen (D) *turn on; palm off (on sb)* A h w	machen	21
sich [D] an|eignen *appropriate; acquire* A h w	atmen	2
aneinander|ge'raten mit + D *come to blows with* s st [ä, ie, a]	*schlafen	27
aneinander|reihen *string together* A h w	machen	21
aneinander|stoßen *collide* s st [ö, ie, o]	stoßen	36
an|ekeln *nauseate* A h w	angeln	1
an|er'kennen (present sometimes **ich anerkenne**, etc.) (**als**) *recognize; accept (as)* A h m [a, a]	brennen	5
an|fachen *arouse* A h w	machen	21
an|fahren *run into; start up* A h (**sein** when intrans.) st [ä, u, a]	tragen	38
an|fallen *attack; arise* A h (**sein** when intrans.) st [ä, iel, a]	*schlafen	27
an|fangen mit + D *begin with* A h st [ä, i, a]	*hängen	12
an|fassen *take hold of* A h w	heizen	14
an|fertigen *make* A h w	machen	21
an|flehen um + A *beg for* A h w	machen	21
an|geben *state; set; show off* A h st [i, a, e]	geben	9
an|gehen *come on; concern* A h (**sein** when intrans.) st [ing, ang]	*hängen	12
an|ge'hören *belong to* D h w	machen	21
angeln (auf + A) *fish (for)* h w	angeln	1
angeln nach + D *fish for* (figurative) h w	angeln	1
an|ge'wöhnen (D) *get (sb) used to* A h w	machen	21
an|greifen *attack* A h st [iff, iff]	greifen	11
an|grenzen an + A *border on* h w	heizen	14
ängstigen *frighten* A h w	machen	21

sich ängstigen um + A/**vor** + D *be*		
anxious about/afraid of h w	machen	21
an|halten *stop; last* A h st [ä, ie, a]	*schlafen	27
an|hängen (an + A) *hang on; hitch up*		
(to) A h st [i, a]	hängen	12
an|häufen *accumulate* A h w	machen	21
an|heften *put up; pin on* A h w	reden	24
an|hören *listen to* A h w	machen	21
sich an|hören *sound* h w	machen	21
an|klagen (G/wegen + G) *accuse (of)*		
A h w	machen	21
an|kleben (an + A) *stick up (on)*		
A h w	machen	21
sich an|kleiden *dress (oneself)* h w	reden	24
an|klopfen (an + A/D) *knock (on)*		
h w	machen	21
an|knüpfen (an + A) *tie on (to); start*		
up A h w	machen	21
an|kommen *arrive;* (**auf** + A) *depend*		
(on) s st [am, o]	kommen	17
an|koppeln an + A *hitch up to*		
A h w	angeln	1
an|kreuzen *put a cross beside* A h w	heizen	14
an|kündigen *announce* A h w	machen	21
an|lächeln *smile at* A h w	angeln	1
an|langen bei/auf/an (all + D) *arrive*		
at s w	machen	21
an|lassen *leave on; start* A h st		
[ä, ie, a]	*schlafen	27
an|lasten (D) *accuse (sb) of* A h w	reden	24
an|laufen *run up; start (of engine)*		
s st [äu, ie, au]	laufen	20
an|legen (an + A) *put (against/by);*		
moor A h w	machen	21
an|lehnen an + A/D *lean on* A h w	machen	21
an|leiten bei + D *instruct in* A h w	reden	24
an|lernen *train* A h w	machen	21
an|liegen *fit tightly* h st [a, e]	sehen	29

an|locken *attract* A h w	machen	21
an|machen *put on; mix* A h w	machen	21
an|malen an + A *paint on* A h w	machen	21
an|melden zu + D/**bei** + D *enrol*		
for/register with A h w	reden	24
sich an|nähern *approach* D h w	angeln	1
an|nehmen *accept* A h st [imm, a,		
omm]	*sprechen	33
an|ordnen *arrange* A h w	atmen	2
an|packen *tackle;* (**an** + D) *grab (by)*		
A h w	machen	21
sich an|passen + D *adapt to* h w	heizen	14
an|pflanzen *grow; cultivate* A h w	heizen	14
an|prallen gegen + A *crash into* s w	machen	21
an|preisen (D) *extol (to sb)* A h st		
[ie, ie]	*schreiben	28
an|probieren (D) *try on (on sb)*		
A h w	informieren	15
an|rechnen (D) *credit (sb) with;*		
charge (sb) for A h w	atmen	2
an|reden mit + D *address as/by* A h w	reden	24
an|regen *stimulate* A h w	machen	21
an|reichern *enrich* A h w	angeln	1
an|reihen an + A *add to* A h w	machen	21
an|reisen *arrive; travel* s w	heizen	21
an|reizen *stimulate* A h w	heizen	14
an|richten *serve; cause* A h w	reden	24
an|rücken (**an** + A) *push (against);*		
advance A h (**sein** when intrans.) w	machen	21
an|rufen *call to; ring* A (also **bei** + D)		
h st [ie, u]	rufen	25
an|rühren *touch* A h w	machen	21
an|sagen *announce* A h w	machen	21
sich [D] **an|schaffen** *get oneself* A h w	machen	21
an|schalten *switch on* A h w	reden	24
an|schauen *look at* A h w	machen	21
an|schlagen (**an** + A) *put up (on)*		
A h st [ä, u, a]	tragen	38

an|schließen an + A/D *connect to;*		
join up to A h st [o, o]	schießen	26
an|schnallen *strap in/on* A h w	machen	21
an|schneiden *broach; cut into* A h st		
[itt, itt]	*streiten	37
an|schreiben *write to;* (**an** + A) *write*		
. . . up (on) A h st [ie, ie]	schreiben	28
an|schreien *shout at* A h st [ie, ie]	*schreiben	28
an|schwellen *swell up* s st [i, o, o]	dreschen	6
an|sehen *look at* A h st [ie, a, e]	sehen	29
an|setzen an + A *position on/against*		
A h w	heizen	14
sich an|siedeln *settle* h w	angeln	1
an|spannen an + A *harness to* A h w	machen	21
an|spielen auf + A *allude to* h w	machen	21
an|spornen *spur on* A h w	machen	21
an|sprechen (**mit** + D/**um** + A)		
address (as/about) A h st [i, a, o]	sprechen	33
an|springen *start* s st [a, u]	klingen	16
an|stacheln zu + D *spur on to* A h w	angeln	1
an|starren *stare at* A h w	machen	21
an|stecken (D) *pin on (sb)* A h w	machen	21
an|stehen nach + D *queue for* h st		
[and, and]	stehen	34
an|steigen *rise; slope up* s st [ie, ie]	schreiben	28
an|stellen *turn on; employ; get up to*		
A h w	machen	21
sich an|stellen nach + D *queue for*		
h w	machen	21
an|stiften *instigate;* (**zu** + D) *incite*		
(to) A h w	reden	24
an|stimmen *strike up* A h w	machen	21
an|stoßen *push* A h st [ö, ie, o]	stoßen	36
an|stoßen an + A *bump into* s st		
[ö, ie, o]	stoßen	36
an|strahlen *illuminate* A h w	machen	21
an|streichen *paint* A h st [i, i]	gleichen	10
sich an|strengen *make an effort* h w	machen	21

an|strömen *stream in* s w	machen	21
an|tasten *break into; encroach on* A h w	reden	24
an|treiben zu + D *drive on to* A h st [ie, ie]	schreiben	28
an|treten *start; form up;* (**gegen** + A) *line up (against)* A h (**sein** when intrans.) st [itt, a, e]	*geben	9
antworten (D) **auf** + A *answer (sb)* h w	reden	24
an|ver'trauen (D) *entrust (sb) with* A h w	machen	21
an|wärmen *warm up* A h w	machen	21
an|weisen (D) *allocate (to sb); instruct* A h st [ie, ie]	*schreiben	28
an|wenden *employ;* (**auf** + A) *apply (to)* A h w/m [a, a]	reden/senden	24/31
an|werben für + A *recruit to* A h st [i, a, o]	sprechen	33
an|wurzeln *take root* s w	angeln	1
an|zahlen *make a down-payment on* A h w	machen	21
an|zapfen *tap* A h w	machen	21
an|zeigen (D) *inform (sb); show; report (to police)* A h w	machen	21
an|ziehen *attract; put on* A h st [og, og]	*kriechen	19
an|zünden *light; set fire to* A h w	reden	24
arbeiten (**an** + D/**bei** + D) *work (at/for); make; do* A h w	reden	24
ärgern *annoy* A h w	angeln	1
sich ärgern über + A *get annoyed at* h w	angeln	1
atmen *breathe* h w	atmen	2
auf|arbeiten *review* A h w	reden	24
auf|atmen *breathe a sigh of relief* h w	atmen	2
auf|bauen *erect;* (**auf** + D) *base (upon)* A h w	machen	21

sich auf|bäumen *rear up* h w	machen	21
auf|be'wahren *store* A h w	machen	21
auf|binden *untie* A h st [a, u]	binden	4
auf|blasen *puff out* A h st [ä, ie, a]	*schlafen	27
auf|bleiben *stay up/open* s st [ie, ie]	schreiben	28
auf|blenden *switch to full beam* A h w	reden	24
auf|blicken von + D *look up from* h w	machen	21
auf|blühen *bloom* s w	machen	21
auf|brausen *flare up* s w	heizen	14
auf|brechen *break open;* (**zu** + D) *start out (on)* A h (**sein** when intrans.) st [i, a, o]	sprechen	33
auf|bringen *raise; introduce* A h m [ach, ach]	*brennen	5
auf|decken *uncover; expose* A h w	machen	21
auf|drängen (D) *force (on sb)* A h w	machen	21
auf|drehen *unscrew* A h w	machen	21
auf|er'stehen *rise (from the dead)* s st [and, and]	stehen	34
auf|fahren *start; flare up* s st [ä, u, a]	tragen	38
auf|fahren auf + A *come up to; run into* s st [ä, u, a]	tragen	38
auf|fallen *stand out* s st [ä, iel, a]	*schlafen	27
auf|fallen (D) **an** + D *strike (sb) about* s st [ä, iel, a]	*schlafen	27
auf|fangen *catch; collect* A h st [ä, i, a]	*hängen	12
auf|fassen als *regard as* A h w	heizen	14
auf|fordern zu + D *invite for* A h w	angeln	1
auf|fressen *swallow up* A h st [i, aß, e]	fressen	8
auf|frischen *freshen up* A h w	machen	21
auf|führen *put on; quote* A h w	machen	21
auf|füllen *fill up; top up* A h w	machen	21
auf|geben *give up; post; set* A h st [i, a, e]	geben	9
auf|gehen *rise; go up;* (**in** + D) *be absorbed (in)* s st [ing, ang]	*hängen	12

auf|gliedern in + A/**nach** + D
subdivide into/by A h w — angeln — 1

auf|haben *have on/open; be open*
A h m [at, att] — *brennen — 5

auf|halten *halt; keep open* A h st
[ä, ie, a] — schlafen — 27

  sich auf|halten mit + D *spend time
on* h st [ä, ie, a] — schlafen — 27

auf|hängen (an + D) *hang (from)*
A h st [i, a] — hängen — 12

auf|heben *pick up; abolish* A h st
[o, o] — kriechen — 19

auf|heitern *brighten up* A h w — angeln — 1

auf|hellen *lighten* A h w — machen — 21

auf|holen *catch up (time)* A h w — machen — 21

auf|hören mit + D *stop* h w — machen — 21

auf|klappen *(fold) open* A h w — machen — 21

auf|klären (über + A) *enlighten
(about)* A h w — machen — 21

auf|kochen *bring to the boil* A h w — machen — 21

auf|kommen *arise* s st [am, o] — kommen — 17

  auf|kommen für + A *pay for* s st
[am, o] — kommen — 17

auf|krempeln *roll up* A h w — angeln — 1

auf|laden auf + A *load (on to)* A h st
[ä, u, a] — tragen — 38

auf|lauern *lie in wait for* D h w — angeln — 1

auf|legen *put on/out; publish* A h w — machen — 21

auf|lesen *pick up* A h st [ie, a, e] — *sehen — 29

auf|leuchten *light up* h/s w — reden — 24

auf|lockern *loosen up* A h w — angeln — 1

auf|lösen *dissolve;* (**in** + A) *resolve
(into)* A h w — heizen — 14

auf|machen (D) *open (to sb)* A h w — machen — 21

auf|muntern *cheer up* A h w — angeln — 1

auf|nehmen *take up; record;* (**in** + A)
admit (into) A h st [imm, a,
omm] — *sprechen — 33

auf|passen auf + A *watch out for; keep an eye on* h w	heizen	14
auf|peitschen *whip up* A h w	machen	21
auf|pumpen *pump up* A h w	machen	21
auf|quellen *swell up* s st [i, o, o]	dreschen	6
sich auf|raffen *pull oneself together* h w	machen	21
auf|ragen *tower up* h w	machen	21
auf|räumen *clear up* A h w	machen	21
aufrecht|er'halten *maintain* A h st [ä, ie, a]	*schlafen	27
auf|regen (über + A) *excite (about)* A h w	machen	21
auf|reißen *tear open; open wide* A h st [i, i]	beißen	3
auf|reizen (zu + D) *incite (to)* A h w	heizen	14
auf|richten *raise; straighten up; give heart to* A h w	reden	24
auf|rollen *roll up; unroll* A h w	machen	21
auf|rufen *call (upon)* A h st [ie, u]	rufen	25
auf|rühren *stir up* A h w	machen	21
auf|rüsten *arm* A h w	reden	24
auf|sagen *recite* A h w	machen	21
auf|saugen *absorb* A h w	machen	21
auf|schieben *postpone; slide open* A h st [o, o]	kriechen	19
auf|schießen *shoot up* s st [o, o]	schießen	26
auf|schlagen *open; turn up; put up* A h st [ä, u, a]	tragen	38
auf|schlagen auf + D/A *hit; strike* s st [ä, u, a]	tragen	38
auf|schließen *unlock* A h st [o, o]	schießen	26
auf|schnallen *unbuckle; strap on* A h w	machen	21
auf|schrauben *unscrew* A h w	machen	21
auf|schreiben *write down; prescribe* A h st [ie, ie]	schreiben	28

auf|schütten auf + A *pour on to* A h w	reden	24
auf|schwellen *swell up* s st [i, o, o]	dreschen	6
auf|sehen (zu + D) *look up (to sb)* h st [ie, a, e]	sehen	29
auf|setzen *put on* A h w	heizen	14
auf|sitzen auf + A *mount* s st [aß, ess]	*fressen	8
auf|spannen *open; stretch out* A h w	machen	21
auf|speichern *store up* A h w	angeln	1
auf|springen (auf + A) *jump up (on to)* s st [a, u]	klingen	16
auf|stapeln *stack up* A h w	angeln	1
auf|stehen *stand up; get up* s st [and, and]	stehen	34
auf|steigen auf + A *get on to* s st [ie, ie]	schreiben	28
auf|stellen (auf + A) *put up (on)* A h w	machen	21
auf|stoßen *kick open;* (auf + A) *bang down (on)* A h st [ö, ie, o]	stoßen	36
auf|streichen (auf + A) *spread (on)* A h st [i, i]	gleichen	10
auf|tanken *fill up* A h w	machen	21
auf|tauchen *surface; emerge* s w	machen	21
auf|tauen *thaw; defrost* A h (**sein** when intrans.) w	machen	21
auf|teilen (unter + A/D) *share out (among)* A h w	machen	21
auf|tischen (D) *serve up (to sb)* A h w	machen	21
auf|tragen (D) *instruct (sb)* h st [ä, u, a]	tragen	38
auf|treiben *raise* A h st [ie, ie]	schreiben	28
auf|treten *appear; behave* s st [itt, a, e]	*geben	9
auf|türmen (zu + D) *pile up (into)* A h w	machen	21
auf|wachen (aus + D) *wake up (from)* s w	machen	21

auf|wachsen *grow up* s st [ä, u, a]	tragen	38
auf|wärmen *warm up* A h w	machen	21
auf|wecken *wake up* A h w	machen	21
auf|weisen *show; exhibit* A h st [ie, ie]	*schreiben	28
auf|wenden *expend* A h w/m [a, a]	reden/senden	24/31
auf|werfen *throw up; raise* A h st [i, a, o]	sprechen	33
auf|wiegen *offset; make up for* A h st [o, o]	kriechen	19
auf|wühlen *churn up* A h w	machen	21
auf|zählen *enumerate* A h w	machen	21
auf|ziehen *pull open; set up; raise* A h st [og, og]	*kriechen	19
auf|zwingen (D) *force (on sb)* A h st [a, u]	klingen	16
aus|arbeiten *develop* A h w	reden	24
aus|bauen *extend; improve* A h w	machen	21
aus|bessern *repair* A h w	angeln	1
aus|beuten *exploit* A h w	reden	24
aus|bilden (**in** + D) *train (in)* A h w	reden	24
aus|bleiben *fail to appear* s st [ie, ie]	schreiben	28
aus|blenden *fade out* A h w	reden	24
aus|brechen (**aus** + D/**in** + A) *break out (of/in)* s st [i, a, o]	sprechen	33
aus|breiten (**über** + A/D) *spread out (over)* A h w	reden	24
aus|brennen *burn out* s m [a, a]	brennen	5
aus|brüten *hatch (out)* A h w	reden	24
aus|bügeln *iron (out)* A h w	angeln	1
aus|dehnen *stretch out;* (**auf** + A) *extend (to)* A h w	machen	21
sich [D] **aus|denken** *think . . . up; imagine* A h m [ach, ach]	*brennen	5
aus|drehen *turn off* A h w	machen	21
aus|drücken *squeeze out; express* A h w	machen	21

auseinander|setzen (D) *explain (to sb)* A h w   heizen   14

aus|fahren *take out; deliver; pull out* A h (**sein** when intrans.) st [ä, u, a]   tragen   38

aus|fallen *drop/turn out; be cancelled* s st [ä, iel, a]   *schlafen   27

aus|fragen (**nach** + D/**über** + A) *question (about)* A h w   machen   21

aus|führen *carry out; export* A h w   machen   21

aus|füllen *fill in/up* A h w   machen   21

aus|geben *give out;* (**für** + A) *spend (on)* A h st [i, a, e]   geben   9

aus|gehen *go out; end* s st [ing, ang]   *hängen   12

aus|gießen (**aus** + D) *pour out (of)* A h st [o, o]   schießen   26

aus|gleichen (**durch** + A) *compensate for (by)* A h st [i, i]   gleichen   10

aus|graben *dig up* A h st [ä, u, a]   tragen   38

aus|grenzen aus + D *exclude from* A h w   heizen   14

aus|halten *stand; endure* A h st [ä, ie, a]   *schlafen   27

aus|hängen *put up* A h w   machen   21

aus|helfen mit + D/**bei** + D *help with* D h st [i, a, o]   sprechen   33

sich aus|kennen (**mit** + D/**in** + D) *know one's way around (sth)* h m [a, a]   brennen   5

aus|kommen mit + D/**ohne** + A *manage on/without* s st [am, o]   kommen   17

aus|kratzen (**aus** + D) *scrape out; scratch out* A h w   heizen   14

aus|kugeln *dislocate* A h w   angeln   1

aus|lachen *laugh at* A h w   machen   21

aus|laden aus + D *unload from* A h st [ä, u, a]   *tragen   38

aus|lassen *leave out;* (**an** + D) *vent
  (on)* A h st [ä, ie, a]   *schlafen   27
  sich aus|lassen über + A *talk/write
  about* h st [ä, ie, a]   *schlafen   27
aus|laufen *run out* s st [äu, ie, au]   laufen   20
aus|legen (D) *lend (sb)* A h w   machen   21
  aus|legen (**für** + A) *pay out (for sb)*
  A h w   machen   21
aus|leihen (D/**an** + D) *lend (sb)* A h
  st [ie, ie]   schreiben   28
  sich [D] **aus|leihen** (**von** + D)
  borrow (from) A h st [ie, ie]   schreiben   28
aus|liefern (D/**an** + A) *hand over (to)*
  A h w   angeln   1
aus|löschen *put out; obliterate* A h w   machen   21
aus|lösen *cause* A h w   heizen   14
aus|machen (**mit** + D) *agree (with);
  make a difference; put out* A h w   machen   21
aus|packen (**aus** + D) *unpack (from)*
  A h w   machen   21
aus|pressen *squeeze (out)* A h w   heizen   14
aus|probieren *try out* A h w   informieren   15
aus|radieren *rub out* A h w   informieren   15
aus|räumen (**aus** + D) *clear out (of)*
  A h w   machen   21
aus|rechnen *work out* A h w   atmen   2
aus|reden (D) *talk (sb) out of* A h w   reden   24
aus|reichen (**zu** + D) *be enough (for)*
  h w   machen   21
aus|reisen aus + D (**nach** + D) *leave
  (for)* s w   heizen   14
aus|reißen *tear out* A h st [i, i]   beißen   3
aus|richten (**auf** + A) *direct
  (towards); tell; pass on* A h w   reden   24
aus|rotten *stamp out* A h w   reden   24
aus|rücken *move out; turn out* s w   machen   21
aus|rufen *call out* A h st [ie, u]   rufen   25
sich aus|ruhen *have a rest* h w   machen   21

aus|rutschen *slip* s w	machen	21
aus|sagen *express; say* A h w	machen	21
aus|schalten *switch off; exclude* A h w	reden	24
aus|schauen nach + D *look out for* h w	machen	21
aus|scheiden *exclude; eliminate* A h st [ie, ie]	*schreiben	28
aus|scheiden aus + D *leave* s st [ie, ie]	*schreiben	28
aus|schenken *pour out; serve* A h w	machen	21
sich aus|schlafen *have a good sleep* h st [ä, ie, a]	schlafen	27
aus|schlagen *reject; kick/swing out* A h st [ä, u, a]	tragen	38
aus|schließen aus + D *exclude from* A h st [o, o]	schießen	26
aus|schmücken *embellish* A h w	machen	21
aus|schöpfen *scoop out;* (**aus** + D) *bale out (of/from)* A h w	machen	21
aus|schreiben *write out* A h st [ie, ie]	schreiben	28
aus|schütten *empty out* A h w	reden	24
aus|schweifen *run riot* s w	machen	21
aus|schwenken *swing out* s w	machen	21
aus|sehen (**nach** + D/**wie**) *look (like)* h st [ie, a, e]	sehen	29
äußern *express* A h w	angeln	1
sich äußern über + A *give one's view on* h w	angeln	1
sich äußern in + D/**durch** + A *be expressed in/through* h w	angeln	1
aus|setzen (D) *expose (to)* A h w	heizen	14
aus|sperren *lock out* A h w	machen	21
aus|spielen gegen + A *play off against* A h w	machen	21
aus|sprechen *express; pronounce* A h st [i, a, o]	sprechen	33
aus|statten mit + D *equip with* A h w	reden	24

aus|stehen *endure; be outstanding*		
A h st [and, and]	stehen	34
aus|steigen aus + D *get out of; alight*		
from s st [ie, ie]	schreiben	28
aus|stellen *display; make out* A h w	machen	21
aus|sterben *die out* s st [i, a, o]	sprechen	33
aus|stoßen *put out;* (**aus** + D) *expel*		
(from) A h st [ö, ie, o]	stoßen	36
aus|strahlen *radiate; broadcast*		
A h w	machen	21
aus|strecken *extend; stretch out*		
A h w	machen	21
aus|strömen *radiate; stream out* A h		
(**sein** when intrans.) w	machen	21
sich [D] **aus|suchen** *choose* A h w	machen	21
aus|tauschen (**gegen** + A) *exchange*		
(for) A h w	machen	21
aus|teilen (**unter** + D/**an** + A)		
distribute (among/to) A h w	machen	21
aus|tilgen *exterminate* A h w	machen	21
aus|tragen *deliver* A h st [ä, u, a]	tragen	38
aus|treten *tread out; wear down*		
A h st [itt, a, e]	*geben	9
aus|treten aus + A *leave* s st		
[itt, a, e]	*geben	9
aus|üben *carry on (trade); hold*		
(power) A h w	machen	21
aus|ver'kaufen *sell out* A h w	machen	21
aus|wählen (**aus** + D/**unter** + D)		
choose (from/from among) A h w	machen	21
aus|wandern (**nach** + D/**in** + A)		
emigrate (to) s w	angeln	1
aus|weichen + D *get out of the way*		
of s st [i, i]	gleichen	10
aus|werten *evaluate* A h w	reden	24
sich aus|wirken auf + A *have an*		
effect on h w	machen	21
aus|zahlen *pay out/off* A h w	machen	21

aus|zeichnen mit + D/**durch** + A
honour with A h w   atmen   2
aus|ziehen (with **haben**) *pull out;*
undress; (with **sein**) *set out;*
(**aus** + D) *move out of* s st [og, og]   *kriechen   19

backen *bake* A h st [ä, u/ackte,
   acken]   *tragen   38
baden *bath; bathe* A h w   reden   24
baggern *excavate; dredge* A h w   angeln   1
bahnen (D) *clear (for sb)* A h w   machen   21
balancieren *balance;* (**über** + A) *pick*
one's way (over) s w   informieren   15
ballen *clench* A h w   machen   21
bändigen *tame* A h w   machen   21
bangen um + A/**vor** + D *be anxious*
about/afraid of h w   machen   21
bannen *captivate; ward off* A h w   machen   21
basieren auf + D *be based on* A h w   informieren   15
basteln *make;* (**an** + D) *be working*
(on); tinker (with) A h w   angeln   1
bauen *build;* (**auf** + A) *rely (on)*
  A h w   machen   21
baumeln an + D *dangle from* h w   angeln   1
bauschen *billow* A h w   machen   21
be'absichtigen *intend* A h w   machen   21
be'achten *heed* A h w   reden   24
be'anspruchen *claim; demand*
  A h w   machen   21
be'anstanden *complain about* A h w   reden   24
be'antragen *apply for* A h w   machen   21
be'antworten (D) *answer (for sb)*
  A h w   reden   24
be'arbeiten *arrange; handle;*
  (**mit** + D) *treat (with)* A h w   reden   24
be'aufsichtigen *supervise* A h w   machen   21
be'auftragen mit + D *entrust with*
  A h w   machen   21

be'bauen *build on;* (**mit** + **D**) *develop*		
(*with*) A h w	machen	21
beben (**vor** + **D**) *tremble (with)* h w	machen	21
sich be'danken (**bei** + **D/für** + **A**) *say*		
thank you (to/for) h w	machen	21
be'dauern *regret; feel sorry for*		
A h w	angeln	1
be'decken mit + **D** *cover with* A h w	machen	21
be'denken *consider* A h m [ach, ach]	*brennen	5
be'deuten *mean* A h w	reden	24
be'dienen *wait on* A h w	machen	21
be'dingen *require* A h w	machen	21
be'drängen (**mit** + **D**) *assail (with);*		
pester (with) A h w	machen	21
be'drohen *threaten; endanger* A h w	machen	21
be'drücken *depress* A h w	machen	21
sich be'eilen (**bei** + **D**) *hurry up*		
(*with*) h w	machen	21
be'eindrucken *impress* A h w	machen	21
be'einflussen *influence* A h w	heizen	14
be'einträchtigen *restrict; spoil* A h w	machen	21
be'enden/be'endigen *finish* A h w	reden/machen	24/21
be'engen *cramp; restrict* A h w	machen	21
be'erdigen *bury* A h w	machen	21
be'fähigen *enable* A h w	machen	21
be'fahren *drive on; use* A h st [ä,		
u, a]	tragen	38
be'fallen *befall; overcome* A h st		
[ä, iel, a]	*schlafen	27
sich be'fassen mit + **D** *concern*		
oneself/deal with h w	heizen	14
be'fehlen *order* D h st [ie, a, o]	*stehlen	35
be'festigen (**mit** + **D/an** + **D**) *fix*		
(*with/to*) A h w	machen	21
sich be'finden *be (situated)* h st		
[a, u]	binden	4
be'flecken *stain* A h w	machen	21
be'fliegen *fly (route)* A h st [o, o]	kriechen	19

be'fördern mit + D/**per** + A *transport*
   by A h w   angeln   1
 be'fördern zu + D *promote (to the*
   post/rank of) A h w   angeln   1
be'frachten mit + D *load with* A h w   reden   24
be'fragen über + A/**nach** + D *question*
   about; ask for A h w   machen   21
be'freien von + A *free from* A h w   machen   21
be'fremden *put off; take aback*
   A h w   reden   24
sich be'freunden mit + D *become*
   friends with h w   reden   24
be'friedigen *satisfy* A h w   machen   21
be'fruchten *fertilize* A h w   reden   24
be'fugen *authorize* A h w   machen   21
be'fürchten *fear* A h w   reden   24
be'fürworten *support* A h w   reden   24
be'gatten *mate with* A h w   reden   24
sich be'geben (in + A) *proceed (into)*
   h st [i, a, e]   geben   9
be'gegnen *meet; counter* D s w   atmen   2
be'gehen *commit* A h st [ing, ang] *hängen   12
be'gehren *desire* A h w   machen   21
be'geistern (für + A) *fire with*
   enthusiasm (for) A h w   angeln   1
be'gießen *water; baste;* (**mit** + D)
   pour . . . over A h st [o, o]   schießen   26
be'ginnen (mit + D) *start (on)* A h
   st [a, o]   *sprechen   33
be'glaubigen *certify;* (**bei** + D)
   accredit (to) A h w   machen   21
be'gleiten (an + D/**auf** + D)
   accompany (on) A h w   reden   24
be'glückwünschen zu + D *congratulate*
   on A h w   machen   21
be'gnadigen *pardon* A h w   machen   21
sich be'gnügen mit + D *make do with*
   h w   machen   21

be'graben *bury* A h st [ä, u, a]	tragen	38
be'greifen *understand* A h st [iff, iff]	greifen	11
be'grenzen (auf + A) *restrict (to)* A h w	heizen	14
be'gründen *give reasons for* A h w	reden	24
be'grüßen *greet; welcome* A h w	heizen	14
be'gutachten *report on; survey* A h w	reden	24
be'halten *keep (on); remember* A h st [ä, ie, a]	*schlafen	27
be'handeln (mit + D/**wegen** + G) *treat (with/for)* A h w	angeln	1
be'harren auf + D *persist in; insist on* h w	machen	21
be'haupten *maintain* A h w	reden	24
sich be'haupten *assert oneself* h w	reden	24
sich be'helfen mit + D *make do with* h st [i, a, o]	sprechen	33
be'helligen *pester* A h w	machen	21
be'herbergen *accommodate* A h w	machen	21
be'herrschen *control; master* A h w	machen	21
be'hexen *bewitch* A h w	heizen	14
be'hindern (in + D) *hinder (in)* A h w	angeln	1
be'hüten vor + D *protect from* A h w	reden	24
bei|be'halten *retain* A h st [ä, ie, a]	*schlafen	27
bei|bringen (D) *teach (sb)* A h m [ach, ach]	*brennen	5
beichten *confess* A h w	reden	24
bei|fügen (D) *enclose (with)* A h w	machen	21
bei|geben (D) *add (to)* A h st [i, a, e]	geben	9
bei|kommen *get the better of; overcome* D s st [am, o]	kommen	17
bei|legen (D) *enclose (with); bestow (on)* A h w	machen	21
bei|liegen (D) *be enclosed (with)* h st [a, e]	sehen	29

bei|springen *rush to the aid of* D s st [a, u]	klingen	16
beißen (in + A/auf + A) *bite (into/ on)* A h st [i, i]	beißen	3
bei|stehen *help; stand by* D h st [and, and]	stehen	34
bei|tragen zu + D *contribute to* A h st [ä, u, a]	tragen	38
bei|treten *join* D s st [itt, a, e]	*geben	9
be'jahen *say yes to; approve of* A h w	machen	21
be'jammern *lament (for)* A h w	angeln	1
be'jubeln *acclaim* A h w	angeln	1
be'kämpfen *combat* A h w	machen	21
bekannt|geben *announce* A h st [i, a, e]	geben	9
bekannt|machen *announce; publish* A h w	machen	21
be'kehren zu + D *convert to* A h w	machen	21
be'kennen *admit* A h m [a, a]	brennen	5
sich be'kennen zu + D *acknowledge* h m [a, a]	brennen	5
sich be'klagen (über + A/bei + D) *complain (about/to)* h w	machen	21
be'kleckern (mit + D) *spill (sth) on* A h w	angeln	1
be'klemmen *oppress* A h w	machen	21
be'kommen *get* A h st [am, o]	kommen	17
be'kräftigen *confirm* A h w	machen	21
sich be'kreuzigen *cross oneself* h w	machen	21
be'laden (mit + D) *load up (with)* A h st [ä, u, a]	*tragen	38
be'lagern *besiege* A h w	angeln	1
be'lasten *load; pollute* A h w	reden	24
be'lästigen *pester* A h w	machen	21
be'leben *enliven* A h w	machen	21
be'legen (mit + D) *cover (with); reserve* A h w	machen	21

be'lehren *enlighten;* (**über** + A)		
inform (about) A h w	machen	21
be'leidigen *insult* A h w	machen	21
be'leuchten *illuminate* A h w	reden	24
be'lichten *expose; light* A h w	reden	24
be'lieben *like* A h w	machen	21
be'liefern mit + D *supply with* A h w	angeln	1
bellen *bark (out)* A h w	machen	21
be'lohnen mit + D/**für** + A *reward*		
with/for A h w	machen	21
be'lüften *ventilate* A h w	reden	24
be'lustigen *amuse* A h w	machen	21
sich be'lustigen über + A *make fun*		
of h w	machen	21
sich be'mächtigen *seize* G h w	machen	21
be'malen *paint* A h w	machen	21
be'mängeln (**an** + D) *criticize*		
(about) A h w	angeln	1
be'merken *notice; remark* A h w	machen	21
be'messen nach + D *measure by*		
A h w	heizen	14
be'mitleiden *pity* A h w	reden	24
sich be'mühen (**um** + A) *try (to help/*		
to obtain) h w	machen	21
be'nachrichtigen von + D *inform of*		
A h w	machen	21
be'nachteiligen *handicap;*		
discriminate against A h w	machen	21
be'nebeln *befuddle* A h w	angeln	1
sich be'nehmen (**wie**) *behave (like)*		
h st [imm, a, omm]	*sprechen	33
be'neiden (**um** + A) *envy (sth)*		
A h w	reden	24
be'nennen (**nach** + D) *name (after/*		
for) A h m [a, a]	brennen	5
be'nötigen *require* A h w	machen	21
be'nutzen/be'nützen (**für** + A/**als**) *use*		
(for/as) A h w	heizen	14

be'obachten (an + D) *observe (about sb)* A h w	reden	24
be'pflanzen mit + D *plant with* A h w	heizen	14
be'raten *advise* A h st [ä, ie, a]	*schlafen	27
be'rauben *rob; (G) deprive (of sth)* A h w	machen	21
sich be'rauschen (an + D) *get drunk (on)* h w	machen	21
be'rechnen *calculate* A h w	atmen	2
be'rechnen (D) mit + D *charge (sb) . . . for* A h w	atmen	2
be'rechtigen zu + D *entitle to* A h w	machen	21
be'reden *talk over; persuade* A h w	reden	24
sich be'reichern an + D *make a lot of money out of* h w	angeln	1
be'reiten (D/für + A) *prepare (for sb)* A h w	reden	24
be'reuen *regret* A h w	machen	21
bergen *rescue; hide* A h st [i, a, o]	sprechen	33
be'richten (D) *report (to sb)* A h w	reden	24
be'richten über + A/von + D *report on* h w	reden	24
bersten *shatter* s st [i, a, o]	*sprechen	33
be'rücksichtigen *consider; make allowances for* A h w	machen	21
be'rufen (in + A) *appoint (to)* A h st [ie, u]	rufen	25
sich be'rufen auf + A *refer to* h st [ie, u]	rufen	25
be'ruhen auf + D *be based on* h w	machen	21
be'ruhigen *calm down; (über + A) reassure (about)* A h w	machen	21
be'rühren *touch* A h w	machen	21
be'sagen *mean* A h w	machen	21
be'sänftigen *calm down* A h w	machen	21
be'schädigen *damage* A h w	machen	21
be'schaffen (D) *obtain (for sb)* A h w	machen	21

be'schäftigen *employ* A h w	machen	21
sich be'schäftigen mit + D *busy*		
oneself with h w	machen	21
be'schämen *shame* A h w	machen	21
be'schatten *shadow; follow secretly*		
A h w	reden	24
be'scheinigen (D) *confirm (to sb)*		
in writing A h w	machen	21
be'schenken *give a present to* A h w	machen	21
be'scheren (mit + D) *give (sth as)*		
a Christmas present to A h w	machen	21
be'schildern *label; sign* A h w	angeln	1
be'schimpfen *swear at* A h w	machen	21
be'schlagen *mist up* s st [ä, u, a]	tragen	38
be'schlagnahmen *confiscate* A h w	machen	21
be'schleunigen *speed up* A h w	machen	21
be'schließen *resolve; end* A h st		
[o, o]	schießen	26
be'schmieren (mit + D) *smear/daub/*		
spread (with) A h w	machen	21
be'schmutzen *make dirty* A h w	heizen	14
be'schneiden *prune* A h st [itt, itt]	*streiten	37
be'schränken auf + A *restrict to*		
A h w	machen	21
be'schreiben *describe* A h st [ie, ie]	schreiben	28
be'schuldigen (G) *accuse (of)*		
A h w	machen	21
be'schützen (vor + D) *protect (from)*		
A h w	heizen	14
sich be'schweren bei + D/über + A		
complain to/about h w	machen	21
be'schwichtigen *pacify* A h w	machen	21
be'schwören *swear to; conjure up*		
A h st [o, o]	*kriechen	19
be'seitigen *remove* A h w	machen	21
be'setzen *occupy;* (mit + D) *fill*		
(with) A h w	heizen	14
be'sichtigen *view; inspect* A h w	machen	21

be'siedeln (mit + D) *settle/populate*		
(with) A h w	angeln	1
be'siegen *defeat* A h w	machen	21
sich be'sinnen *think things over;*		
change one's mind h st [a, o]	sprechen	33
sich be'sinnen auf + A *remember*		
h st [a, o]	sprechen	33
be'sitzen *own* A h st [aß, ess]	*fressen	8
be'sorgen *get; take care of* A h w	machen	21
be'spielen *make a recording on*		
(tape, etc.) A h w	machen	21
be'sprechen *discuss* A h st [i, a, o]	sprechen	33
sich be'sprechen über + A *confer*		
about h st [i, a, o]	sprechen	33
be'spritzen *splash* A h w	heizen	14
besser|gehen (impers.: **es geht** D		
besser) *feel better* D s st [ing, ang]	*hängen	12
sich bessern *mend one's ways* h w	angeln	1
be'stärken (in + D) *confirm (in)*		
A h w	machen	21
be'stätigen (als) *confirm (as)* A h w	machen	21
be'stäuben *pollinate* A h w	machen	21
be'staunen *marvel at* A h w	machen	21
be'stechen *bribe; win over* A h st		
[i, a, o]	sprechen	33
be'stecken mit + D *stick . . . on*		
A h w	machen	21
be'stehen *exist* h st [and, and]	stehen	34
be'stehen auf + D *insist on* h st		
[and, and]	stehen	34
be'stehen aus + D/in + D *consist*		
of/in h st [and, and]	stehen	34
be'stehen vor + D *stand up to* h st		
[and, and]	stehen	34
bestehen|bleiben *persist* s st [ie, ie]	schreiben	28
be'steigen *mount* A h st [ie, ie]	schreiben	28
be'stellen (bei + D) *order (from)*		
A h w	machen	21

be'stellen (D) *pass . . . on (to sb)*
 A h w   machen   21
be'sticken *embroider* A h w   machen   21
be'stimmen *determine;* (**für** + A)
 intend (for) A h w   machen   21
be'strafen (**für** + A/**wegen** + G) *punish*
 (for) A h w   machen   21
be'strahlen *floodlight; irradiate* A h w   machen   21
be'streichen (**mit** + D) *spread (with)*
 A h st [i, i]   gleichen   10
be'streiten *dispute; finance* A h st
 [itt, itt]   streiten   37
be'streuen mit + D *sprinkle with*
 A h w   machen   21
be'stürzen *dismay* A h w   heizen   14
be'suchen *visit; attend (e.g. school)*
 A h w   machen   21
sich be'tätigen *busy oneself;* (**als**) *act*
 (as) h w   machen   21
be'täuben *deaden* A h w   machen   21
sich be'teiligen an + D *participate in*
 h w   machen   21
beten (**für** + A/**um** + A) *pray (for)*
 h w   reden   24
be'teuern *affirm; protest* A h w   angeln   1
be'tonen *stress* A h w   machen   21
be'trachten *look at;* (**als**) *regard (as)*
 A h w   reden   24
be'tragen *amount to* N h st [ä, u, a]   tragen   38
 sich be'tragen (D + **gegenüber**)
 behave (towards) h st [ä, u, a]   tragen   38
be'treffen *concern; affect* A h st
 [i, af, o]   *sprechen   33
be'treiben *tackle; pursue* A h st
 [ie, ie]   schreiben   28
be'treten *walk on to/into* A h st
 [itt, a, e]   *geben   9
be'treuen *look after* A h w   machen   21

sich be'trinken *get drunk* h st [a, u]	klingen	16
be'trügen *deceive;* (**um** + A) *swindle*		
(out of) A h st [o, o]	kriechen	19
betteln (bei + D) **um** + A *beg (sb)*		
for h w	angeln	1
beugen *bend; conjugate* A h w	machen	21
be'unruhigen *worry (sb)* A h w	machen	21
be'urlauben *give leave of absence to*		
A h w	machen	21
be'urteilen *assess* A h w	machen	21
be'völkern *populate* A h w	angeln	1
be'vollmächtigen *authorize* A h w	machen	21
bevor|stehen *be about to happen to*		
D h st [and, and]	stehen	34
be'vorzugen (**vor** + D) *prefer (to)*		
A h w	machen	21
be'wachen *guard* A h w	machen	21
be'waffnen (mit + D) *arm (with)*		
A h w	atmen	2
be'wahren vor + D *preserve from*		
A h w	machen	21
sich be'währen als *prove to be* N h w	machen	21
be'wältigen *deal with; cope with*		
A h w	machen	21
be'wässern *irrigate* A h w	angeln	1
be'wegen *move;* (**zu** + D) *persuade*		
(into) (st in this meaning)	machen/	
A h w/s [o, o]	kriechen	21/19
be'weinen *mourn* A h w	machen	21
be'weisen *prove* A h st [ie, ie]	*schreiben	28
sich be'werben um + A *apply for* h st		
[i, a, o]	sprechen	33
be'werfen mit + D *pelt with* A h st		
[i, a, o]	sprechen	33
be'werten (mit + D) *value (at)*		
A h w	reden	24
be'willigen (D) *award (to sb)* A h w	machen	21
be'wirken *bring about* A h w	machen	21

be'wirten *feed;* (mit + D) *serve*		
(with) A h w	reden	24
be'wohnen *live in* A h w	machen	21
sich be'wölken *cloud over* h w	machen	21
be'wundern (wegen + G/für + A)		
admire (for) A h w	angeln	1
be'zahlen (A/für + A) *pay (for sth)*		
A h w	machen	21
be'zähmen *restrain* A h w	machen	21
be'zaubern *enchant* A h w	angeln	1
be'zeichnen (als) *describe (as)* A h w	atmen	2
be'zeugen *testify to* A h w	machen	21
be'ziehen *cover; move/take in;*		
(auf + A) *apply (to)* A h st		
[og, og]	*kriechen	19
sich be'ziehen auf + A *refer to* h st		
[og, og]	*kriechen	19
be'ziffern auf + A *estimate at* A h w	angeln	1
be'zwecken *aim at* A h w	machen	21
be'zweifeln *doubt* A h w	angeln	1
be'zwingen *conquer; control* A h st		
[a, u]	klingen	16
biegen *bend; turn* A h (sein when		
intrans.) st [o, o]	kriechen	19
bieten *offer;* (für + A/auf + A) *bid*		
(for) A h st [o, o]	*kriechen	19
bilden (aus + D) *form (from); mould*		
A h w	reden	24
billigen *approve* A h w	machen	21
binden (an + D/zu + D) *tie (to/into)*		
A h st [a, u]	binden	4
bitten um + A/zu + D *ask for/to* A h		
st [at, et]	*geben	9
blähen *swell* A h w	machen	21
blamieren *disgrace* A h w	informieren	15
blasen *blow* A h st [ä, ie, a]	*schlafen	27
blättern *flake (off)* s w	angeln	1
blättern in + D *leaf through* h w	angeln	1

bleiben *stay;* (D) *remain (for sb)*		
N s st [ie, ie]	schreiben	28
bleichen *bleach; become bleached*		
A h w	machen	21
blenden *dazzle* A h w	reden	24
blicken *look; glance* h w	machen	21
blinken *indicate (when driving);*		
gleam h w	machen	21
blinzeln *blink; wink* h w	angeln	1
blitzen *flash* (impers.: **es blitzt** *there's*		
lightning) h w	heizen	14
blockieren *blockade; jam* A h w	informieren	15
blödeln *fool about* h w	angeln	1
blöken *bleat; low* h w	machen	21
blühen *bloom; flower* h w	machen	21
bluten (aus + D) *bleed (from)* h w	reden	24
bocken *refuse (to go on)* h w	machen	21
bohren (in + A) *bore (into)* A h w	machen	21
bohren in + D *drill (tooth)* h w	machen	21
bombardieren *bomb* A h w	informieren	15
borgen (D) *lend (to sb)* A h w	machen	21
borgen von + D *borrow from* A h w	machen	21
bowlen *bowl* h w	machen	21
boxen (gegen + A) *box (sb/against*		
sb) h w	heizen	14
braten *fry; roast; bake* A h st		
[ä, ie, a]	*schlafen	27
brauchen *need; take (time)* A h w	machen	21
brauen *brew* A h w	machen	21
bräunen *tan; brown* A h w	machen	21
brausen *roar; shower; race* h w	heizen	14
brechen (mit + D) *break (with)* A h		
(**sein** when intrans.) st [i, a, o]	sprechen	33
bremsen *brake* A h w	heizen	14
brennen *burn;* (**auf** + A) *be bent (on)*		
A h m [a, a]	brennen	5
bringen (D) *bring (to sb); take (to*		
sb); broadcast A h m [ach, ach]	*brennen	5

bringen (A) **um** + A *do (sb) out of*		
h m [ach, ach]	*brennen	5
brühen *brew; make* A h w	machen	21
brüllen *roar;* (**vor** + D/**nach** + D)		
bellow (with/to) A h w	machen	21
brummen *buzz; drone* A h w	machen	21
brüskieren *offend* A h w	informieren	15
brutalisieren *brutalize* A h w	informieren	15
brüten *brood;* (**über** + D) *ponder*		
(over) h w	reden	24
buchen *book; enter* A h w	machen	21
buchstabieren *spell* A h w	informieren	15
sich bücken (**nach** + D) *bend down*		
(for sth) h w	machen	21
bügeln *iron* A h w	angeln	1
buhlen um + A *court* h w	machen	21
bummeln *stroll* s w	angeln	1
bumsen *bang* A h w	heizen	14
bündeln *bundle up* A h w	angeln	1
bürgen für + A *vouch for; guarantee*		
h w	machen	21
bürsten *brush* A h w	reden	24
büßen A/**für** + A *atone for* h w	heizen	14
campen *camp* h w	machen	21
changieren *shimmer* h w	informieren	15
charakterisieren *characterize* A h w	informieren	15
checken *check; examine* A h w	machen	21
chiffrieren *(en)code* A h w	informieren	15
chloren/chlorieren *chlorinate* A h w	machen/	
	informieren	21/15
choreographieren *choreograph*		
A h w	informieren	15
christianisieren *Christianize* A h w	informieren	15
computerisieren *computerize* A h w	informieren	15
cutten *edit; cut* A h w	reden	24
dabei|bleiben *stick to it* s st [ie, ie]	schreiben	28

dabei|haben *have around; have with one* A h m [at, att, a]   *brennen   5

da|bleiben *stay there* s st [ie, ie]   schreiben   28

dagegen|setzen *object* A h w   heizen   14

dagegen|sprechen *be against it* h st [i, a, o]   sprechen   33

daher|kommen *turn up* s st [am, o]   kommen   17

daher|reden *blather on; talk/say off the cuff* A h w   reden   24

sich dahin|bewegen *move off* h w   machen   21

dahin|sagen *say . . . without thinking* A h w   machen   21

dahinter|stehen *stand by it/them* h st [and, and]   stehen   34

dahin|ziehen *drift by* s st [og, og]   *kriechen   19

dämmen *retain; keep in* A h w   machen   21

dämmern *become light; become dark; doze* h w   angeln   1

dampfen (vor + D) *steam (with)* (with **haben**); *steam off* (with **sein**) w   machen   21

dämpfen *steam; deaden* A h w   machen   21

daneben|gehen *miss* s st [ing, ang]   *hängen   12

danken (für + A) *thank (for)* D h w   machen   21

daran|gehen *set about it* s st [ing, ang]   *hängen   12

dar|bieten *proffer; present* A h st [o, o]   *kriechen   19

darein|reden *interrupt* D h w   reden   24

dar|legen (D) *explain (to sb)* A h w   machen   21

dar|stellen *represent; act* A h w   machen   21

darüber|liegen *be higher* h st [a, e]   sehen   29

darüber|stehen *be above such things* h st [and, and]   stehen   34

darunter|liegen *be lower* h st [a, e]   sehen   29

sich darunter|mischen *mingle with them* h w   machen   21

da|stehen *stand there* h st [and, and]   stehen   34

datieren (aus + D) *date (from)*
A h w — informieren — 15
dauern *last* h w — angeln — 1
davon|fahren (D) *leave; leave (sb)*
behind s st [ä, u, a] — tragen — 38
davon|kommen (mit + D) *escape*
(with) s st [am, o] — kommen — 17
davon|laufen *run away* s st [äu, ie,
au] — laufen — 20
sich davon|machen (mit + D) *make*
off (with) h w — machen — 21
dazu|geben *add* A h st [i, a, e] — geben — 9
dazu|ge'hören *go with it/them* h w — machen — 21
dazu|kommen *come too; turn up* s st
[am, o] — kommen — 17
dazu|rechnen *add on; also consider*
A h w — atmen — 2
dazu|tun *add; help with* A h st [at, a] — tun — 39
dazu|ver'dienen *earn on the side*
A h w — machen — 21
dazwischen|kommen (D) *complicate*
matters (for sb) s st [am, o] — kommen — 17
dazwischen|reden *interrupt* h w — reden — 24
dazwischen|treten *intervene* s st
[itt, a, e] — *geben — 9
debattieren *debate;* (**über** + A/**mit**
+ D) *discuss (sth/with sb)*
A h w — informieren — 15
dechiffrieren *decode* A h w — informieren — 15
decken *cover; spread* A h w — machen — 21
 sich decken mit + D *coincide with*
h w — machen — 21
defilieren *march past;* (**vor** + D)
parade (before) h/s w — informieren — 15
definieren *define* A h w — informieren — 15
degradieren (zu + D) *demote (to)*
A h w — informieren — 15
dehnen *stretch (out)* A h w — machen — 21

deklarieren (als) *declare (to be)*
   A h w   informieren   15
dekorieren (mit + D) *decorate (with)*
   A h w   informieren   15
delegieren (an + A) *delegate (to)*
   A h w   informieren   15
demaskieren *expose* A h w   informieren   15
demokratisieren *democratize* A h w   informieren   15
demolieren *wreck* A h w   informieren   15
demonstrieren (für + A/gegen + A)
   demonstrate (for/against) A h w   informieren   15
demontieren *dismantle; eradicate*
   A h w   informieren   15
demütigen *humiliate; humble* A h w   machen   21
denken (an + A/über + A) *think*
   (of/about) A h m [ach, ach]   *brennen   5
 denken von + D *think of; believe of*
   A h m [ach, ach]   *brennen   5
 sich [D] denken *imagine* A h m
   [ach, ach]   *brennen   5
denunzieren (bei + D) *inform against*
   (to) A h w   informieren   15
deponieren (bei + D) *deposit with*
   A h w   informieren   15
deprimieren *depress* A h w   informieren   15
desinfizieren *disinfect* A h w   informieren   15
destillieren *distil;* **(zu + D)** *condense*
   (into) A h w   informieren   15
detaillieren *explain in detail* A h w   informieren   15
deuteln an + D *quibble about* h w   angeln   1
deuten (auf + A) *point (at/to);*
   interpret A h w   reden   24
dezimieren *decimate* A h w   informieren   15
dichten *seal; write (poetry)* A h w   reden   24
dicht|machen *close down* A h w   machen   21
dienen (in + D/mit + D/zu + D/als)
   serve (in/with/to/as) D h w   machen   21
diffamieren *defame* A h w   informieren   15

differenzieren (zwischen + D)
  differentiate (between) h w   informieren 15
diktieren *dictate* A h w   informieren 15
dirigieren *conduct; run* A h w   informieren 15
diskontieren *give a discount on*
  A h w   informieren 15
diskutieren A/**über** + A *discuss* h w   informieren 15
disponieren über + A *have at one's*
  disposal h w   informieren 15
disqualifizieren *disqualify* A h w   informieren 15
sich distanzieren von + A *disassociate*
  oneself from h w   informieren 15
dividieren (durch + A) *divide (by)*
  A h w   informieren 15
dokumentieren *record* A h w   informieren 15
dolmetschen (bei + D) *act as*
  interpreter (at) h w   machen 21
dominieren *predominate* h w   informieren 15
donnern *thunder;* (**an** + A/**gegen** + A)
  hammer (on) h w   angeln 1
dosieren *measure out* A h w   informieren 15
dozieren (über + A/**an** + D) *lecture*
  (on/at) h w   informieren 15
dramatisieren *dramatize* A h w   informieren 15
drängeln *push; pester* A h w   angeln 1
drängen *push;* (**auf** + A/**zu** + D) *press*
  (for/to) A h w   machen 21
  sich drängen *throng; push one's way*
  h w   machen 21
drehen *turn; film;* (**um** + A) *revolve*
  (around) A h w   machen 21
  drehen an + D *fiddle with* h w   machen 21
dreschen *thresh* A h st [i, o, o]   dreschen 6
dressieren *train (animals)* A h w   informieren 15
driften *drift* s w   reden 24
drillen (in + A) *drill (in)* A h w   machen 21
dringen in + A/**durch** + A *penetrate*
  s st [a, u]   klingen 16

dringen auf + A *insist on* h st [a, u]	klingen	16
drohen (mit + D) *threaten (with)* D h w	machen	21
dröhnen *roar;* **(von** + D) *resound (with)* h w	machen	21
drosseln *throttle back; cut down* A h w	angeln	1
drucken *print* A h w	machen	21
drücken (auf + A/**aus** + D) *press (on); squeeze (out of); depress* A h w	machen	21
sich drücken vor + D *get out of* h w	machen	21
sich ducken *duck;* **(vor** + D) *humble oneself (before)* h w	machen	21
sich duellieren (um + A) *fight a duel (over)* h w	informieren	15
duften nach + D *smell of* h w	reden	24
dulden *tolerate; put up with* A h w	reden	24
düngen *fertilize* A h w	machen	21
dunkeln *darken* A h w	angeln	1
dünsten *steam; braise; stew* A h w	reden	24
durch|arbeiten *work through/out* A h w	reden	24
durch|blättern/durch'blättern *leaf through* A h w	angeln	1
durch|blicken *look through* A h w	machen	21
durch|boxen *force through* A h w	heizen	14
sich durch|boxen *battle through* h w	heizen	14
durch|brechen *break through; appear* s st [i, a, o]	sprechen	33
durch'brechen *break through* A h st [i, a, o]	sprechen	33
durch|brennen *burn out; blow (fuse)* s m [a, a]	brennen	5
durch|bringen *get . . . through* A h m [ach, ach]	*brennen	5
durch|denken *think through* A h m [ach, ach]	*brennen	5

sich durch|drängen durch + A *force* *one's way through* h w	machen	21
durch|dringen durch + A *penetrate;* *come through* s st [a, u]	klingen	16
durch'dringen *penetrate* A h st [a, u]	klingen	16
durcheinander|bringen *get into a* *muddle* A h m [ach, ach]	*brennen	5
durcheinander|ge'raten *get into a* *muddle* s st [ä, ie, a]	*schlafen	27
durch|fahren durch + A *drive* *(straight) through* s st [ä, u, a]	tragen	38
durch'fahren *travel through* A h st [ä, u, a]	tragen	38
durch|fallen *fall through;* **(in** + D/**bei** + D) *fail (in)* s st [ä, iel, a]	*schlafen	27
sich durch|finden durch + A *find one's* *way through/around* h st [a, u]	binden	4
durch'fliegen *fly through; skim through* A h st [o, o]	kriechen	19
durch|fliegen *fly non-stop* s st [o, o]	kriechen	19
durch|fließen durch + A *flow through* s st [o, o]	schießen	26
durch'forschen *search thoroughly* A h w	machen	21
durch|fressen *eat through* A h st [i, a, e]	fressen	8
durch|führen *carry out/through* A h w	machen	21
durch|führen durch + A/**unter** + D *go* *through/under* h w	machen	21
durch|geben (in + D) *announce (on)* A h st [i, a, e]	geben	9
durch|gehen (durch + A/**bis zu** + D) *go right through (through/to)* s st [ing, ang]	*hängen	12
durch|greifen (gegen + A) *take drastic* *action (against)* h st [iff, iff]	greifen	11
durch|halten *hold out; stand* A h st [ä, ie, a]	*schlafen	27

durch|helfen durch + A *help through*
  D h st [i, a, o]   sprechen   33
sich durch|kämpfen durch + A *battle*
  through h w   machen   21
durch|kommen durch + A *come*
  through; get through s st [am, o]   kommen   17
durch'kreuzen *thwart* A h w   heizen   14
  durch|kreuzen *cross out* A h w   heizen   14
durch|lassen durch + A *let through/in*
  A h st [ä, ie, a]   *schlafen   27
durch|laufen durch + A *run/go through*
  s st [äu, ie, au]   laufen   20
  durch'laufen *cover (distance)* A h st
  [äu, ie, au]   laufen   20
durch'leben *live through* A h w   machen   21
durch|lesen *read through* A h st
  [ie, a, e]   *sehen   29
durch'leuchten *probe; X-ray* A h w   reden   24
durch'löchern *make holes in;* (**mit**
  + D) *riddle (with)* A h w   angeln   1
durch'nässen *soak; drench* A h w   heizen   14
durch|pausen *trace* A h w   heizen   14
durch'queren *travel across/through*
  A h w   machen   21
durch|regnen (impers.) *rain in* h w   atmen   2
durch|reichen durch + A *hand through*
  A h w   machen   21
durch|reisen *pass through* s w   heizen   14
durch|reißen *tear in two* A h st
  [i, i]   beißen   3
durch|schalten *connect; put through*
  A h w   reden   24
durch'schauen *see through;*
  understand A h w   machen   21
durch|schlafen *sleep through* h st
  [ä, ie, a]   schlafen   27
durch|schlagen durch + A *come*
  through s st [ä, u, a]   tragen   38

sich durch|schleichen *slip through* h st		
[i, i]	gleichen	10
durch|sehen *look through* A h st		
[ie, a, e]	sehen	29
durch|setzen *carry through* A h w	heizen	14
sich durch|setzen gegen + A *assert*		
oneself against h w	heizen	14
durch|sickern *seep through; leak out*		
s w	angeln	1
durch|streichen *delete* A h st [i, i]	gleichen	10
durch|strömen durch + A *stream*		
through s w	machen	21
durch|suchen *search through* A h w	machen	21
durch'suchen nach + D *search for*		
A h w	machen	21
durch|wählen *dial direct* h w	machen	21
durch|wühlen nach + D *ransack (for)*		
A h w	machen	21
durch|ziehen *pull through* A h st		
[og, og]	*kriechen	19
durch'ziehen *run through* A h st		
[og, og]	*kriechen	19
dürfen *be allowed to; may* h m [a, u, u]	dürfen	7
dürsten (nach + D) *thirst (for)*		
(impers.: **es dürstet mich** *I am*		
thirsty) h w	reden	24
sich duschen *take a shower* h w	machen	21
duzen *say 'du' to; be on familiar*		
terms with A h w	heizen	14
ebnen *level; smooth* A h w	atmen	2
ehren mit + D *honour with* A h w	machen	21
eifern für + A/**gegen** + A *agitate*		
for/against h w	angeln	1
sich eignen (als) *be suitable (as)*		
h w	angeln	1
eilen (with **sein**) *hurry;* (with **haben**)		
be urgent w	machen	21

ein|arbeiten *train;* **(in** + A)
incorporate (into) A h w   reden   24
  sich ein|arbeiten in + A *familiarize*
oneself with h w   reden   24
ein|äschern *reduce to ashes; cremate*
A h w   angeln   1
ein|atmen *breathe in* A h w   atmen   2
ein|bauen *build in; incorporate* A h w   machen   21
ein|be'rufen *call (up); convene* A h st
[ie, u]   rufen   25
ein|betten in + A *embed in* A h w   reden   24
ein|beulen *dent* A h w   machen   21
ein|be'ziehen in + A *include in* A h st
[og, og]   *kriechen   19
ein|biegen (in + A) *turn (into [e.g.*
street]) s st [o, o]   kriechen   19
sich [D] ein|bilden *imagine; imagine*
wrongly A h w   reden   24
ein|binden *bind; link in* A h st [a, u]   binden   4
ein|blenden *insert; fade in* A h w   reden   24
ein|brechen in + A/**bei** + D *break in;*
burgle; invade usually s st [i, a, o]   sprechen   33
ein|bringen *bring in* A h m [ach, ach]   *brennen   5
ein|bürgern *naturalize; introduce*
A h w   angeln   1
ein|büßen *lose; forfeit* A h w   heizen   14
ein|dämmern *doze off* s w   angeln   1
ein|deutschen *Germanize* A h w   machen   21
ein|drängen (auf + A) *crowd in*
(upon) s w   machen   21
ein|dringen (in + A) *penetrate (into)*
s st [a, u]   klingen   16
  ein|dringen auf + A *press; urge* s st
[a, u]   klingen   16
ein|drücken *smash in* A h w   machen   21
ein|engen *restrict* A h w   machen   21
ein|fädeln (in + A) *thread (into)*
A h w   angeln   1

ein|fahren in + A *arrive at; pull in;* *bring in* A h (**sein** when intrans.) st [ä, u, a]	tragen	38
ein|fallen (D) *occur (to sb)* s st [ä, iel, a]	*schlafen	33
ein|fallen in + A *join in* s st [ä, iel, a]	*schlafen	33
ein|färben *dye* A h w	machen	21
sich ein|finden *arrive; meet;* (**bei** + D) *report (to sb)* h st [a, u]	binden	4
ein|flechten in + A *weave into* A h st [i, o, o]	dreschen	6
ein|fliegen *fly in* A h (**sein** when intrans.) st [o, o]	kriechen	19
ein|frieren *freeze (up); deep-freeze* h (**sein** when intrans.) st [o, o]	kriechen	19
ein|fügen in + A *fit into* A h w	machen	21
sich ein|fühlen (**in** + A) *empathize* *(with sb)* h w	machen	21
ein|führen (**in** + A) *import (into);* *introduce (into); install (into)* A h w	machen	21
ein|geben *feed in* A h st [i, a, e]	geben	9
ein|gehen *arrive; close down;* (**in** + A) *enter (into)* s st [ing, ang]	*hängen	12
ein|gehen auf + A *agree to; respond* *to* s st [ing, ang]	*hängen	12
ein|ge'stehen *admit; confess* A h st [and, and]	stehen	34
sich ein|ge'wöhnen *settle down* h w	machen	21
ein|gießen (**in** + A) *pour (in); pour* *out* A h st [o, o]	schießen	26
ein|gliedern in + A *incorporate in;* *include in* A h w	angeln	1
ein|graben in + A *bury in; plant in* A h st [ä, u, a]	tragen	38
ein|greifen (**in** + A) *intervene (in)* h st [iff, iff]	greifen	11

sich ein|haken (bei + D) *link arms*
  (with) h w   machen   21
ein|halten *keep (to)* A h st [ä, ie, a]   *schlafen   27
ein|handeln (für + A/**gegen** + A)
  barter (for) A h w   angeln   1
ein|holen *catch up with; haul in* A h w   machen   21
ein|hüllen in + A *wrap up in; shroud*
  in A h w   machen   21
sich einigen (auf + A/**über** + A/**mit**
  + D) *agree (on/about/with)* h w   machen   21
ein|kalkulieren *take into account*
  A h w   informieren 15
ein|kassieren *collect (money)* A h w   informieren 15
ein|kaufen *shop; buy* A h w   machen   21
ein|klammern *bracket* A h w   angeln   1
ein|kleiden *kit out* A h w   reden   24
ein|knicken *bend* A h w   machen   21
ein|kochen *preserve; bottle* A h w   machen   21
ein|kreisen *encircle* A h w   heizen   14
ein|laden (auf + A) *invite (for)* A h
  st [ä, u, a]   *tragen   38
  ein|laden (in + A) *load (into)* A h
  st [ä, u, a]   *tragen   38
ein|lassen *admit;* (**in** + A) *set (into)*
  A h st [ä, ie, a]   *schlafen   27
  sich ein|lassen mit + D/**auf** + A *get*
  mixed up with/in h st [ä, ie, a]   *schlafen   27
ein|laufen *come in; shrink* s st
  [äu, ie, au]   laufen   20
sich ein|leben *settle down* h w   machen   21
ein|legen (in + A) *put (in); pickle;*
  inlay A h w   machen   21
ein|leiten *start; introduce* A h w   reden   24
ein|lenken *give way* (with **haben**);
  (**in** + A) *turn (into)* (with **sein**) w   machen   21
ein|leuchten (D) *be clear (to sb)* h w   reden   24
ein|lösen *cash (cheque)* A h w   heizen   14
ein|machen *preserve; bottle* A h w   machen   21

ein|marschieren in + A *invade* s w	informieren	15
ein|mauern *wall in* A h w	angeln	1
sich ein|mischen (in + A) *interfere* *(in); butt in* h w	machen	21
ein|münden in + A *flow into; lead into* h/s w	reden	24
ein|nehmen *take (up); occupy* A h st [imm, a, omm]	*sprechen	33
ein|ordnen *arrange; classify* A h w	atmen	2
sich ein|ordnen *fit in; get in lane* h w	atmen	2
ein|packen (in + A) *pack (in); wrap up* A h w	machen	21
ein|pflanzen *plant; implant* A h w	heizen	14
ein|prägen (D) *impress on (sb);* **(in** + A) *stamp (into)* A h w	machen	21
ein|quartieren (in + D/**bei** + D) *billet (in/with)* A h w	informieren	15
ein|rahmen *frame* A h w	machen	21
ein|räumen (in + A) *put away (in); admit* A h w	machen	21
ein|rechnen *include* A h w	atmen	2
ein|reden (D) *talk (sb) into believing* A h w	reden	24
ein|regulieren (auf + A) *set (to/at)* A h w	informieren	15
ein|reiben in + A *rub in* A h st [ie, ie]	schreiben	28
ein|reichen *submit; hand in* A h w	machen	21
sich ein|reihen in + A *join* h w	machen	21
ein|richten *equip; furnish; set up* A h w	reden	24
sich ein|richten auf + A *prepare (for)* h w	reden	24
ein|rollen *roll up* A h w	machen	21
ein|rosten *go rusty* s w	reden	24
ein|rücken in + A *march into* s w	machen	21
ein|sacken *subside* s w	machen	21
ein|salzen *salt* A h w	heizen	14

ein|sammeln *pick up; collect* A h w	angeln	1
ein|schalten *switch on; call in* A h w	reden	24
ein|schärfen (D) *impress (on sb)*		
A h w	machen	21
ein|schätzen *judge* A h w	heizen	14
ein|schenken (D) *pour out (for sb)*		
A h w	machen	21
ein|schieben (**in** + A) *put (in); insert*		
A h st [o, o]	kriechen	19
ein|schießen in + A *inject/insert into*		
A h st [o, o]	schießen	26
sich ein|schiffen nach + D *embark for*		
h w	machen	21
ein|schlafen *fall asleep* s st [ä, ie, a]	schlafen	27
ein|schläfern *put to sleep* A h w	angeln	1
ein|schlagen (**in** + A) *knock (into);*		
take up; strike A h st [ä, u, a]	tragen	38
sich ein|schleichen *creep in* h st		
[i, i]	gleichen	10
ein|schließen (**in** + D) *lock up (in)*		
A h st [o, o]	schießen	26
ein|schließen (**in** + A) *include (in)*		
A h st [o, o]	schießen	26
sich ein|schmeicheln bei + D		
ingratiate oneself with h w	angeln	1
ein|schneiden *cut into* A h st [itt, itt]	*streiten	37
ein|schränken *curb;* (**in** + D) *restrict*		
(in) A h w	machen	21
ein|schreiben *register; enter; write*		
down A h st [ie, ie]	schreiben	28
ein|schreiten *intervene;* (**gegen** + A)		
take action (against) s st [itt, itt]	streiten	37
ein|schüchtern *intimidate* A h w	angeln	1
ein|schwenken (**in** + A) *turn (into);*		
fall into line s w	machen	21
ein|sehen *realize* A h st [ie, a, e]	sehen	29
ein|senden (**D/an** + A) *send in (to)*		
A h w/m [a, a]	reden/senden	24/31

ein|setzen *begin; set in* h w	heizen	14
ein|setzen in + A *put in; insert into;* *appoint to* A h w	heizen	14
sich ein|setzen für + A *do what one* *can for* h w	heizen	14
ein|sinken in + D *sink into* h st [a, u]	klingen	16
ein|sortieren in + A *sort/tidy away* *into* A h w	informieren	15
ein|spannen *harness* A h w	machen	21
ein|sparen *cut down/save on* A h w	machen	21
ein|sperren *lock up* A h w	machen	21
ein|springen für + A *stand in for* s st [a, u]	klingen	16
ein|spritzen *inject; (D) inject (sb)* *with* A h w	heizen	14
ein|stecken (in + A) *stick (into); plug* *in* A h w	machen	21
sich [D] ein|stecken *pocket* A h w	machen	21
ein|stehen für + A *vouch/take* *responsibility for* h st [and, and]	stehen	34
ein|steigen in + A *get in/on* s st [ie, ie]	schreiben	28
ein|stellen *put away; employ; adjust;* *close; abandon* A h w	machen	21
sich ein|stellen auf + A *adjust* *oneself to* h w	machen	21
ein|stimmen in + A *join in* h w	machen	21
ein|stoßen *smash in* A h st [ö, ie, o]	stoßen	36
ein|streichen mit + D *spread with* A h st [i, i]	gleichen	10
ein|strömen *pour in* s w	machen	21
ein|studieren *rehearse* A h w	informieren	15
ein|stufen *classify* A h w	machen	21
ein|stürzen *collapse* s w	heizen	14
ein|tauchen *immerse; dive* A h (**sein** *when intrans.*) w	machen	21
ein|tauschen gegen + A *exchange for* A h w	machen	21

ein|teilen *divide up; plan (out)*		
A h w	machen	21
ein|tragen *enter; bring in* A h st		
[ä, u, a]	tragen	38
ein|treffen *arrive; come true* s st		
[i, af, o]	*sprechen	33
ein|treiben *collect; drive in* A h st		
[ie, ie]	schreiben	28
ein|treten in + A *enter* s st [itt, a, e]	*geben	9
ein|treten *kick in* A h st [itt, a, e]	*geben	9
ein|treten für + A *stand up for* s st		
[itt, a, e]	*geben	9
ein|üben *practise* A h w	machen	21
sich ein|ver'leiben *assimilate* h w	machen	21
ein|wandern in + A *(im)migrate*		
(in)to s w	angeln	1
ein|weichen *soak* A h w	machen	21
ein|weihen *open; dedicate;* (**in** + A)		
initiate (into) A h w	machen	21
ein|wenden gegen + A *object to* A h		
w/m [a, a]	reden/senden	24/31
ein|werfen *insert; throw in; smash*		
A h st [i, a, o]	sprechen	33
ein|wickeln in + A *wrap up in* A h w	angeln	1
ein|willigen in + A *consent to* h w	machen	21
ein|wirken auf + A *influence* h w	machen	21
sich ein|wurzeln *take root* h w	angeln	1
ein|zahlen *pay in; deposit* A h w	machen	21
ein|zäunen *fence in* A h w	machen	21
ein|ziehen *pull/draw in; move in (to*		
house) A h (**sein** *when intrans.*) st		
[og, og]	*kriechen	19
eis|laufen *ice-skate* s st [äu, ie, au]	laufen	20
eitern *suppurate* h w	angeln	1
ekeln *disgust* (impers.: **mich ekelt vor**		
+ D . . . *disgusts me*) A h w	angeln	1
sich ekeln vor + D *find . . . repulsive*		
h w	angeln	1

elektrifizieren *electrify* A h w	informieren	15
sich emanzipieren von + D		
emancipate oneself from h w	informieren	15
emp'fangen *receive* A h st [ä, i, a]	*hängen	12
emp'fehlen (D) *recommend (to sb)*		
A h st [ie, a, o]	*stehlen	35
emp'finden (für + A/**als)** *feel (for/to*		
be) A h st [a, u]	binden	4
empören *fill with indignation* A h w		
(past part. **empört**)	machen	21
sich empören über + A *become*		
incensed about h w (past part.		
empört)	machen	21
empor|kommen *rise* s st [am, o]	kommen	17
enden *end; terminate* h w	reden	24
sich engagieren für + A *commit*		
oneself to h w	informieren	15
ent'arten zu + D/**in** + A *degenerate*		
into s w	reden	24
ent'behren *do without* A h w	machen	21
ent'binden (A) *deliver (sb's) baby;*		
release A h st [a, u]	binden	4
ent'blößen *uncover* A h w	heizen	14
ent'decken *discover* A h w	machen	21
ent'ehren *dishonour* A h w	machen	21
ent'eisen *de-ice* A h w	heizen	14
ent'erben *disinherit* A h w	machen	21
ent'fallen *escape (the mind)* D s st		
[ä, iel, a]	*schlafen	27
ent'fallen auf + A *be allotted to* s st		
[ä, iel, a]	*schlafen	27
ent'falten *unfold; expound* A h w	reden	24
sich ent'färben *fade* h w	machen	21
ent'fernen *remove* A h w	machen	21
sich ent'fernen *go away* h w	machen	21
ent'fesseln *unleash* A h w	angeln	1
ent'flammen *arouse; flare up* A h		
(**sein** when intrans.) w	machen	21

ent'fliegen *fly away/off* s st [o, o]	kriechen	19
ent'fliehen *escape from* D s st [o, o]	kriechen	19
ent'fremden (D) *alienate (from)* A h w	reden	24
ent'führen *kidnap; hijack* A h w	machen	21
entgegen|arbeiten *work against* D h w	reden	24
entgegen|bringen *show (love etc.)* D h m [ach, ach]	*brennen	5
entgegen|gehen *be heading for* D s st [ing, ang]	*hängen	12
entgegen|kommen *come to meet; comply with* D s st [am, o]	kommen	17
entgegen|sehen *look forward to* D h st [ie, a, e]	sehen	29
entgegen|setzen (D) *oppose (sth) with* A h w	heizen	14
entgegen|stehen *stand in the way of* D h st [and, and]	stehen	34
entgegen|treten *stand up to; answer* D s st [itt, a, e]	*geben	9
entgegen|wirken *oppose* D h w	machen	21
ent'gegnen (D) *retort (to)* A h w	atmen	2
ent'gehen *escape; escape one's notice* D s st [ing, ang]	*hängen	12
ent'halten *contain* A h st [ä, ie, a]	*schlafen	27
sich ent'halten *abstain/refrain from* G h st [ä, ie, a]	*schlafen	27
ent'hüllen *reveal* A h w	machen	21
ent'kommen *escape from* D s st [am, o]	kommen	17
ent'korken *uncork* A h w	machen	21
ent'kräften *weaken* A h w	reden	24
ent'kriminalisieren *legalize* A h w	informieren	15
ent'laden *unload* A h st [ä, u, a]	*tragen	38
ent'larven als *expose as* A h w	machen	21
ent'lassen aus + D *release from* A h st [ä, ie, a]	*schlafen	27

ent'lasten *ease; relieve* A h w	reden	24
ent'laufen *run away from* D s st		
[äu, ie, au]	laufen	20
ent'leihen *borrow* A h st [ie, ie]	schreiben	28
ent'lohnen für + A *pay for* A h w	machen	21
ent'lüften *ventilate* A h w	reden	24
ent'mannen *castrate; emasculate*		
A h w	machen	21
ent'mensch(lich)en *dehumanize*		
A h w	machen	21
ent'militarisieren *demilitarize* A h w	informieren	15
ent'mutigen *discourage* A h w	machen	21
ent'nehmen (D) *take (from);*		
understand (from) A h st		
[imm, a, omm]	*sprechen	33
ent'nerven *be nerve-racking for*		
A h w	machen	21
sich ent'puppen als *turn out to be*		
h w	machen	21
ent'rätseln *decipher* A h w	angeln	1
ent'reißen (D) *snatch (from sb)*		
A h st [i, i]	beißen	3
ent'rümpeln *clear out* A h w	angeln	1
ent'rüsten über + A *make indignant*		
at A h w	reden	24
ent'schädigen für + A *compensate for*		
A h w	machen	21
ent'schärfen *deactivate; defuse* A h w	machen	21
ent'scheiden (über + A) *decide (on)*		
A h st [ie, ie]	*schreiben	28
sich ent'scheiden für + A/**gegen** + A		
decide in favour of/against h st		
[ie, ie]	*schreiben	28
ent'schlafen *pass away* s st [ä, ie, a]	schlafen	27
sich ent'schließen *decide;* (**zu** + D)		
make up one's mind (to) h st [o, o]	schießen	26
ent'schlüpfen *slip away* s w	machen	21
ent'schuldigen *excuse* A h w	machen	21

sich ent'schuldigen (bei + **D/für** + **A/** **wegen** + **G)** *apologize (to/for/for)*		
h w	machen	21
ent'senden *dispatch* A h w/m [a, a]	reden/senden	24/31
ent'setzen *horrify* A h w	heizen	14
sich entsetzen vor + **D** *be horrified*		
at h w	heizen	14
sich ent'sinnen **G/an** + **A** *recollect*		
h st [a, o]	sprechen	33
ent'sorgen *dispose of* A h w	machen	21
ent'spannen *relax* A h w	machen	21
ent'sprechen *correspond to; comply*		
with D h st [i, a, o]	sprechen	33
ent'springen *spring from* D s st [a, u]	klingen	16
ent'stauben *dust* A h w	machen	21
ent'stehen aus + **D** *arise from* s st		
[and, and]	stehen	34
ent'stellen *distort* A h w	machen	21
ent'tarnen als *reveal as* A h w	machen	21
ent'täuschen *disappoint* A h w	machen	21
ent'wachsen *outgrow* D s st [ä, u, a]	*tragen	38
ent'waffnen *disarm* A h w	atmen	2
ent'wässern *drain* A h w	angeln	1
ent'weichen *escape* s st [i, i]	gleichen	10
ent'weihen *desecrate* A h w	machen	21
ent'werfen *design* A h st [i, a, o]	sprechen	33
ent'werten *cancel* A h w	reden	24
ent'wickeln *produce; develop*		
A h w	angeln	1
sich ent'wickeln (aus + **D/zu** + **D)**		
develop (from/into) h w	angeln	1
ent'wirren *unravel* A h w	machen	21
ent'wöhnen *wean* A h w	machen	21
ent'würdigen *degrade* A h w	machen	21
ent'wurzeln *uproot* A h w	angeln	1
ent'ziehen (D) *take away (from)*		
A h st [og, og]	*kriechen	19
ent'ziffern *decipher* A h w	angeln	1

ent'zücken *delight* A h w	machen	21
ent'zünden *kindle* A h w	reden	24
sich ent'zünden *catch fire; become*		
inflamed h w	reden	24
sich ent'zweien mit + D *fall out with*		
h w	machen	21
er'ahnen *guess* A h w	machen	21
er'arbeiten *work for/on* A h w	reden	24
er'barmen *move to pity* A h w	machen	21
sich er'barmen *take pity on* G h w	machen	21
er'bauen *build; edify* A h w	machen	21
er'beben *shake* s w	machen	21
erben *inherit* A h w	machen	21
er'betteln *get by begging* A h w	angeln	1
er'beuten *carry off* A h w	reden	24
er'bittern *enrage* A h w	angeln	1
er'blicken *catch sight of; see* A h w	machen	21
er'blinden *go blind* s w	reden	24
sich er'brechen *vomit* h st [i, a, o]	sprechen	33
er'bringen *produce* A h m [ach, ach]	*brennen	5
er'denken *make up; invent* A h m		
[ach, ach]	*brennen	5
er'dichten *manufacture; fabricate*		
A h w	reden	24
sich er'dreisten *have the audacity* h w	reden	24
er'drosseln *strangle* A h w	angeln	1
er'drücken *crush; overwhelm* A h w	machen	21
er'dulden *endure* A h w	reden	24
sich er'eifern über + A *get excited*		
about h w	angeln	1
sich er'eignen *happen* h w	atmen	2
er'fahren (von + D/**durch** + A) *find*		
out (from/through) A h st		
[ä, u, a]	tragen	38
er'fassen *grasp; seize* A h w	heizen	14
er'finden *invent* A h st [a, u]	binden	4
er'folgen *be forthcoming* s w	machen	21
er'fordern *demand* A h w	angeln	1

er'forschen *discover; explore* A h w	machen	21
er'fragen *ascertain* A h w	machen	21
er'freuen *please* A h w	machen	21
sich er'freuen *enjoy (e.g. health)* G h w	machen	21
sich er'freuen an + D *take pleasure in* h w	machen	21
er'frieren *freeze (to death)* s st [o, o]	kriechen	19
er'frischen *refresh* A h w	machen	21
er'füllen *grant; fill; fulfil* A h w	machen	21
er'gänzen *complete;* (**durch** + A/**um** + A) *extend (with)* A h w	heizen	14
er'geben *result in* A h st [i, a, e]	geben	9
sich er'geben (**D/in** + A) *surrender (to); submit (to)* h st [i, a, e]	geben	9
sich er'geben aus + D *arise from* h st [i, a, e]	geben	9
er'gehen *go* (impers.: **es ergeht mir . . .** *it's going . . . for me*) s st [ing, ang]	*hängen	12
sich er'gießen (**in** + A) *pour out (into)* h st [o, o]	schießen	26
er'greifen *grasp; seize; take up* A h st [iff, iff]	greifen	11
er'gründen *fathom* A h w	reden	24
er'halten *receive; preserve* A h st [ä, ie, a]	*schlafen	27
er'härten *strengthen* A h w	reden	24
er'heben *raise* A h st [o, o]	kriechen	19
sich er'heben (**gegen** + A/**über** + A) *rise (against/above)* h st [o, o]	kriechen	19
er'heitern *cheer up* A h w	angeln	1
er'hellen *light up* A h w	machen	21
er'hitzen *heat* A h w	heizen	14
sich [D] **er'hoffen von** + D *expect from* A h w	machen	21
er'höhen *raise* A h w	machen	21
sich er'holen *relax;* (**von** + D) *recover*		

(from) h w	machen	21
er'innern an + A *remind of* A h w	angeln	1
sich er'innern an + A *remember* h w	angeln	1
sich er'kälten *catch cold* h w	reden	24
er'kämpfen *win* A h w	machen	21
er'kaufen *buy; win (through sacrifice)* A h w	machen	21
er'kennen an + D *recognize by* A h m [a, a]	brennen	5
er'klären (D) *explain (to sb); declare* A h w	machen	21
er'klingen *ring out* s st [a, u]	klingen	16
er'kranken (**an** + D) *become ill (with)* s w	machen	21
sich er'kundigen nach + D *enquire about* h w	machen	21
er'langen *obtain* A h w	machen	21
er'lassen *enact* A h st [ä, ie, a]	*schlafen	27
er'lauben (D) *allow (sb)* A h w	machen	21
er'läutern *explain* A h w	angeln	1
er'leben *experience* A h w	machen	21
er'ledigen *deal with; finish off* A h w	machen	21
er'leichtern *make easier; relieve* A h w	angeln	1
er'leiden *suffer* A h st [itt, itt]	*streiten	37
er'leuchten *light up* A h w	reden	24
er'liegen *succumb to* D s st [a, e]	sehen	29
er'löschen *die out* s st [i, o, o]	dreschen	6
er'lösen (**von** + D) *rescue (from)* A h w	heizen	14
er'mächtigen *authorize* A h w	machen	21
er'mahnen *admonish* A h w	machen	21
er'mäßigen *reduce* A h w	machen	21
er'messen *gauge* A h st [i, a, e]	fressen	8
er'mitteln *ascertain* A h w	angeln	1
er'möglichen (D) *make possible (for sb)* A h w	machen	21
er'morden *murder* A h w	reden	24

er'müden *make/become tired* A h **(sein** when intrans.) w	reden	24
er'muntern *encourage* A h w	angeln	1
er'mutigen *encourage* A h w	machen	21
er'nähren *feed* A h w	machen	21
sich er'nähren von + D *live on* h w	machen	21
er'nennen zu + D *appoint (to the post of)* A h m [a, a]	brennen	5
er'neuern *replace; renovate* A h w	angeln	1
er'niedrigen *reduce; humiliate* A h w	machen	21
ernten *harvest; win* A h w	reden	24
er'obern *conquer* A h w	angeln	1
er'öffnen *open; (D) reveal (to sb)* A h w	atmen	2
er'örtern *discuss* A h w	angeln	1
er'pressen (mit + D) *blackmail (with)* A h w	heizen	14
er'proben (an + A) *test (on)* A h w	machen	21
er'raten *guess* A h st [ä, ie, a]	*schlafen	27
er'rechnen *calculate* A h w	atmen	2
er'regen *annoy; arouse* A h w	machen	21
sich er'regen über + A *get excited about* h w	machen	21
er'reichen *reach* A h w	machen	21
er'richten *erect; build* A h w	reden	24
er'ringen *gain; win* A h st [a, u]	klingen	16
er'röten (vor + D/**über** + A) *blush (with/at)* s w	reden	24
er'säufen *drown* A h w	machen	21
er'schaffen *create* A h st [uf, a]	*tragen	38
er'schallen *resound* s w/st [o, o] (usually weak except past part. **erschollen**)	machen/ kriechen	21/19
er'scheinen *appear* s st [ie, ie]	schreiben	28
er'schießen *shoot (dead)* A h st [o, o]	schießen	26
er'schlaffen *become limp; weaken* s w	machen	21

er'schlagen *strike dead; kill* A h st [ä, u, a]	tragen	38
sich [D] er'schleichen *get hold of (deviously)* A h st [i, i]	gleichen	10
er'schließen *open up, develop; deduce* A h st [o, o]	schießen	26
er'schöpfen *exhaust* A h w	machen	21
er'schrecken *frighten* A h w	machen	21
er'schrecken **über** + A/**vor** + D *be scared by* s st [i, ak, o]	*sprechen	33
sich er'schrecken *get a fright* h w/st [i, ak, o]	machen/ *sprechen	21/33
er'schüttern *shake* A h w	angeln	1
er'schweren *make more difficult;* (**durch** + A) *hinder (by)* A h w	machen	21
sich [D] er'schwindeln (**von** + D) *swindle (sb) out of* A h w	angeln	1
er'setzen (**durch** + A) *replace (by)* A h w	heizen	14
er'sparen *save; spare* A h w	machen	21
er'starren *set; grow stiff* s w	machen	21
er'statten (**über** + A) *report (on); reimburse* A h w	reden	24
er'staunen *astonish* A h w	machen	21
er'stechen *stab (to death)* A h st [i, a, o]	sprechen	33
er'stehen *rise* s st [and, and]	stehen	34
er'steigen *climb* A h st [ie, ie]	schreiben	28
er'sticken *suffocate;* (**an** + D) *choke (on)* A h (**sein** when intrans.) w	machen	21
er'strahlen *shine; glow* s w	machen	21
er'streben *strive for* A h w	machen	21
sich er'strecken *stretch;* (**bis an** + A) *extend (as far as)* h w	machen	21
sich er'strecken **auf** + A *include; affect* h w	machen	21
er'stürmen *storm* A h w	machen	21
er'tappen (**bei** + D) *catch (at)* A h w	machen	21

er'teilen *give; grant* A h w	machen	21
er'tönen *sound; ring out* s w	machen	21
er'tragen *bear* A h st [ä, u, a]	tragen	38
er'tränken *drown* A h w	machen	21
sich [D] **er'träumen** *dream of* A h w	machen	21
er'trinken *be drowned* s st [a, u]	klingen	16
sich er'tüchtigen *keep fit* h w	machen	21
er'übrigen *spare* A h w	machen	21
er'wachen (aus + D) *awake (from)* s w	machen	21
er'wachsen (aus + D) *grow (out of/ from)* s st [ä, u, a]	*tragen	38
er'wägen *consider* A h st [o, o]	kriechen	19
er'wähnen *mention* A h w	machen	21
er'wärmen *warm;* **(für** + A) *win over (to)* A h w	machen	21
er'warten (von + D) *expect (of)* A h w	reden	24
er'wecken *(a)wake; arouse* A h w	machen	21
er'weichen *soften* A h **(sein** when intrans.) w	machen	21
er'weisen *prove; show* A h st [ie, ie]	*schreiben	28
er'weitern *widen; extend* A h w	angeln	1
er'werben *earn; win; acquire* A h st [i, a, o]	sprechen	33
er'widern auf + A *reply to* A h w	angeln	1
er'wischen *catch; grab* A h w	machen	21
er'würgen *strangle* A h w	machen	21
er'zählen (D) **über** + A/**von** + D *tell (sb) about* A h w	machen	21
er'zeugen *produce* A h w	machen	21
er'ziehen *educate; bring up* A h st [og, og]	*kriechen	19
er'zielen *achieve; score* A h w	machen	21
sich [D] **er'zwingen (von** + D) *force (out of sb)* A h st [a, u]	klingen	16
essen *eat* A h st [i, a, ge]	*fressen	8
etablieren *set up; establish* A h w	informieren	15

evakuieren *evacuate* A h w	informieren	15
sich exaltieren *get over-excited* h w	informieren	15
exerzieren *drill* A h w	informieren	15
existieren *exist* h w	informieren	15
expedieren *dispatch* A h w	informieren	15
experimentieren mit + D *experiment* *with/on* h w	informieren	15
explodieren *explode* s w	informieren	15
exportieren *export* A h w	informieren	15
fabrizieren *knock together* A h w	informieren	15
fabulieren *spin yarns* h w	informieren	15
fächeln *fan* A h w	angeln	1
sich fächern *fan out* h w	angeln	1
fachsimpeln *talk shop* h w	angeln	1
fädeln (auf + A) *thread (on to)* A h w	angeln	1
fahnden nach + D *search for* h w	reden	24
fahren *drive; run;* (**mit** + D) *go (by/ at)* A h (**sein** when intrans.) st [ä, u, a]	tragen	38
sich fahren *handle* h st [ä, u, a]	tragen	38
fahren|lassen *let go* A h st [ä, ie, a]	*schlafen	27
fallen (in + A/**auf** + A) *fall (into/on)* s st [ä, iel, a]	*schlafen	27
fällen *fell; pass (sentence)* A h w	machen	21
fallen|lassen (past part. **fallen(ge)lassen**) *abandon; let fall* A h st [ä, ie, a]	*schlafen	27
fälschen *forge* A h w	machen	21
falten *fold* A h w	reden	24
fangen *catch; capture* A h st [ä, i, a]	*hängen	12
färben *dye* A h w	machen	21
sich färben *change colour; turn* h w	machen	21
farcieren *stuff* A h w	informieren	15
fasern *fray* h w	angeln	1
fassen *grasp;* (**nach** + D) *reach (for)* A h w	heizen	14

fassen an + A *touch* h w	heizen	14
fasten *fast* h w	reden	24
faszinieren *fascinate* A h w	informieren	15
fauchen *hiss; snarl* h w	machen	21
faulen *rot; go bad* usually s w	machen	21
faulenzen *laze about* h w	heizen	14
fausten *punch* A h w	reden	24
favorisieren *favour* A h w	informieren	15
faxen *fax* A h w	heizen	14
fechten *fence* A h st [i, o, o]	*dreschen	6
federn *fit with springs; be springy* A h w	angeln	1
fegen (**von** + D) *brush (from); sweep up* A h w	machen	21
fehlen *lack; be missing* (impers.: **es fehlt an** + D *there's a lack of*; **mir fehlt** + N *I lack . . .*) h w	machen	21
feiern *celebrate* A h w	angeln	1
feilen *file* A h w	machen	21
feilschen um + A *haggle over* h w	machen	21
fern|halten von + D *keep away from* A h st [ä, ie, a]	*schlafen	27
fern|sehen *watch television* h st [ie, a, e]	sehen	29
fertigen *make* A h w	machen	21
fertig|machen *wear (sb) out* A h w	machen	21
fertig|stellen *complete* A h w	machen	21
fesseln (**an** + A) *tie/chain up (to); fascinate* A h w	angeln	1
fest|binden (**an** + D) *tie up (to)* A h st [a, u]	binden	4
fest|bleiben *stand firm* s st [ie, ie]	schreiben	28
sich fest|fahren *get stuck; get bogged down* h st [ä, u, a]	tragen	38
fest|frieren *freeze up* s st [o, o]	kriechen	19
sich fest|haken an + D *get caught on* h w	machen	21

fest|halten *hold on to; capture; record*		
A h st [ä, ie, a]	*schlafen	27
festigen *consolidate* A h w	machen	21
fest|klammern (an + D) *peg up (on)*		
A h w	angeln	1
sich fest|klammern an + D *cling on*		
to h w	angeln	1
fest|kleben (an + D) *stick (on to)*		
A h w	machen	21
sich fest|laufen *run aground; get*		
bogged down h st [äu, ie, au]	laufen	20
fest|legen *fix; arrange* A h w	machen	21
fest|liegen *be fixed; be stuck* h st		
[a, e]	sehen	29
fest|machen *fix; arrange; moor*		
A h w	machen	21
fest|nageln (an + D/**auf** + A) *nail*		
down (to) A h w	angeln	1
fest|setzen *fix; lay down* A h w	heizen	14
fest|sitzen *be stuck* h st [aß, ess]	*fressen	8
fest|stehen *be definite* h st [and, and]	stehen	34
fest|stellen *establish; confirm* A h w	machen	21
fest|ziehen *pull tight* A h st [og, og]	*kriechen	19
fetten *grease* A h w	reden	24
feuern (auf + A) *fire (at)* A h w	angeln	1
fiebern *have a fever;* (**nach** + D) *long*		
(for) h w	angeln	1
filmen *film* A h w	machen	21
filtern *filter* A h w	angeln	1
filtrieren *filter* A h w	informieren	15
finanzieren *finance* A h w	informieren	15
finden *find* A h st [a, u]	binden	4
sich finden *turn up; work out* h st		
[a, u]	binden	4
fingern *fiddle;* (**an** + D/**nach** + D)		
fumble (with/for) A h w	angeln	1
fingieren *fake* A h w	informieren	15
fischen *fish; fish for* A h w	machen	21

fischen nach + D *fish for (e.g. compliments)* h w	machen	21
fixieren *fix one's gaze on* A h w	informieren	15
sich fixieren auf + A/**an** + D *devote oneself to* h w	informieren	15
flach|legen *floor* A h w	machen	21
flackern *flicker* h w	angeln	1
flaggen *put out flags (on)* A h w	machen	21
flambieren *flambé* A h w	informieren	15
flammen *blaze* h w	machen	21
flanieren *stroll* s w	informieren	15
flankieren *flank* A h w	informieren	15
flattern *flutter* (with **sein**); *shake* (with **haben**) w	angeln	1
flechten *plait; weave* A h st [i, o, o]	*dreschen	6
flecken *stain* A h w	machen	21
fleddern *plunder; rob* A h w	angeln	1
flehen bei + D/**um** + A *plead with/for* h w	machen	21
fletschen (A/**mit** + D) *bare (teeth)* h w	machen	21
flicken *mend* A h w	machen	21
fliegen *fly* A s (if trans., usually **haben**) st [o, o]	kriechen	19
fliehen vor + D *flee from* s st [o, o]	kriechen	19
fliehen aus + D *escape from* s st [o, o]	kriechen	19
fließen *flow* s st [o, o]	schießen	26
flimmern *shimmer* s w	angeln	1
flirten *flirt* h w	reden	24
florieren *flourish* h w	informieren	15
flöten *whistle* A h w	reden	24
flott|machen *get . . . going* A h w	machen	21
fluchen auf + A/**über** + A *swear at* h w	machen	21
flüchten vor + D *flee from* s w	reden	24
flüstern (D) *whisper (to sb)* A h w	angeln	1

folgen (aus + D) *follow (from)*
  D s w   machen   21
 folgen auf + A *come after* s w   machen   21
folgern aus + D *deduce from* A h w   angeln   1
foltern *torture* A h w   angeln   1
fönen *blow-dry* A h w   machen   21
forcieren *intensify* A h w   informieren   15
fordern *demand; make demands on*
  A h w   angeln   1
fördern *promote* A h w   angeln   1
formalisieren *formalize* A h w   informieren   15
formen *form; mould* A h w   machen   21
formieren *form; draw up* A h w   informieren   15
formulieren *formulate* A h w   informieren   15
forschen nach + D/**in** + D *search for;*
  research into h w   machen   21
fort|be'stehen *remain (in existence)*
  h st [and, and]   stehen   34
fort|be'wegen *move (along)* A h w   machen   21
fort|bilden *give further training to*
  A h w   reden   24
fort|bleiben *stay away; fail to come*
  s st [ie, ie]   schreiben   28
sich fort|erben auf + A *be passed on*
  to h w   machen   21
fort|fahren (in + D) *continue (with)*
  s st [ä, u, a]   tragen   38
fort|fallen *be removed* s st [ä, iel, a] *schlafen   27
fort|führen *lead away; continue*
  A h w   machen   21
fort|gehen *leave; go on* s st [ing, ang] *hängen   12
fort|kommen *get away; get on* s st
  [am, o]   kommen   17
fort|laufen *run away; continue* s st
  [äu, ie, au]   laufen   20
fort|legen *put aside* A h w   machen   21
fort|nehmen *take away* A h st [imm,
  a, omm]   *sprechen   33

sich fort|pflanzen *reproduce oneself;* *spread* h w	heizen	14
fort|reißen *sweep away* A h st [i, i]	beißen	3
fort|schreiben *update* A h st [ie, ie]	schreiben	28
fort|schreiten *progress* s st [itt, itt]	streiten	37
fort|setzen *continue* A h w	heizen	14
fort|treiben *drive away* A h st [ie, ie]	schreiben	28
fort|wollen *want to get away; want to* *move* h m [i, o, o]	*sollen	32
fotografieren *photograph* A h w	informieren	15
fragen nach + D/**um** + A *ask for/* *about* A h w	machen	21
sich fragen (ob) *wonder (whether)* h w	machen	21
frankieren *frank* A h w	informieren	15
freien um + A *court; woo* h w	machen	21
frei|geben *release;* (D) *give (sb) time* *off* A h st [i, a, e]	geben	9
frei|halten *keep clear; treat (to* *drinks)* A h st [ä, ie, a]	*schlafen	27
frei|kämpfen *liberate* A h w	machen	21
frei|kaufen *ransom* A h w	machen	21
frei|kommen (aus + D) *be released* *(from)* s st [am, o]	kommen	17
frei|lassen *set free* A h st [ä, ie, a]	*schlafen	27
frei|legen *uncover* A h w	machen	21
frei|machen *frank; stamp* A h w	machen	21
frei|setzen *release* A h w	heizen	14
frei|sprechen (von + D) *acquit (of)* A h st [i, a, o]	sprechen	33
frei|stehen *be vacant* h st [and, and]	stehen	34
frei|stehen *be possible for* (**es steht** **mir frei** *I'm free to*) D h st [and, and]	stehen	34
frequentieren *frequent* A h w	informieren	15
fressen *eat (of animals)* A h st [i, a, e]	fressen	8

freuen *please* (**es freut mich** *I'm pleased*) A h w	machen	21
sich freuen auf + A *look forward to* h w	machen	21
sich freuen an + D *take pleasure in* h w	machen	21
sich freuen über + A *be pleased at* h w	machen	21
frieren *feel cold; freeze; be freezing* (also impers.: **mich friert (es)** *I am cold*) A h st [o, o]	kriechen	19
frisieren *do (sb's) hair* A h w	informieren	15
fritieren *deep-fry* A h w	informieren	15
froh'locken *rejoice* h w	machen	21
frömmeln *affect piety* h w	angeln	1
fronen *do forced labour; slave* h w	machen	21
frönen *indulge; devote oneself to* D h w	machen	21
frösteln *feel chilly* (also impers.: **es fröstelt mich** *I feel chilly*) h w	angeln	1
sich frottieren *rub oneself down* h w	informieren	15
frotzeln *tease;* (**über** + A) *make fun (of sb)* h w	angeln	1
frühstücken *breakfast* h w	machen	21
fuchsen *vex* A h w	heizen	14
sich fuchsen über + A *be annoyed about* h w	heizen	14
fügen *set;* (**zu** + D) *add (to)* A h w	machen	21
sich fügen *fall into line with* D h w	machen	21
sich fügen in + A *fit into* h w	machen	21
fühlen (**nach** + D) *feel (for)* A h w	machen	21
führen (**an** + D/**nach** + D) *lead (by/to); run; bear* A h w	machen	21
sich führen *behave* h w	machen	21
füllen *fill;* (**in** + A) *pour (into)* A h w	machen	21
fummeln an + D *fiddle with* h w	angeln	1
fundieren *underpin* A h w	informieren	15
fungieren als *function as* h w	informieren	15

funkeln *sparkle* h w	angeln	1
funken *broadcast* A h w	machen	21
funktionieren *work* h w	informieren	15
fürchten (**für** + A/**um** + A) *fear (for)* A h w	reden	24
sich fürchten (**vor** + D) *be afraid (of)* h w	reden	24
furnieren (**mit** + D) *veneer (with/in)* A h w	informieren	15
fußen auf + D *be based on* h w	heizen	14
füttern (**mit** + D) *feed (with)* A h w	angeln	1
gabeln *fork* A h w	angeln	1
gackern *cluck; cackle* h w	angeln	1
gaffen *gape* h w	machen	21
gähnen *yawn* h w	machen	21
galoppieren *gallop* usually **sein** w	informieren	15
gammeln *loaf* h w	angeln	1
garantieren (D) *guarantee (sb)* A h w	informieren	15
garantieren für + A *guarantee (sth)* h w	informieren	15
garen *cook* A h w	machen	21
gären *ferment* A h w/st [o, o]	machen/ kriechen	21/19
garnieren mit + D *garnish with; decorate with* A h w	informieren	15
gastieren *give a guest performance* h w	informieren	15
(sich) gaunern *swindle; cheat* h w	angeln	1
sich ge'bärden *behave* h w	reden	24
ge'bären *bear; give birth to* A h st [a, o]	*stehlen	35
geben (D) *give (to sb)* (**es gibt** + A *there is/are*) A h st [i, a, e]	geben	9
ge'bieten (D) *command (sb)* A h st [o, o]	*kriechen	19
ge'bieten über + A *have command over* h st [o, o]	*kriechen	19

ge'brauchen (zu + D) *use (for)* A h w	machen	21
ge'deihen *thrive* s st [ie, ie]	schreiben	28
ge'denken *intend* A h m [ach, ach]	*brennen	5
ge'denken *remember* G h m [ach, ach]	*brennen	5
sich ge'dulden *be patient* h w	reden	24
gefährden *endanger* A h w (past part. gefährdet)	reden	24
ge'fallen *please* D h st [ä, iel, a]	*schlafen	27
ge'fallen an + D *be pleasing about* h st [ä, iel, a]	*schlafen	27
gefangen|halten *hold prisoner* A h st [ä, ie, a]	*schlafen	27
gefangen|nehmen *take prisoner* A h st [imm, a, omm]	*sprechen	33
ge'frieren *freeze* s st [o, o]	kriechen	19
gegeneinander|halten *compare* A h st [ä, ie, a]	*schlafen	27
gegeneinander|prallen *collide* s w	machen	21
gegeneinander|schlagen *bang together* A h (**sein** when intrans.) st [ä, u, a]	tragen	38
gegeneinander|stellen *put side by side; compare* A h w	machen	21
gegen|steuern *take countermeasures* h w	angeln	1
sich [D]/einander gegenüber|liegen *face one another* h st [a, e]	sehen	29
gegenüber|stehen *stand facing; confront* D h st [and, and]	stehen	34
gegenüber|stellen (D) *confront (with)* A h w	machen	21
gegenüber|treten *face (up to)* D s st [itt, a, e]	*geben	9
gegen|zeichnen *countersign* A h w	atmen	2
geheim|halten *keep secret* A h st [ä, ie, a]	*schlafen	27

gehen *go; walk; work; be all right*
s st [ing, ang]   *hängen   12
  gehen um + A *be a matter of* s st
[ing, ang]   *hängen   12
  gehen nach + D *go by (sb/sth)* s st
[ing, ang]   *hängen   12
sich gehen|lassen *let oneself go; lose*
control h st [ä, ie, a]   *schlafen   27
ge'horchen *obey; respond to* D h w   machen   21
ge'hören *belong to* D h w   machen   21
  ge'hören zu + D *be one of; be part*
of h w   machen   21
  ge'hören in + A *belong in* h w   machen   21
  sich ge'hören *be fitting; be good*
manners h w   machen   21
geifern *slaver* h w   angeln   1
geigen *(play the) fiddle* h w   machen   21
geißeln *castigate* A h w   angeln   1
geistern *wander (like a ghost)* h w   angeln   1
geizen (**mit** + D) *be mean (with)*
h w   heizen   14
ge'langen an + A/**zu** + D *arrive at;*
attain s w   machen   21
ge'lingen *succeed* (also impers. + D:
es gelingt mir *I succeed*) s st
[a, u]   klingen   16
gellen *ring out;* (**von** + D) *ring*
(with) h w   machen   21
gelten (D/**für** + A) *be valid (for);*
apply (to); be directed (at) h st
[i, a, o]   *sprechen   33
ge'lüsten nach + D *make . . . crave*
for (impers.: **es gelüstet mich nach**
I crave for) A h w   reden   24
genehmigen *approve* A h w (past
part. **genehmigt**)   machen   21
ge'nesen (**von** + D) *recover (from)*
s st [a, e]   *fressen   8

sich genieren (wegen + G/vor + D)
  feel embarrassed (about/in the
  presence of) h w   informieren   15
ge'nießen *enjoy* A h st [o, o]   schießen   26
genügen **(D/für + A)** *be enough/*
  adequate (for) h w (past part.
  genügt)   machen   21
gerade|halten *hold up; hold straight*
  A h st [ä, ie, a]   *schlafen   27
gerade|stehen *stand up straight;* **(für**
  + A) *answer (for)* h st [and, and]   stehen   34
ge'raten *get; turn out* s st [ä, ie, a]   *schlafen   27
 ge'raten in + A *be caught in; get into*
  s st [ä, ie, a]   *schlafen   27
 ge'raten nach + D *take after* s st
  [ä, ie, a]   *schlafen   27
 ge'raten zu + D *turn into; become*
  s st [ä, ie, a]   *schlafen   27
gerben *tan* A h w   machen   21
gering|schätzen *have a low opinion of;*
  disregard A h w   heizen   14
ge'rinnen *clot; coagulate* s st [a, o]   sprechen   33
ge'schehen **(D)** *happen (to sb)* s st
  [ie, a, e]   sehen   29
sich gesellen zu + D *join* h w (past
  part. **gesellt)**   machen   21
gestalten *fashion; shape* A h w (past
  part. **gestaltet)**   reden   24
 sich gestalten *turn out* h w (past
  part. **gestaltet)**   reden   24
ge'statten **(D)** *permit (sb)* A h w   reden   24
ge'stehen **(D)** *confess (to sb)* A h st
  [and, and]   stehen   34
gestikulieren *gesticulate* h w   informieren   15
gesunden *recover* s w (past part.
  gesundet)   reden   24
sich ge'trauen *dare* h w   machen   21
ge'währen **(D)** *grant (to sb)* A h w   machen   21

gewährleisten *guarantee* A h w (past part. **gewährleistet**)	reden	24
gewichten *evaluate* A h w (past part. **gewichtet**)	reden	24
ge'winnen *win;* (für + A) *win over (to)* A h st [a, o]	*sprechen	33
ge'wittern *thunder and lighten* h w	angeln	1
ge'wöhnen (an + A) *accustom (to)* A h w	machen	21
gießen (in + A/über + A) *pour (into/over)* A h st [o, o]	schießen	26
gipfeln in + D *culminate in* h w	angeln	1
gipsen *plaster* A h w	heizen	14
girren *coo* h w	machen	21
glänzen (vor + D/mit + D) *shine (with/at)* h w	heizen	14
glätten *smooth out; calm* A h w	reden	24
glatt|gehen *go smoothly* s st [ing, ang]	*hängen	12
glatt|machen *smooth out; level* A h w	machen	21
glauben (D) *believe (sb)* A h w	machen	21
glauben an + A *believe in* h w	machen	21
gleich|bleiben *stay the same* s st [ie, ie]	schreiben	28
gleichen *resemble; equal* D h st [i, i]	gleichen	10
gleich|kommen (an + D) *equal (in)* D s st [am, o]	kommen	17
gleich|machen *make equal* A h w	machen	21
gleich|schalten *bring into line* A h w	reden	24
gleich|setzen (D/mit + D) *equate (with)* A h w	heizen	14
gleich|stehen (D) *be equal (with)* h st [and, and]	stehen	34
gleich|stellen (D/mit + D) *put on an equal footing (with)* A h w	machen	21
es gleich|tun (D) an + D/in + D *match (sb)* in h st [at, a]	tun	39
gleich|ziehen *draw level* h st [og, og]	*kriechen	19
gleiten *glide; slide* s st [itt, itt]	streiten	37

gliedern *structure;* (**in** + A) *divide (into)* A h w	angeln	1
glimmen *glow* h w/st [o, o]	machen/ kriechen	21/19
glimmern *glisten* h w	angeln	1
glitzern *sparkle* h w	angeln	1
glossieren *commentate on* A h w	informieren	15
glotzen *goggle* h w	heizen	14
glucken *brood; cluck* h w	machen	21
glücken *be successful for* D s w	machen	21
gluckern *gurgle* h w	angeln	1
glucksen *chuckle* h w	heizen	14
glühen *glow;* (**vor** + D) *be fired (with)* h w	machen	21
gongen *sound a gong* h w	machen	21
gönnen (D) *not begrudge (sb)* A h w	machen	21
sich [D] **gönnen** *treat oneself to* A h w	machen	21
graben (**nach** + D/**in** + A) *dig (for/in)* A h st [ä, u, a]	tragen	38
grabschen (**nach** + D) *grab (at)* A h w	machen	21
graduieren *graduate; calibrate* A h w	informieren	15
sich grämen über + A/**um** + A/**wegen** + G *worry about* h w	machen	21
grasen *graze* h w	heizen	14
grassieren *be rampant* h w	informieren	15
grätschen *straddle* A h w	machen	21
gratulieren (**zu** + D) *congratulate (on)* D h w	informieren	15
grauen vor + D *fill with dread of* (impers. + D: **mir graut (es) vor** + D *I dread . . .*) D h w	machen	21
graulen (**aus** + D) *drive out (of)* (impers. + A/D: **mich/mir grault (es) vor** + D *I dread . . .*) A h w	machen	21

graupeln *hail; sleet* (impers.: **es graupelt** *it's hailing; it's sleeting*) h w   angeln   1

grausen vor + D *fill with dread of* (impers. + A/D: **mich/mir graust (es) vor** + D *I dread . . .*) A/D h w   heizen   14

gravieren (auf + A) *engrave (on)* A h w   informieren   15

greifen (an + D) *seize (by)* A h st [iff, iff]   greifen   11

  greifen nach + D/**in** + A *reach for/ into* h st [iff, iff]   greifen   11

  greifen zu + D *resort to* h st [iff, iff]   greifen   11

grenzen an + A *border on; verge on* h w   heizen   14

grillen *grill; have a barbecue* A h w   machen   21

grinsen *grin* h w   heizen   14

grollen *rumble; be sullen* h w   machen   21

groß|tun mit + D *boast about* h st [at, a]   tun   39

grübeln über + D *ponder over* h w   angeln   1

grummeln *rumble; mumble* h w   angeln   1

gründen *found;* (**auf** + A) *base (on)* A h w   reden   24

  gründen auf + D/**in** + D *be based on* h w   reden   24

grünen *turn green (again)* h w   machen   21

grunzen *grunt* A h w   heizen   14

gruppieren *arrange* A h w   informieren   15

gruseln *make one's flesh creep* (impers.: **es gruselt mich/mir** *my flesh creeps*) A/D h w   angeln   1

grüßen *greet; salute; say hello* A h w   heizen   14

gucken *look* h w   machen   21

gurgeln *gargle; gurgle* h w   angeln   1

gurren *coo* h w   machen   21

gut|gehen *turn out well* (impers. + D:
  es geht mir gut *I'm well*) s st
  [ing, ang]   *hängen   12
gut|machen *make good; make up*
  A h w   machen   21
gut|sagen für + A *vouch for* h w   machen   21
gut|schreiben (D) *credit (sb) with*
  A h st [ie, ie]   schreiben   28
gut|tun (D) *do (sb) good* h st [at, a]   tun   39

haaren *moult* h w   machen   21
haben *have* A h m [at, att, a]   *brennen   5
hacken *hoe; chop;* (**nach** + D) *peck*
  (at) A h w   machen   21
haften (**an** + D/**auf** + D) *stick (to)*
  h w   reden   24
 haften für + A *be responsible for* h w   reden   24
haften|bleiben (**an** + D/**auf** + D) *stick*
  (to) s st [ie, ie]   schreiben   28
hageln *hail;* (**auf** + A) *rain down (on)*
  h w   angeln   1
häkeln *crochet* A h w   angeln   1
haken (**an** + A) *hook (on to); be*
  stuck A h w   machen   21
halbieren *cut in half; halve* A h w   informieren   15
hallen (**von** + D) *reverberate (with)*
  h w   machen   21
halten (**an** + D) *hold (by); keep*
  A h st [ä, ie, a]   *schlafen   27
 halten für + A *consider to be* A h st
  [ä, ie, a]   *schlafen   27
 halten von + D *think of* A h st
  [ä, ie, a]   *schlafen   27
 halten *stop; last; hold up;* (**auf** + A)
  attach importance (to) h st
  [ä, ie, a]   *schlafen   27
 sich halten *keep going; last;* (**an** + A)
  stay (with) h st [ä, ie, a]   *schlafen   27

halt|machen (vor + D) *stop (at)*
   h w   machen   21
hämmern (gegen + A) *hammer (on)*
   A h w   angeln   1
hamstern *hoard* A h w   angeln   1
handeln (mit + D) *trade (in/with);*
   haggle; act h w   angeln   1
  handeln von + D/**über** + A *be about*
   h w   angeln   1
  sich handeln um + A *be a matter*
   of h w   angeln   1
handhaben *handle* A h w   machen   21
hangeln *move hand over hand* s w angeln   1
hängen (an + D) *hang (from); cling*
   (to); depend (on) h st [i, a]   hängen   12
  hängen (an + A/**auf** + A) *hang (on)*
   A h w   machen   21
hängen|bleiben (an + D/**in** + D) *get*
   caught/stuck (on/in) s st [ie, ie] schreiben   28
hängen|lassen *leave behind* A h st
   [ä, ie, a]   *schlafen   27
  sich hängen|lassen *let oneself go*
   h st [ä, ie, a]   *schlafen   27
hänseln *tease* A h w   angeln   1
hantieren (an + D/**mit** + D) *be busy*
   (on/with) h w   informieren   15
hapern an + D *be a shortage of; be a*
   problem with (impers.: **es hapert**
   bei mir an + D *I'm short of*) h w angeln   1
harken *rake* A h w   machen   21
harmon(is)ieren mit + D *harmonize*
   with h w   informieren   15
harren G/**auf** + A *await* h w   machen   21
härten *harden* A h w   reden   24
haspeln *wind* A h w   angeln   1
hassen (an + D) *hate (about)* A h w heizen   14
hasten *hurry* s w   reden   24
hätscheln *fondle; pamper* A h w   angeln   1

hauchen (auf + A/gegen + A) *breathe*
  (on) A h w   machen   21
hauen *knock;* **(in + A)** *cut (in)*
  A h w   machen   21
 hauen (auf + A) *hit/punch (on)* h   machen/
  w/st [ieb, au]   *laufen 21/20
 hauen mit + D *bump sth* s w   machen   21
 sich hauen *fight* h w   machen   21
häufeln *heap up* A h w   angeln   1
häufen (auf + A) *pile (on to)* A h w machen   21
haus|halten mit + D *be economical*
  with h st [ä, ie, a]   *schlafen   27
hausieren (mit + D) *hawk (sth)*
  around h w   informieren 15
häuten *flay* A h w   reden   24
havarieren *crash* s w   informieren 15
heben *raise* A h st [o, o]   kriechen   19
hecheln *pant* h w   angeln   1
hechten *dive headlong* s w   reden   24
heften (an + A/in + A) *pin/fix (on/*
  into) A h w   reden   24
 sich heften auf + A *be fixed on*
  h w   reden   24
hegen *look after; harbour* A h w   machen   21
heiligen *bless; observe* A h w   machen   21
heilig|halten *keep (sacred)* A h st
  [ä, ie, a]   *schlafen   27
heim|be'gleiten *see home* A h w reden   24
heim|bringen *bring home* A h m
  [ach, ach]   *brennen   5
heim|fahren *drive home* A h **(sein**
  when intrans.) st [ä, u, a]   tragen   38
heim|führen *take home* A h w   machen   21
heim|gehen *go home; pass away* s st
  [ing, ang]   *hängen   12
heim|kehren (aus + D) *return home*
  (from) s w   machen   21
heim|kommen *come home* s st [am, o] kommen   17

heim|schicken *send home* A h w	machen	21
heim|suchen *strike; afflict* A h w	machen	21
heim|zahlen (D) *pay (sb) back for* A h w	machen	21
heiraten *marry* A h w	reden	24
heißen (**nach** + D) *be called (after); mean; bid* A h st [ie, ei]	heißen	13
heiß|laufen *overheat* s st [äu, ie, au]	laufen	20
heizen *heat; have the heating on* A h w	heizen	14
helfen (**bei** + D) *help (with)* D h st [i, a, o]	*sprechen	33
hemmen *slow down; check; hamper* A h w	machen	21
herab|hängen (**von** + D) *hang down (from)* h st [i, a]	hängen	12
herab|lassen *lower; let down* A h st [ä, ie, a]	*schlafen	27
sich herab|lassen *condescend* h st [ä, ie, a]	*schlafen	27
herab|mindern *disparage* A h w	angeln	1
herab|sehen (**auf** + A) *look down (on)* h st [ie, a, e]	sehen	29
herab|setzen *reduce; cut* A h w	heizen	14
herab|sinken *sink;* (**auf** + A) *settle (on)* s st [a, u]	klingen	16
herab|stürzen (**von** + D) *plummet down (from)* s w	heizen	14
sich herab|stürzen (**von** + D) *throw oneself (from/off)* h w	heizen	14
herab|würdigen *belittle* A h w	machen	21
sich heran|arbeiten an + A *work one's way towards* h w	reden	24
heran|bringen an + A *introduce to* A h m [ach, ach]	*brennen	5
heran|fahren (**an** + A) *drive up (to)* s st [ä, u, a]	tragen	38

heran|führen an + A *bring up to; lead to* A h w	machen	21
heran|gehen an + A *go up to; tackle* s st [ing, ang]	*hängen	12
heran|kommen an + A *draw near to; get hold of; equal* s st [am, o]	kommen	17
heran|reichen an + A *measure up to* h w	machen	21
heran|reifen (zu + D) *mature (into)* h w	machen	21
heran|rücken *draw up;* (**an** + A) *advance (towards)* A h w	machen	21
sich heran|tasten an + A *grope one's way towards* h w	reden	24
heran|tragen (an + A) *bring over (to)* A h st [ä, u, a]	tragen	38
heran|treten an + A *approach; assail* s st [itt, a, e]	*geben	9
heran|wachsen (an + A) *grow up (into)* h st [ä, u, a]	*tragen	38
heran|wagen (an + A) *venture near (to)* h w	machen	21
heran|ziehen (an + A) *draw up (to)* A h st [og, og]	*kriechen	19
sich herauf|arbeiten *work one's way up* h w	reden	24
herauf|be'schwören *provoke* A h w	machen	21
herauf|bringen *bring up* A h m [ach, ach]	*brennen	5
herauf|dringen (von + D/**aus** + D) *rise/drift up (from)* s st [a, u]	klingen	16
herauf|kommen (auf + A) *come up (on to)* s st [am, o]	kommen	17
herauf|setzen *increase* A h w	heizen	14
herauf|steigen *climb (up); rise* s st [ie, ie]	schreiben	28
herauf|ziehen *pull up; approach* A h (**sein** when intrans.) st [og, og]	*kriechen	19

heraus|arbeiten *bring out;* (**aus** + D)
develop (from) A h w .... reden ... 24

heraus|bekommen *get back;* (**aus** + D)
get . . . (out of) A h st [am, o] ... kommen ... 17

sich heraus|bilden *develop* h w ... reden ... 24

heraus|bitten *ask to come outside*
A h st [a, e] .... *geben ... 9

heraus|brechen *wrench out; erupt*
A h (**sein** when intrans.) st
[i, a, o] .... sprechen ... 33

heraus|bringen (**aus** + D) *bring out
(of); launch* A h m [ach, ach] ... *brennen ... 5

heraus|drücken (**aus** + D) *squeeze out
(of)* A h w .... machen ... 21

heraus|fahren (**aus** + D) *drive out
(of)* A h (**sein** when intrans.) st
[ä, u, a] .... tragen ... 38

heraus|finden *find out;* (**aus** + D) *pick
out (from)* A h st [a, u] .... binden ... 4

(sich) heraus|finden (**aus** + D) *find
one's way out (of)* h st [a, u] .... binden ... 4

heraus|fliegen (**aus** + D) *be thrown
out (of)* s st [o, o] .... kriechen ... 19

heraus|fordern *challenge; provoke*
A h w .... angeln ... 1

heraus|führen *lead out* A h w ... machen ... 21

heraus|geben *hand out/back; publish;
give change* A h st [i, a, e] ...... geben ... 9

heraus|gehen (**aus** + D) *go/come out
(of)* s st [ing, ang] .... *hängen ... 12

heraus|greifen **aus** + D *pick from*
A h st [iff, iff] .... greifen ... 11

sich heraus|halten (**aus** + D) *keep out
(of)* h st [ä, ie, a] .... *schlafen ... 27

heraus|heben (**aus** + D) *lift out (of)*
A h st [o, o] .... kriechen ... 19

heraus|helfen (**aus** + D) *help out (of)*
D h st [i, a, o] .... sprechen ... 33

heraus|holen (aus + D) *bring/get out (of); make up* A h w	machen	21
heraus|kommen (aus + D) *come/get out (of); get over* s st [am, o]	kommen	17
heraus|lesen aus + D *read into; pick out from* A h st [ie, a, e]	*sehen	29
heraus|locken (aus + D) *entice out (of)* A h w	machen	21
sich heraus|lügen aus + D *lie one's way out of* h st [o, o]	kriechen	19
heraus|nehmen (aus + D) *take out (of)* A h st [imm, a, omm]	*sprechen	33
heraus|pressen (aus + D) *wring out (from)* A h w	heizen	14
sich heraus|putzen *get dressed up* h w	heizen	14
heraus|ragen aus + D *jut/stand out from; rise above* h w	machen	21
heraus|reißen (aus + D) *pull up (from); tear away (from)* A h st [i, i]	beißen	3
heraus|rücken mit + D *come out with* s w	machen	21
heraus|rufen (aus + D) *call out (of)* A h st [ie, u]	rufen	25
heraus|rutschen (aus + D) *slip out (of)* s w	machen	21
heraus|schauen (aus + D) *look out (of); be showing* h w	machen	21
heraus|schießen (aus + D) *spurt out (of)* s st [o, o]	schießen	26
heraus|schlagen *knock out;* **(aus** + D) *leap out (of)* A h (**sein** when intrans.) st [ä, u, a]	tragen	38
heraus|schleichen (aus + D) *sneak out (of)* s st [i, i]	gleichen	10
heraus|schleudern (aus + D) *fling out (of)* A h w	angeln	1

heraus|schlüpfen (aus + D) *slip out (of)* s w	machen	21
heraus|schrauben *unscrew* A h w	machen	21
heraus|schreiben (aus + D) *copy out (from)* A h st [ie, ie]	schreiben	28
heraus|schreien *give vent to* A h st [ie, ie]	*schreiben	28
heraus|springen (aus + D) *jump out (of)* s st [a, u]	klingen	16
heraus|sprudeln (aus + D) *bubble out (of)* s w	angeln	1
heraus|stellen *put/set out; emphasize* A h w	machen	21
sich heraus|stellen (als) *turn out (to be)* h w	machen	21
heraus|strecken (aus + D/zu + D) *stick out (of)* A h w	machen	21
heraus|streichen *point out;* **(aus + D)** *delete (from)* A h st [i, i]	gleichen	10
heraus|strömen (aus + D) *pour out (of); escape (from)* s w	machen	21
heraus|stürzen (aus + D) *rush out (of)* s w	heizen	14
heraus|suchen *pick out* A h w	machen	21
heraus|tragen *carry out(side)* A h st [ä, u, a]	tragen	38
heraus|treten (aus + D) *come/stand out (from)* s st [itt, a, e]	*geben	9
heraus|wirtschaften aus + D *make a profit on* A h w	reden	24
heraus|ziehen (aus + D) *pull/move out (of)* A h **(sein** when intrans.**)** st [og, og]	*kriechen	19
herbei|eilen *hurry over* s w	machen	21
herbei|führen *produce; cause* A h w	machen	21
herbei|holen *fetch; send for* A h w	machen	21
herbei|kommen *come up* s st [am, o]	kommen	17

sich herbei|lassen *condescend* h st		
[ä, ie, a]	*schlafen	27
herbei|laufen *come running up* s st		
[äu, ie, au]	laufen	20
herbei|rufen *call (over)* A h st [ie, u]	rufen	25
herbei|schaffen *bring; get* A h w	machen	21
herbei|strömen *come flocking* s w	machen	21
herbei|winken *beckon over* A h w	machen	21
herbei|wünschen *long for* A h w	machen	21
herbei|ziehen *draw (up)* A h st		
[og, og]	*kriechen	19
her|be'kommen *get (from)* A h st		
[am, o]	kommen	17
her|be'stellen *ask . . . to come*		
A h w	machen	21
her|bringen *bring here* A h m		
[ach, ach]	*brennen	5
herein|brechen über + A *break over;*		
engulf s m [ach, ach]	*brennen	5
herein|bringen (in + A) *bring in(to)*		
A h m [ach, ach]	*brennen	5
herein|drängen (in + A) *push one's*		
way in(to) s w	machen	21
herein|fallen (auf + A) *be taken in*		
(by) s st [ä, iel, a]	*schlafen	27
herein|führen *show in* A h w	machen	21
herein|holen *bring in* A h w	machen	21
herein|kommen *come/get in* s st		
[am, o]	kommen	17
herein|lassen (in + A) *let in(to)* A h		
st [ä, ie, a]	*schlafen	27
herein|nehmen in + A *bring into;*		
include in A h st [imm, a, omm]	*sprechen	33
herein|reichen in + A *hand in; come*		
right into A h w	machen	21
herein|rufen *call in* A h st [ie, u]	rufen	25
herein|schleichen (in + A) *creep*		
in(to) s st [i, i]	gleichen	10

herein|sehen in + A *look in; look into*		
h st [ie, a, e]	sehen	29
herein|sehen bei + D *drop in on* h		
st [ie, a, e]	sehen	29
herein|strömen (**in** + A) *pour in(to)*		
s w	machen	21
herein|stürmen (**in** + A) *come*		
storming in(to) s w	machen	21
herein|stürzen (**in** + A) *rush in(to)*		
s w	heizen	14
herein|tragen (**in** + A) *carry in(to)*		
A h st [ä, u, a]	tragen	38
sich herein|wagen *venture in* h w	machen	21
her|fahren *come/drive here* A h (**sein**		
when intrans.) st [ä, u, a]	tragen	38
her|fahren hinter + D/**vor** + D *drive*		
along behind/in front of s st		
[ä, u, a]	tragen	38
her|fallen über + A *fall upon; set*		
upon s st [ä, iel, a]	*schlafen	27
her|finden *find one's way here* h st		
[a, u]	binden	4
her|führen *bring here* A h w	machen	21
her|geben *hand over; produce* A h st		
[i, a, e]	geben	9
sich her|geben für + A *get involved*		
in h st [i, a, e]	geben	9
her|gehen neben + D/**vor** + D/**hinter**		
+ D *walk along beside/in front of/*		
behind s st [ing, ang]	*hängen	12
her|halten *do; suffice* h st [ä, ie, a]	*schlafen	27
her|holen *fetch* A h w	machen	21
her|jagen hinter + D *pursue* s w	machen	21
her|kommen *come (here); come from*		
s st [am, o]	kommen	17
her|laufen neben + D/**vor** + D/**hinter**		
+ D *run along beside/in front of/*		
after s st [äu, ie, au]	laufen	20

her|leiten von + D/**aus** + D *derive from* A h w	reden	24
her|nehmen *find; obtain* A h st [imm, a, omm]	*sprechen	33
her|reichen *pass; hand* A h w	machen	21
her|richten *get ready* A h w	reden	24
herrschen (über + A) *reign/rule (over)* h w	machen	21
her|rufen (hinter + D) *call (after); call over* A h st [ie, u]	rufen	25
her|rühren von + D *come from; stem from* h w	machen	21
her|schaffen *get; bring here* A h w	machen	21
her|schicken (hinter + D) *send (after); send here* A h w	machen	21
sich her|schleichen hinter + D *creep along behind* h st [i, i]	gleichen	10
her|sehen *look here/this way* h st [ie, a, e]	sehen	29
her|sehen hinter + D *follow with one's eyes* h st [ie, a, e]	sehen	29
her|sein *be . . . ago;* (**von** + D) *be (from)* s st [ist, war, wes]	sein	30
her|stellen *manufacture; establish; put (over) here* A h w	machen	21
her|stürzen hinter + D *rush after* s w	heizen	14
her|tragen *carry/bring here* A h st [ä, u, a]	tragen	38
her|treiben vor + D *drive along in front of* A h st [ie, ie]	schreiben	28
herüber|bringen *bring over* A h m [ach, ach]	*brennen	5
herüber|fahren *drive over* A h (**sein** when intrans.) st [ä, u, a]	tragen	38
herüber|fliegen *fly over* A s st [o, o]	kriechen	19
herüber|geben *hand over* A h st [i, a, e]	geben	9
herüber|holen *bring over* A h w	machen	21

herüber|kommen *come/get over* s st
[am, o]   kommen   17
herüber|laufen *run over* s st [äu, ie,
au]   laufen   20
herüber|reichen *hand over;* (**über** + A)
reach (across) A h w   machen   21
herüber|schicken *send over* A h w   machen   21
herüber|schwimmen *swim/float across*
s st [a, o]   sprechen   33
herüber|sehen (**zu** + D) *look across*
(at) h st [ie, a, e]   sehen   29
herüber|wehen zu + D *blow towards*
h w   machen   21
herüber|ziehen *pull over; win over*
A h st [og, og]   *kriechen   19
sich herum|drehen *turn right round*
h w   machen   21
herum|fahren um + A *drive round* s st
[ä, u, a]   tragen   38
herum|führen um + A *take round; go*
round A h w   machen   21
herum|gehen *go round; walk about*
s st [ing, ang]   *hängen   12
herum|kommen um + A *avoid; get*
around s st [am, o]   kommen   17
herum|laufen *go round; walk about*
s st [äu, ie, au]   laufen   20
herum|reisen *travel about* s w   heizen   14
herum|sitzen *sit around* h st [aß,
ess]   *fressen   8
sich herum|sprechen *get around* h st
[i, a, o]   sprechen   33
herum|streichen *roam about;* (**um**
+ A) *prowl (round)* s st [i, i]   gleichen   10
herum|trampeln auf + D *trample all*
over; walk all over s w   angeln   1
herum|wickeln um + A *wrap round*
A h w   angeln   1

herum|wirbeln *whirl round* A h (**sein** when intrans.) w	angeln	1
herum|wühlen in + D *rummage in(to)* h w	machen	21
herunter|brennen *burn down* s m [a, a]	brennen	5
herunter|bringen *bring down; ruin* A h m [ach, ach]	*brennen	5
herunter|drücken *force down; reduce* A h w	machen	21
herunter|fahren *drive/bring down* A h (**sein** when intrans.) st [ä, u, a]	tragen	38
herunter|fallen *fall down;* (**von** + D) *fall (off)* s st [ä, iel, a]	*schlafen	27
herunter|fliegen *fly down* s st [o, o]	kriechen	19
herunter|gehen (**auf** + A) *come down (to)* s st [ing, ang]	*hängen	12
herunter|heben (**von** + D) *lift down (from)* A h st [o, o]	kriechen	19
herunter|klappen *pull/turn down; close* A h w	machen	21
herunter|kommen (**von** + D) *come down (from)* s st [am, o]	kommen	17
herunter|lassen (**an** + D) *lower (by)* A h st (ä, ie, a)	*schlafen	27
herunter|nehmen (**von** + D) *take down (from)* A h st [imm, a, omm]	*sprechen	33
herunter|schießen *shoot down; hurtle down* A h (**sein** when intrans.) st [o, o]	schießen	26
herunter|schlagen *knock off; turn down* A h st [ä, u, a]	tragen	38
herunter|schlucken *swallow (down)* A h w	machen	21
herunter|schrauben *turn down; reduce* A h w	machen	21

herunter|sehen (auf + A) *look down (on)* h st [ie, a, e]	sehen	29
herunter|steigen *climb down* s st [ie, ie]	schreiben	28
herunter|stürzen (von + D) *fall/plunge down (from)* s w	heizen	14
herunter|tragen *carry down* A h st [ä, u, a]	tragen	38
herunter|werfen *throw down* A h st [i, a, o]	sprechen	33
herunter|ziehen *pull down; drag down* A h st [og, og]	*kriechen	19
hervor|bringen *bring out;* **(aus + D)** *produce (from)* A h m [ach, ach]	*brennen	5
hervor|gehen aus + D *emerge from* s st [ing, ang]	*hängen	12
hervor|heben *emphasize* A h st [o, o]	kriechen	19
hervor|holen (aus + D) *get out (of)* A h w	machen	21
hervor|kommen (aus + D/unter + D) *come out (from/from under)* s st [am, o]	kommen	17
hervor|locken (aus + D) *lure out (of)* A h w	machen	21
hervor|quellen (aus + D) *pour out (of)* s st [i, o, o]	dreschen	6
hervor|ragen *stand out;* **(aus + D)** *project (from)* h w	machen	21
hervor|rufen *call out/back; elicit* A h st [ie, u]	rufen	25
hervor|springen *jut out;* **(hinter + D)** *jump out (from behind)* s st [a, u]	klingen	16
hervor|stechen *stand out;* **(aus + D)** *stick out (of)* h st [i, a, o]	sprechen	33
hervor|stehen *protrude* h st [and, and]	stehen	34
hervor|stürzen (hinter + D) *rush out (from behind)* s w	heizen	14

hervor|treten *stand out;* **(aus + D/ hinter + D)** *step out (from/from behind)* s st [itt, a, e]	*geben	9
sich hervor|tun (als) *distinguish oneself (as)* h st [at, a]	tun	39
sich hervor|wagen (aus + D) *dare to come out (of)* h w	machen	21
hervor|zaubern *conjure up* A h w	angeln	1
hervor|ziehen (hinter + D/unter + D) *pull out (from behind/from under)* A h st [og, og]	*kriechen	19
her|ziehen (vor + D/hinter + D/neben + D) *walk along (in front of/ behind/beside)* s st [og, og]	*kriechen	19
hetzen *hunt; rush; stir up hatred;* **(auf + A)** *set on (to)* A h **(sein** when intrans.) w	heizen	14
heucheln *feign; be hypocritical* A h w	angeln	1
heulen (vor + D) *howl (with)* h w	machen	21
hexen *conjure up; work magic* A h w	heizen	14
hier|be'halten *keep here* A h st [ä, ie, a]	*schlafen	27
hier|bleiben *stay here* s st [ie, ie]	schreiben	28
hierher|bitten *ask to come here* A h st [a, e]	*geben	9
hierher|bringen *bring here* A h m [ach, ach]	*brennen	5
hierher|ge'hören *belong here; be relevant* h w	machen	21
hierher|kommen *come/get here* s st [am, o]	kommen	17
hierher|schicken *send here* A h w	machen	21
hieven *heave* A h w	machen	21
hinab|blicken *look down* h w	machen	21
hinab|senken *lower* A h w	machen	21
hinab|steigen *climb down* s st [ie, ie]	schreiben	28

hinab|ziehen *drag down* A h st		
[og, og]	*kriechen	19
hin|arbeiten auf + A *work towards*		
h w	reden	24
hinauf|blicken *look up* h w	machen	21
hinauf|fahren *drive up* s st [ä, u, a]	tragen	38
hinauf|gehen *go up; lead up* s st [ing,*		
ang]	*hängen	12
hinauf|helfen *help up* D h st [i, a, o]	sprechen	33
hinauf|klettern (A/**auf** + A) *climb*		
(up) s w	angeln	1
hinauf|kommen *come/get up* s st [am,*		
o]	kommen	17
hinauf|laufen *run up* s st [äu, ie, au]	laufen	20
hinauf|reichen *pass up;* (**bis** + D)		
reach up (to) A h w	machen	21
hinauf|schicken *send up* A h w	machen	21
hinauf|schnellen *shoot up* s w	machen	21
hinauf|sehen *look up* h st [ie, a, e]	sehen	29
hinauf|setzen (**auf** + D) *put up (on);*		
increase A h w	heizen	14
hinauf|steigen *climb/go up* s st [ie, ie]	schreiben	28
hinauf|tragen *carry up* A h st [ä, u,*		
a]	tragen	38
hinauf|werfen auf + A *throw up on to*		
A h st [i, a, o]	sprechen	33
sich hinauf|winden an + D *creep/climb*		
up h st [a, u]	binden	4
hinauf|ziehen *pull up; move up* A h		
(**sein** when intrans.) st [og, og]	*kriechen	19
hinaus|be'fördern *throw out* A h w	angeln	1
sich hinaus|be'geben *go out* h st		
[i, a, e]	geben	9
sich hinaus|beugen *lean out* h w	machen	21
hinaus|blicken (**aus** + D) *look out*		
(of) h w	machen	21
hinaus|bringen (**aus** + D) *take out*		
(of) A h m [ach, ach]	*brennen	5

hinaus|drängen aus + D *push . . . out of; push one's way out of* A h (**sein** when intrans.) w	machen	21
hinaus|eilen (aus + D) *hurry out (of)* s w	machen	21
hinaus|fahren (aus + D) *drive out (of); shoot out (of)* A h (**sein** when intrans.) st [ä, u, a]	tragen	38
hinaus|fahren über + A *go past* s st [ä, u, a]	tragen	38
hinaus|fallen (aus + D) *fall out (of)* s st [ä, iel, a]	*schlafen	27
hinaus|finden (aus + D) *find one's way out (of)* h st [a, u]	binden	4
hinaus|fliegen (aus + D) *fly out (of); be thrown out (of)* s st [o, o]	kriechen	19
hinaus|führen (aus + D) *show/lead out (of); get out (of)* A h w	machen	21
hinaus|führen über + A *go beyond* h w	machen	21
hinaus|gehen (aus + D) *go out (of)* s st [ing, ang]	*hängen	12
hinaus|gehen auf + A *open on to* s st [ing, ang]	*hängen	12
hinaus|gehen über + A *go beyond* s st [ing, ang]	*hängen	12
hinaus|ge'langen (aus + D) *get out (of)* s w	machen	21
hinaus|ge'langen über + A *progress beyond* s w	machen	21
hinaus|greifen über + A *go beyond* h st [iff, iff]	greifen	11
hinaus|halten (zu + D) *hold out (of)* A h st [ä, ie, a]	*schlafen	27
hinaus|hängen (aus + D) *hang out (of)* A h w [st when intrans.: i, a]	machen/ hängen	21/12
hinaus|heben aus + D *lift out of/ down from* A h st [o, o]	kriechen	19

hinaus|jagen (aus + D) *drive out (of); race out (of)* A h **(sein** when intrans.) w	machen	21
hinaus|kommen (aus + D) *come/get out (of)* s st [am, o]	kommen	17
hinaus|kommen über + A *get beyond* s st [am, o]	kommen	17
hinaus|lassen (aus + D) *let out (of)* A h st [ä, ie, a]	*schlafen	27
hinaus|laufen (aus + D) *run out (of)* s st [äu, ie, au]	laufen	20
hinaus|laufen auf + A *lead to* s st [äu, ie, au]	laufen	20
sich hinaus|lehnen (zu + D) *lean out (of)* h w	machen	21
hinaus|nehmen (aus + D) *take out (of)* A h st [imm, a, omm]	*sprechen	33
hinaus|ragen über + A *project over; stand out from* h w	machen	21
hinaus|reichen (aus + D) *pass out (of)* A h w	machen	21
hinaus|reichen bis zu + D *stretch as far as* h w	machen	21
hinaus|reichen über + A *go beyond* h w	machen	21
hinaus|rennen (aus + D) *run out (of)* s m [a, a]	brennen	5
hinaus|rücken *move out; postpone* A h w	machen	21
hinaus|schaffen (aus + D) *get out (of)* A h w	machen	21
hinaus|scheuchen *chase out* A h w	machen	21
hinaus|schicken *send out* A h w	machen	21
hinaus|schieben (aus + D) *push out (of); postpone* A h st [o, o]	kriechen	19
hinaus|schießen (aus + D) *shoot out (of)* s st [o, o]	schießen	26

hinaus|schießen über + A *shoot past*		
s st [o, o]	schießen	26
hinaus|schleichen (aus + D) *steal out*		
(of) s st [i, i]	gleichen	10
hinaus|schmuggeln (aus + D) *smuggle*		
out (of) A h w	angeln	1
hinaus|schwimmen *swim out* s st		
[a, o]	sprechen	33
hinaus|sehen *look out* h st [ie, a, e]	sehen	29
hinaus|setzen *put out(side)* A h w	heizen	14
sich hinaus|stehlen (aus + D) *steal*		
out (of) h st [ie, a, o]	stehlen	35
hinaus|steigen (aus + D) *climb out*		
(of) s st [ie, ie]	schreiben	28
hinaus|stellen *put out(side)* A h w	machen	21
hinaus|strecken *stick out* A h w	machen	21
hinaus|strömen *pour out* s w	machen	21
hinaus|stürzen (aus + D) *fall (out*		
of); rush out (of) s w	heizen	14
hinaus|tragen *carry out; spread* h st		
[ä, u, a]	tragen	38
sich hinaus|trauen *venture out* h w	machen	21
hinaus|treiben (aus + D) *drive out*		
(of) A h st [ie, ie]	schreiben	28
hinaus|treiben *drift out* s st [ie, ie]	schreiben	28
hinaus|treten *step out (of)* s st [itt,		
a, e]	*geben	9
hinaus|wachsen über + A *grow taller*		
than; surpass s st [ä, u, a]	*tragen	38
sich hinaus|wagen (aus + D/**in** + A)		
venture out (of/into) h w	machen	21
hinaus|weisen (aus + D) *order out*		
(of); imply A h st [ie, ie]	*schreiben	28
hinaus|werfen (aus + D) *throw out*		
(of) A h st [i, a, o]	sprechen	33
hinaus|ziehen *pull/drive out; prolong;*		
delay; move/get out A h (**sein**		
when intrans.) st [og, og]	*kriechen	19

sich hinaus|ziehen *extend; drag on;* *be delayed* h st [og, og]	*kriechen	19
hinaus|zögern *delay* A h w	angeln	1
hindern (an + D) *stop (from)* A h w	angeln	1
hin|deuten (auf + A/**zu** + D) *point* *(to)* h w	reden	24
hin|drängen zu + D *push towards;* *push one's way towards* A h (**sein** *when intrans.*) w	machen	21
sich hindurch|finden (durch + A) *find* *one's way through* h st [a, u]	binden	4
hindurch|gehen (durch + A) *walk/go* *through* s st [ing, ang]	*hängen	12
hindurch|sehen (durch + A) *see* *through* h st [ie, a, e]	sehen	29
hindurch|ziehen (durch + A) *pull* *through; move through* A h (**sein** *when intrans.*) st [og, og]	*kriechen	19
hin|eilen (zu + D/**über** + A) *hurry* *(to/across)* s w	machen	21
sich hinein|be'geben in + A *enter* h st [i, a, e]	geben	9
hinein|blicken (in + A) *look in(to)* h w	machen	21
hinein|bohren in + A *drill/bore in(to)* A h w	machen	21
hinein|bringen in + A *bring in;* *introduce into* A h m [ach, ach]	*brennen	5
sich hinein|denken in + A *think one's* *way into* h m [ach, ach]	*brennen	5
hinein|drängen in + A *push into* A h w	machen	21
hinein|fahren (in + A) *drive in(to);* *slip into* A h (**sein** *when intrans.*) st [ä, u, a]	tragen	38
hinein|fallen in + A *fall into* s st [ä, iel, a]	*schlafen	27

sich hinein|finden in + A *get used to; come to terms with* h st [a, u]	binden	4
hinein|fliegen in + A *fly/be thrown into* s st [o, o]	kriechen	19
hinein|gehen (in + A) *go in(to)* s st [ing, ang]	*hängen	12
hinein|ge'raten in + A *get into* s st [ä, ie, a]	*schlafen	27
hinein|gießen (in + A) *pour in(to)* A h st [o, o]	schießen	26
hinein|helfen (in + A) *help (on with/ into)* D h st [i, a, o]	sprechen	33
hinein|jagen (in + A) *chase in(to)* A h w	machen	21
hinein|kommen (in + A) *come/get in(to)* s st [am, o]	kommen	17
hinein|kriechen (in + A) *crawl in(to)* s st [o, o]	kriechen	19
hinein|lassen (in + A) *let in(to)* A h st [ä, ie, a]	*schlafen	27
hinein|laufen (in + A) *run in(to)* s st [äu, ie, au]	laufen	20
hinein|legen (in + A) *put in(to)* A h w	machen	21
hinein|leuchten (in + A) *shine a light in(to); throw light (on)* h w	reden	24
hinein|manövrieren in + A *manœuvre/ get into* A h w	informieren	15
hinein|passen (in + A) *fit in(to); fit (in with)* h w	heizen	14
hinein|pfuschen in + A *meddle in* h w	machen	21
hinein|pressen in + A *press/stamp/ force into* A h w	heizen	14
hinein|pumpen (in + A) *pump in(to)* A h w	machen	21
hinein|reden in + A *break into; interfere in* h w	reden	24

hinein|regnen (in + A) *rain in(to)*
h w | atmen | 2

hinein|reichen *pass in;* (in + A) *reach/
extend (into)* A h w | machen | 21

hinein|reißen in + A *drag into* A h st
[i, i] | beißen | 3

hinein|rufen *call in* A h st [ie, u] | rufen | 25

hinein|schaffen (in + A) *get in(to)*
A h w | machen | 21

hinein|schießen (in + A) *shoot in(to)*
s st [o, o] | schießen | 26

hinein|schlagen (in + A) *knock/cut
in(to)* A h st [ä, u, a] | tragen | 38

hinein|schleichen (in + A) *creep
in(to)* s st [i, i] | gleichen | 10

hinein|schlingen (in sich) *devour* A h
st [a, u] | klingen | 16

hinein|schlüpfen (in + A) *slip in(to)*
s w | machen | 21

hinein|schmuggeln (in + A) *smuggle
in(to)* A h w | angeln | 1

hinein|schreiben (in + A) *write in* A
h st [ie, ie] | schreiben | 28

hinein|schütten (in + A) *pour in(to)*
A h w | reden | 24

hinein|sehen (in + A) *look in(to)* h
st [ie, a, e] | sehen | 29

hinein|setzen (in + A) *put in(to)*
A h w | heizen | 14

hinein|spielen *make a contribution*
h w | machen | 21

hinein|sprechen in + A *speak into* h s
[i, a, o] | sprechen | 33

hinein|stecken in + A *put into* A
h w | machen | 21

hinein|stoßen (in + A) *push/thrust
in(to)* A h (**sein** when intrans.) st
[ö, ie, o] | stoßen | 36

hinein|stürzen (in + A) *fall in(to);*
burst in(to); hurl in(to) A h (**sein**
when intrans.) w   heizen   14

hinein|tragen (in + A) *carry/bring*
in(to) A h st [ä, u, a]   tragen   38

hinein|treiben in + A *drive/carry/*
force into A h st [ie, ie]   schreiben   28

sich hinein|versetzen in + A *put*
oneself into (e.g. position) h w   heizen   14

hinein|wachsen in + A *grow into* s st
[ä, u, a]   *tragen   38

sich hinein|wagen (in + A) *venture*
in(to) h w   machen   21

hinein|werfen (in + A) *throw in(to);*
cast (at) A h st [i, a, o]   sprechen   33

hinein|ziehen (in + A) *pull/drag/draw*
in(to); march in(to); drift in(to)
A h (**sein** when intrans.) st [og,
og]   *kriechen   19

hinein|zwingen in + A *force into* A h
st [a, u]   klingen   16

hin|fahren *go there; take there* A h
(**sein** when intrans.) st [ä, u, a]   tragen   38

hin|fahren (mit + D) über + A *run*
(e.g. fingers) over s st [ä, u, a]   tragen   38

hin|fallen *fall down* s st [ä, iel, a]   *schlafen   27

hin|finden (zu + D) *find one's way*
(to) h st [a, u]   binden   4

hin|fliegen *fly there/off/to* s st [o, o] kriechen   19

hin|führen (zu + D) *take (to); lead*
(to) A h w   machen   21

sich hin|geben (D) *abandon oneself*
(to) h st [i, a, e]   geben   9

hin|gehen (zu + D) *go (to); pass* s st
[ing, ang]   *hängen   12

hin|ge'langen *get there;* (**zu** + D) *get*
(to) s w   machen   21

hin|ge'raten *get there* s st [ä, ie, a]   *schlafen   27

hin|gleiten *glide along* s st [itt, itt]	streiten	37
hin|halten (D) *hold out (to sb); keep waiting* A h st [ä, ie, a]	*schlafen	27
hin|hauen *fall heavily* s st [ieb, au]	*laufen	20
hinken *limp;* (**auf** + D/**mit** + D) *walk with a limp (in)* s w	machen	21
sich hin|knien *kneel down* h w	*machen	21
hin|kommen *get there; belong* s st [am, o]	kommen	17
hin|laufen (**zu** + D) *run/walk (to); run/walk there* s st [äu, ie, au]	laufen	20
hin|legen *put/lay out; lay down* A h w	machen	21
sich hin|legen *lie down* h w	machen	21
hin|leiten (**zu** + D) *lead (to); lead there* A h w	reden	24
hin|lenken (**zu** + D/**auf** + A) *steer (to/towards)* A h w	machen	21
hin|nehmen *accept* A h st [imm, a, omm]	*sprechen	33
hin|neigen (**zu** + D) *incline (to/towards)* A h w	machen	21
hin|reichen *be enough;* (**bis zu** + D) *reach (as far as)* h w	machen	21
hin|reichen (D) *pass (to sb)* A h w	machen	21
hin|reisen *travel there* s w	heizen	14
hin|reißen *enrapture;* (**zu** + D) *drive (to sth)* A h st [i, i]	beißen	3
hin|richten *execute* A h w	reden	24
hin|rücken *move over* A (**sein** when intrans.) h w	machen	21
hin|sagen *say wihout thinking* A h w	machen	21
hin|schaffen *get . . . there* A h w	machen	21
hin|schicken *send (off)* A h w	machen	21
hin|schieben (D) *push over (to)* A h st [o, o]	kriechen	19
hin|schielen (**zu** + D) *steal a glance (at)* h w	machen	21
hin|schlagen *strike* A h st [ä, u, a]	tragen	28

sich hin|schleichen *creep over* h st [i, i]	gleichen	10
sich hin|schleppen (**zu** + D) *drag oneself along (to); drag on* h w	machen	21
hin|schreiben *write (down)* A h st [ie, ie]	schreiben	28
hin|sehen *look (at it)* h st [ie, a, e]	sehen	29
hin|setzen *put down; seat* A h w	heizen	14
sich hin|setzen *sit down* h w	heizen	14
hin|starren zu + D/**nach** + D *stare at* h w	machen	21
hin|stellen *put; put down;* (**als**) *make out (to be)* A h w	machen	21
sich hin|stellen *stand (up); park* h w	machen	21
hin|steuern zu + D/**auf** + A *steer towards/aim at* A h (**sein** when intrans.) w	angeln	1
hin|strecken (D) *hold out (to)* A h w	machen	21
sich hin|strecken (**bis an** + A) *stretch (as far as); lie down at full length* h w	machen	21
hin|strömen (**zu** + D) *flow (to); flock (to)* s w	machen	21
hin|stürzen *fall down;* (**zu** + D) *rush (towards)* s w	heizen	14
hintan|setzen *put last* A h w	heizen	14
hintenüber|fallen *fall over backwards* s st [ä, iel, a]	*schlafen	27
hintenüber|kippen *tip over backwards* s w	machen	21
hinter'bringen (D) *tip (sb) off about* A h m [ach, ach]	*brennen	5
hintereinander|fahren *ride one behind the other* s st [ä, u, a]	tragen	38
hintereinander|gehen *walk in single file* s st [ing, ang]	*hängen	12
hinter'fragen *examine* A h w	machen	21

hinter'gehen *deceive* A h st [ing, ang]	*hängen	12
hinterher|blicken *gaze after* D h w	machen	21
hinterher|fahren (D) *drive along behind (sb)* s st [ä, u, a]	tragen	38
hinterher|gehen (D) *walk along behind (sb)* s st [ing, ang]	*hängen	12
hinterher|hinken (D) *hobble along behind (sb); lag behind (sth)* s w	machen	21
hinterher|kommen *come after* s st [am, o]	kommen	17
hinterher|laufen (D) *run after (sb)* s st [äu, ie, au]	laufen	20
hinterher|schicken (D) *send on (to sb)* A h w	machen	21
hinter'lassen *leave (behind); bequeath* A h st [ä, ie, a]	*schlafen	27
hinter'legen bei + D *deposit with* A h w	machen	21
hinter'treiben *foil; prevent* A h st [ie, ie]	schreiben	28
hinter'ziehen *misappropriate* A h st [og, og]	*kriechen	19
hin|tragen (**zu** + D) *take (to); take there* A h st [ä, u, a]	tragen	38
hin|treiben (**zu** + D) *drive (to); drift off/there* A h (**sein** when intrans.) st [ie, ie]	schreiben	28
hin|treten (**vor** + D) *go up (to)* s st [itt, a, e]	*geben	9
hinüber|blicken (**zu** + D/**nach** + D) *look across (at)* h w	machen	21
hinüber|bringen (**auf** + A/**zu** + D) *take over (to)* A h m [ach, ach]	*brennen	5
hinüber|fahren (**über** + A) *drive across* A h (**sein** when intrans.) st [ä, u, a]	tragen	38
hinüber|führen (**über** + A) *lead/take across* A h w	machen	21

hinüber|führen an + A/**nach** + D *lead across to* h w	machen	21
hinüber|gehen (zu + D) *go across (to)* s st [ing, ang]	*hängen	12
hinüber|helfen (über + A) *help across* D h st [i, a, o]	sprechen	33
hinüber|kommen (über + A) *get across* s st [am, o]	kommen	17
hinüber|lassen *let across* A h st [ä, ie, a]	*schlafen	27
hinüber|reichen (D) *extend across; pass over (to)* A h w	machen	21
hinüber|rufen *call over* A h st [ie, u]	rufen	25
hinüber|schicken *send over* A h w	machen	21
hinüber|schwimmen *swim across* s st [a, o]	sprechen	33
hinüber|sehen (zu + D/**nach** + D) *look across (at)* h st [ie, a, e]	sehen	29
hinüber|springen über + A *jump over; clear* s st [a, u]	klingen	16
hinüber|steigen über + A *climb over* s st [ie, ie]	schreiben	28
hinüber|wechseln (zu + D) *go over (to)* A h/s w	angeln	1
hinüber|werfen *throw over; cast across* A h st [i, a, o]	sprechen	33
hinüber|ziehen (über + A) *draw across; go across* A h (**sein** when intrans.) st [og, og]	*kriechen	19
hin- und her|be'wegen *move to and fro* A h w	machen	21
hin- und her|fahren *travel back and forth* s st [ä, u, a]	tragen	38
hin- und her|gehen *walk up and down* s st [ing, ang]	*hängen	12
hin- und her|pendeln *commute* s w	angeln	1
sich hinunter|be'geben *go down* h st [i, a, e]	geben	9

hinunter|blicken (auf + A) *look down (on)* h w	machen	21
hinunter|bringen *take down* A h m [ach, ach]	*brennen	5
hinunter|fahren *drive down* A h (**sein** when intrans.) st [ä, u, a]	tragen	38
hinunter|fallen *fall down* s st [ä, iel, a]	*schlafen	27
hinunter|führen *lead down* A h (**sein** when intrans.) w	machen	21
hinunter|gehen *go down* s st [ing, ang]	*hängen	12
hinunter|jagen *chase down; race down* A h (**sein** when intrans.) w	machen	21
hinunter|kippen *tip down; knock back* A h w	machen	21
hinunter|klettern *climb down* s w	angeln	1
hinunter|kommen *come down* s st [am, o]	kommen	17
hinunter|lassen *let down; lower* A h st [ä, ie, a]	*schlafen	27
hinunter|laufen *run down; walk down* s st [äu, ie, au]	laufen	20
hinunter|reichen (bis auf + A/bis zu + D) *reach down (to); pass down* A h w	machen	21
hinunter|rutschen *slide down* s w	machen	21
hinunter|schlingen *gulp down* A h st [a, u]	klingen	16
hinunter|schlucken *swallow; choke back* A h w	machen	21
hinunter|sehen (auf + A) *look down (on)* h st [ie, a, e]	sehen	29
hinunter|springen *jump/run down* s st [a, u]	klingen	16
hinunter|spülen (A) *flush . . . down (sth)* A h w	machen	21
hinunter|stürzen *plunge down* s w	heizen	14
hinunter|stürzen von + D *fling off* A h w	heizen	14

hinunter|tragen *carry down* A h st [ä, u, a]	tragen	38
hinunter|werfen *throw down* A h st [i, a, o]	sprechen	33
hinunter|ziehen *move down; pull down* A h (**sein** when intrans.) st [og, og]	*kriechen	19
sich hinunter|ziehen *extend down* h st [og, og]	*kriechen	19
sich hin|wagen *venture there* h w	machen	21
hinweg|brausen über + A *roar over* s w	heizen	14
hinweg|gehen über + A *pass over* s st [ing, ang]	*hängen	12
hinweg|helfen über + A *help to get over* D h st [i, a, o]	sprechen	33
hinweg|kommen über + A *get over* s st [am, o]	kommen	17
hinweg|lesen (über + A) *read (past sth) without noticing* h st [ie, a, e]	*sehen	29
hinweg|sehen über + A *look past; overlook* h st [ie, a, e]	sehen	29
sich hinweg|setzen über + A *disregard* h w	heizen	14
hinweg|täuschen über + A *mislead about* A h w	machen	21
hinweg|trösten über + A *console for* A h w	reden	24
hinweisen auf + A *point to; refer to* h st [ie, ie]	*schreiben	28
hinweisen (A) auf + A *point out (to sb)* A h st [ie, ie]	*schreiben	28
sich hin|wenden zu + D *turn to/ towards* h m [a, a]	senden	31
hin|werfen *throw down; dash off; remark casually* A h st [i, a, o]	sprechen	33
hin|wirken auf + A *work towards* h w	machen	21
hin|zählen *count out* A h w	machen	21

hin|zeigen zu + D *point to/towards* h w	machen	21
hin|ziehen (zu + D) *pull (towards); attract (to); delay* A h st [og, og]	*kriechen	19
hin|ziehen zu + D *move to* s st [og, og]	*kriechen	19
sich hin|ziehen (über + A) *drag on (for); be delayed* h st [og, og]	*kriechen	19
hin|zielen auf + A *aim/be aimed at* h w	machen	21
hinzu|be'kommen *get in addition* A h st [am, o]	kommen	17
sich [D] hinzu|denken *add in one's imagination* A h m [ach, ach]	*brennen	5
hinzu|dichten *add out of one's head* A h w	reden	24
hinzu|fügen *add* A h w	machen	21
hinzu|geben (D) *give (sb) in addition; add* A h st [i, a, e]	geben	9
sich hinzu|ge'sellen D/**zu** + D *join* h w	machen	21
hinzu|kommen *come along; turn up* s st [am, o]	kommen	17
hinzu|kommen zu + D *join; be added to* s st [am, o]	kommen	17
hinzu|nehmen *add* A h st [imm, a, omm]	*sprechen	33
hinzu|setzen (zu + D) *add (to)* A h w	heizen	14
hinzu|ver'dienen *earn extra* A h w	machen	21
hinzu|zählen *add (on)* A h w	machen	21
hinzu|ziehen *consult* A h st [og, og]	*kriechen	19
hissen *hoist* A h w	heizen	14
hobeln A/**an** + D *plane* h w	angeln	1
hoch|achten *respect* A h w	reden	24
sich hoch|arbeiten *work one's way up* h w	reden	24
hoch|biegen *bend up* A h st [o, o]	kriechen	19
hoch|blicken *look up* h w	machen	21

hoch|bringen *bring up; make well*		
again A h m [ach, ach]	*brennen	5
hoch|drehen *wind up; rev up* A h w	machen	21
hoch|fahren (aus + D) *start up*		
(from); flare up s st [ä, u, a]	tragen	38
hoch|fliegen *fly up* s st [o, o]	kriechen	19
hoch|gehen *go up; blow up* s st [ing,		
ang]	*hangen	12
hoch|halten *hold up; uphold* A h st		
[ä, ie, a]	*schlafen	27
hoch|heben *lift up* A h st [o, o]	kriechen	19
hoch|klappen *fold/lift/turn up* A h w	machen	21
hoch|krempeln *roll up* A h w	angeln	1
hoch|nehmen *pick up; send up* A h st		
[imm, a, omm]	*sprechen	33
hoch|ragen *tower up* h w	machen	21
hoch|reißen *throw up* A h st [i, i]	beißen	3
hoch|schießen *send up; shoot up* A h		
(**sein** when intrans.) st [o, o]	schießen	26
hoch|schlagen *turn up; leap up* A h		
(**sein** when intrans.) st [ä, u, a]	tragen	38
hoch|schnellen *leap up* s w	machen	21
hoch|schrauben *force up; increase* A		
h w	machen	21
hoch|spielen *blow up (out of*		
proportion) A h w	machen	21
hoch|springen (an + D) *jump up (at)*		
s st [a, u]	klingen	16
hoch|stapeln *perpetrate frauds; make*		
empty boasts h w	angeln	1
hoch|steigen *climb; rise (up)* s st		
[ie, ie]	schreiben	28
hoch|stellen *put/turn up* A h w	machen	21
hoch|stemmen *lift* A h w	machen	21
hoch|tragen *carry up* A h st [ä, u, a]	tragen	38
hoch|treiben *force up* A h st [ie, ie]	schreiben	28
hoch|werfen *throw up; toss* A h st		
[i, a, o]	sprechen	33

hoch|winden *wind up* A h st [a, u]	binden	4
hoch|ziehen *pull/put up; raise; hunch* A h st [og, og]	*kriechen	19
sich hoch|ziehen an + D *pull oneself up by* h st [og, og]	*kriechen	19
hocken *squat; sit around* h w	machen	21
hoffen (auf + A) *hope (for); put one's trust (in)* A h w	machen	21
höher|schrauben *force up* A h w	machen	21
höhlen *hollow out* A h w	machen	21
höhn'lächeln/höhn|lächeln *smile scornfully* h w	angeln	1
höhn'lachen/höhn|lachen *laugh scornfully* h w	machen	21
höhn|sprechen *fly in the face of* D h st [i, a, o]	sprechen	33
hökern *run a street stall* h w	angeln	1
holen *fetch; get* A h w	machen	21
sich [D] holen *get; win; catch* A h w	machen	21
holpern *jolt; stumble* s w	angeln	1
honorieren *pay (for); appreciate; honour* A h w	informieren	15
hoppeln (über + A) *hop (over); bump (over)* s w	angeln	1
horchen auf + A *listen to* h w	machen	21
hören (über + A/**von** + D) *hear (about/from); listen to* A h w	machen	21
hören an + D *tell by* A h w	machen	21
hören auf + A *listen to; heed; answer to* h w	machen	21
horsten *nest* h w	reden	24
horten *hoard* A h w	reden	24
huldigen *pay tribute to; be addicted to* D h w	machen	21
humpeln *walk with a limp* usually **sein** w	angeln	1
hungern *go hungry;* (**nach** + D) *hunger (for)* h w	angeln	1

hupen *hoot; sound one's horn* h w	machen	21
hüpfen *hop; bounce; leap* s w	machen	21
huren (mit + D) *fornicate (with)* h w	machen	21
huschen *slip; steal; dart* s w	machen	21
hüsteln *give a slight cough* h w	angeln	1
husten *cough (up)* A h w	reden	24
hüten *look after; guard* A h w	reden	24
sich hüten *take care not to;* (**vor** + D) *be on one's guard (against)* h w	reden	24
hypnotisieren *hypnotize* A h w	informieren	15
idealisieren *idealize* A h w	informieren	15
identifizieren (mit + D) *identify (with)* A h w	informieren	15
ignorieren *ignore* A h w	informieren	15
illuminieren *illuminate* A h w	informieren	15
illustrieren *illustrate* A h w	informieren	15
imitieren *imitate* A h w	informieren	15
immigrieren *immigrate* s w	informieren	15
immunisieren (gegen + A) *immunize (against)* A h w	informieren	15
impfen *vaccinate; inoculate* A h w	machen	21
imponieren (durch + A) *impress (by)* D h w	informieren	15
importieren *import* A h w	informieren	15
imprägnieren *impregnate* A h w	informieren	15
improvisieren (über + A) *improvise (on)* h w	informieren	15
indoktrinieren *indoctrinate* A h w	informieren	15
industrialisieren *industrialize* A h w	informieren	15
infiltrieren *infiltrate* A h w	informieren	15
informieren (über + A) *inform (about)* A h w	informieren	15
inhaftieren *take into custody* A h w	informieren	15
inhalieren *inhale* A h w	informieren	15
injizieren *inject* A h w	informieren	15
inkriminieren *incriminate* A h w	informieren	15

inserieren (A/**wegen** + G) **in** + D
  advertise (sth) in h w   informieren   15
inspirieren *inspire* A h w   informieren   15
inspizieren *inspect* A h w   informieren   15
installieren *install; set up* A h w   informieren   15
instruieren (**über** + A) *inform (about)*
  A h w   informieren   15
instrumentieren *orchestrate;*
  instrument A h w   informieren   15
inszenieren *stage; direct* A h w   informieren   15
integrieren *integrate* A h w   informieren   15
intensivieren *intensify* A h w   informieren   15
interessieren *interest* A h w   informieren   15
  sich interessieren für + A *be*
  interested in h w   informieren   15
internieren *intern* A h w   informieren   15
interpolieren *interpolate* A h w   informieren   15
interpretieren *interpret* A h w   informieren   15
interpunktieren *punctuate* A h w   informieren   15
interviewen *interview* A h w   machen   21
intonieren *start to sing/play* A h w   informieren   15
intrigieren (**gegen** + A) *scheme*
  (against) h w   informieren   15
investieren (**in** + A) *invest (in)*
  A h w   informieren   15
irisieren *be iridescent* h w   informieren   15
ironisieren *ironize; satirize* A h w   informieren   15
irre|führen *mislead; deceive* A h w   machen   21
irre|leiten *misdirect* A h w   reden   24
irre|machen *disconcert;* (**in** + D)
  shake (in) A h w   machen   21
irren *wander* s w   machen   21
  sich irren (**in** + D/**bei** + D) *be*
  mistaken (about) h w   machen   21
irritieren *irritate; disturb; put off*
  A h w   informieren   15
isolieren (**von** + D) *isolate (from);*
  insulate A h w   informieren   15

jagen (A/**auf** + A) *hunt; chase; shoot* h w	machen	21
jagen (with **sein**) *race; rush;* (**nach** + D) (with **haben**) *chase (after)* h w	machen	21
sich jähren *have an anniversary* (**X jährt sich zum zehntenmal** *it's X's tenth anniversary*) h w	machen	21
jammern *wail; moan;* (**über** + A) *grumble (about)* h w	angeln	1
jammern nach + D *cry out for* h w	angeln	1
jäten *weed* A h w	reden	24
jauchzen *cheer;* (**vor** + D) *shout (with)* h w	heizen	14
jaulen *howl* h w	machen	21
jetten *jet* s w	reden	24
jodeln *yodel* A h w	angeln	1
joggen *jog* h/s w	machen	21
johlen *yell; howl* A h w	machen	21
jonglieren (**mit** + D) *juggle (with)* A h w	informieren	15
jubeln *applaud;* (**über** + A) *cheer (at); rejoice (over)* h w	angeln	1
jucken *itch; make itch* (impers.: **es juckt mich** *I itch; I am itching to*) A h w	machen	21
jungen *give birth; produce young* h w	machen	21
justieren *adjust* A h w	informieren	15
kacheln *tile* A h w	angeln	1
kahl|fressen *strip bare* A h st [i, a, e]	fressen	8
kahl|scheren *shave sb's head; shear bald* A h s [o, o]	kriechen	19
kalauern *tell corny jokes* h w	angeln	1
kalben *calve* h w	machen	21
kalken *whitewash* A h w	machen	21
kalkulieren *calculate; cost* A h w	informieren	15

kalt|bleiben *remain unmoved* s st [ie, ie] — schreiben — 28

kämmen *comb* A h w — machen — 21

kämpfen (mit + D/gegen + A) *fight (with/against)* A h w — machen — 21

kämpfen um + A/für + A *fight for = in order to get/for = on behalf of* h w — machen — 21

sich kämpfen *fight one's way* h w — machen — 21

kampieren *camp (down)* h w — informieren — 15

kanalisieren *channel; canalize* A h w — informieren — 15

kandidieren für + A *stand (as a candidate) for* h w — informieren — 15

kanonisieren *canonize* A h w — informieren — 15

kanten *tilt* A h w — reden — 24

kapern *capture; seize* A h w — angeln — 1

kapieren *understand; get* A h w — informieren — 15

kapitalisieren *capitalize* A h w — informieren — 15

kapitulieren (vor + D) *surrender (to); give up (in the face of)* h w — informieren — 15

sich kaprizieren auf + A *be committed to* h w — informieren — 15

kaputt|machen *break; destroy* A h w — machen — 21

karambolieren (mit + D) *crash (into)* h/s w — informieren — 15

kargen mit + D *be mean with* h w — machen — 21

karikieren *caricature* A h w — informieren — 15

karren *cart* A h w — machen — 21

kartographieren *map* A h w — informieren — 15

kassieren *collect; receive* A h w — informieren — 15

kassieren bei + D *settle up with* h w — informieren — 15

kastrieren *castrate* A h w — informieren — 15

katapultieren *catapult; eject* A h w — informieren — 15

kategorisieren *categorize* A h w — informieren — 15

katzbuckeln (vor + D) *toady (to)* h w — angeln — 1

kauen (an + D) *chew (on)* A h w — machen — 21

kauern *crouch (down)* h w — angeln — 1

sich kauern an + A *huddle up to* h w — angeln — 1

kaufen (D) *buy (for sb); shop* A h w	machen	21
kegeln *play skittles; bowl; score*		
A h w	angeln	1
kehren *turn; sweep* A h w	machen	21
sich kehren (**gegen** + A) *turn*		
(against); (**an** + D) *pay attention*		
(to) h w	machen	21
kehrt|machen *turn in one's tracks* h w	machen	21
keifen *nag; scold* h w	machen	21
keilen (**in** + A) *drive (into); wedge*		
(into); kick A h w	machen	21
keimen *germinate; awaken* h w	machen	21
keltern *press (e.g. grapes)* A h w	angeln	1
kennen (**an** + D/**als**) *know (by/as)*		
A h m [a, a]	brennen	5
kennen|lernen *get/come to know;*		
meet A h w	machen	21
kennzeichnen *label; characterize*		
A h w	atmen	2
kentern *capsize* s w	angeln	1
kerben *notch* A h w	machen	21
ketten (**an** + A) *chain (to); bind (to)*		
A h w	reden	24
keuchen *pant* h w	machen	21
kichern *giggle* h w	angeln	1
kidnappen *kidnap* A h w	machen	21
kippen *tip (over); fall; overturn* A h		
(**sein** when intrans.) w	machen	21
kitten *cement; stick; patch up* A h w	reden	24
kitzeln *tickle* (impers.: **es kitzelt**		
mich, zu . . ., *I feel an urge to . . .*)		
A h w	angeln	1
klaffen *gape; yawn* h w	machen	21
kläffen *yap* h w	machen	21
klagen *moan;* (**über** + A) *complain*		
(about) h w	machen	21
klagen gegen + A *sue* h w	machen	21
klammern *clip; staple* A h w	angeln	1

sich klammern an + A *cling to; be pedantic about* h w	angeln	1
klappen (nach oben/nach unten) *turn (up/down); tilt; work out* A h w	machen	21
klappen (mit + D) *bang (sth)* h w	machen	21
klappern *rattle* h w	angeln	1
klären *clear (up)* A h w	machen	21
klar|machen *make clear* A h w	machen	21
klar|sehen *understand (the matter)* h st [ie, a, e]	sehen	29
klar|spülen *rinse* A h w	machen	21
klar|stellen *clear up; clarify* A h w	machen	21
klatschen (gegen + A) *slap (against); clap* A h/s w	machen	21
kleben (an + D) *stick (to); stick together* A h w	machen	21
kleben (von + D/**vor** + D) *be sticky (with)* h w	machen	21
kleben|bleiben *remain stuck* s st [ie, ie]	schreiben	28
kleckern *make a mess; spill* A h w	angeln	1
klecksen *make a stain/blot* h w	heizen	14
kleiden *dress; clothe; suit* A h w	reden	24
klein|hacken *chop up* A h w	machen	21
klein|machen *cut up small* A h w	machen	21
klein|schneiden *cut up small* A h st [itt, itt]	*streiten	37
klein|stellen *turn down* A h w	machen	21
klemmen *tuck; get caught; stick* A h w	machen	21
klettern (auf + A) *climb (up)* s w	angeln	1
klicken *click* h w	machen	21
klimatisieren *air-condition* A h w	informieren	15
klimpern (mit + D) *jingle* h w	angeln	1
klingeln (nach + D) *ring (for)* (impers.: **es klingelt** *the bell/the phone's ringing*) h w	angeln	1

klingen *ring out;* (**wie**) *sound (like)*		
h st [a, u]	klingen	16
klirren *clink; rattle* h w	machen	21
klopfen (**an** + A) *knock (at); beat*		
A h w	machen	21
klügeln (**an** + D) *ponder (over)* h w	angeln	1
klumpen *go lumpy* h w	machen	21
knabbern (**an** + D) *nibble (at)* h w	angeln	1
knacken *creak; crack; break into*		
A h w	machen	21
knallen *ring out; bang* A h w	machen	21
knarren *creak* h w	machen	21
knattern *clatter* h w	angeln	1
knebeln *gag* A h w	angeln	1
kneifen A/**in** + A *pinch* h st [iff, iff]	greifen	11
kneten *knead;* (**aus** + D) *model*		
(from) A h w	reden	24
knicken *snap; crease* A h (**sein** when		
intrans.) w	machen	21
knicksen (**vor** + D) *curtsy (to)* h w	heizen	14
knien *kneel* h w	*machen	21
knipsen *clip; snap* A h w	heizen	14
knirschen *crunch* h w	machen	21
knirschen mit + D *grind (e.g. teeth)*		
h w	machen	21
knistern (**mit** + D) *rustle; crackle* h w	angeln	1
knittern *crease; crumple* A h w	angeln	1
knobeln (**um** + A) *play dice (for)* h w	angeln	1
knöpfen *button (up)* A h w	machen	21
knospen *bud* h w	machen	21
knoten *knot; tie* A h w	reden	24
knuffen (**in** + A) *poke (in)* A h w	machen	21
knüllen *crumple; crease* A h w	machen	21
knüpfen (**an** + A) *tie/attach (to);*		
knot A h w	machen	21
knüppeln *cudgel; club* A h w	angeln	1
knurren *growl; rumble;* (**über** + A)		
grumble (about) A h w	machen	21

knuspern (an + D) *nibble (at)* A h w — angeln — 1
kochen *boil; cook; make (e.g. hot drink)* A h w — machen — 21
ködern *lure* A h w — angeln — 1
kodieren *(en)code* A h w — informieren — 15
kohlen *smoulder; exaggerate* h w — machen — 21
kokettieren (mit + D) *flirt (with)* h w — informieren — 15
kollaborieren (mit + D) *collaborate (with)* h w — informieren — 15
kollern (with **sein**) *roll;* (with **haben**) *rumble* w — angeln — 1
kollidieren (mit + D) *collide (with); conflict (with)* h w — informieren — 15
kolonisieren *colonize; reclaim* A h w — informieren — 15
kolorieren *colour; embellish* A h w — informieren — 15
kombinieren (mit + D/zu + D) *combine (with/into)* A h w — informieren — 15
kommandieren *command; order* A h w — informieren — 15
kommen (in + A) *come (into); get (into)* s st [am, o] — kommen — 17
kommen aus + D *be a native of* s st [am, o] — kommen — 17
kommen um + A *lose* s st [am, o] — kommen — 17
kommen zu + D *get around to* s st [am, o] — kommen — 17
kommentieren *annotate; comment on* A h w — informieren — 15
kommerzialisieren *commercialize* A h w — informieren — 15
kompensieren (mit + D/durch + A) *compensate for (by)* A h w — informieren — 15
komplizieren *complicate* A h w — informieren — 15
komponieren *compose* A h w — informieren — 15
komprimieren *compress; condense* A h w — informieren — 15
kompromittieren *compromise* A h w — informieren — 15

kondolieren (D) **zu** + D *offer one's condolences (to sb) on* h w	informieren	15
konferieren über + A *confer on/about* h w	informieren	15
konfirmieren *confirm (in church)* A h w	informieren	15
konfrontieren (**mit** + D) *confront (with)* A h w	informieren	15
konjugieren *conjugate* A h w	informieren	15
konkretisieren *put into concrete terms* A h w	informieren	15
konkurrieren (**mit** + D/**um** + A) *compete (with/for)* h w	informieren	15
können *can; be able to; know (how to)* A h m [a, o, o]	können	18
konservieren *preserve* A h w	informieren	15
konspirieren (**gegen** + A) *conspire (against)* h w	informieren	15
konstatieren *establish; detect; state* A h w	informieren	15
konsternieren *fill with consternation* A h w	informieren	15
konstituieren *constitute; set up* A h w	informieren	15
konstruieren *design; construct; fabricate* A h w	informieren	15
konsultieren *consult* A h w	informieren	15
kontern mit + D *counter(-attack) with* A h w	angeln	1
kontrastieren (**mit** + D) *form a contrast (with)* h w	informieren	15
kontrollieren (**auf** + A) *check (for); control* A h w	informieren	15
konvertieren (**in** + A) *convert (into); be converted* A h (sometimes **sein** when intrans.) w	informieren	15
sich konzentrieren (**auf** + A) *concentrate (on)* h w	informieren	15
konzipieren *draft; conceive* A h w	informieren	15

kooperieren (mit + D) *co-operate* *(with)* h w	informieren	15
koordinieren *co-ordinate* A h w	informieren	15
köpfen *decapitate* A h w	machen	21
kopieren *(photo)copy* A h w	informieren	15
koppeln (an + A/**mit** + D) *link up* *(to); combine (with)* A h w	angeln	1
korrelieren mit + D *correlate with* h w	informieren	15
korrespondieren mit + D *correspond* *with/to* h w	informieren	15
korrigieren *correct* A h w	informieren	15
korrumpieren *corrupt* A h w	informieren	15
kosten (D/A) *cost (sb); taste; try* A h w	reden	24
kosten von + D *have a taste of* h w	reden	24
sich **kostümieren** *dress up* h w	informieren	15
krabbeln *crawl* s w	angeln	1
krachen *crash; ring out; creak* h w	machen	21
krächzen *caw; squawk* h w	heizen	14
kräftigen *invigorate* A h w	machen	21
krähen *crow* h w	machen	21
krallen in + A *dig into* A h w	machen	21
sich **krallen an** + A *clutch (tightly); dig one's claws into* h w	machen	21
krampfen *have cramp; be convulsed* h w	machen	21
sich **krampfen in** + A *dig (one's fingers) into* h w	machen	21
kränkeln *be in poor health* h w	angeln	1
kranken an + D *suffer from* h w	machen	21
kränken *hurt (sb's feelings)* A h w	machen	21
kratzen *scratch;* (**aus** + D/**von** + D) *scrape (out of/off)* A h w	heizen	14
kraulen (with **haben** or **sein**) *do the crawl;* (with **haben**) *tickle* A w	machen	21
kräuseln *ruffle; frizz* A h w	angeln	1
krausen *wrinkle (up); crease* A h w	heizen	14

kreieren *create* A h w	informieren	15
kreischen *screech* h w	machen	21
kreiseln *gyrate* h/s w	angeln	1
kreisen (um + A) *revolve (around)*		
h/s w	heizen	14
krempeln *roll* A h w	angeln	1
krepieren *explode* s w	informieren	15
kreuzen *cross; cruise; tack* A h		
(usually **sein** when intrans.) w	heizen	14
sich kreuzen *cross; intersect;* (**mit**		
+ D) *clash (with)* h w	heizen	14
kreuzigen *crucify* A h w	machen	21
kribbeln *tickle; tingle; swarm* (also		
impers.: **es kribbelt mir/mich in**		
+ D *I've a tickle in*) h w	angeln	1
kriechen *crawl;* (**vor** + D) *grovel (to)*		
s st [o, o]	kriechen	19
kriegen *get* A h w	machen	21
kriminalisieren *make . . . turn to*		
crime; present (sth) as criminal		
A h w	informieren	15
kringeln *curl (up)* A h w	angeln	1
kriseln *come to a crisis* (impers.: **es**		
kriselt in + D *there's trouble in*)		
h w	angeln	1
sich kristallisieren *crystallize* h w	informieren	15
kritisieren *criticize* A h w	informieren	15
kritteln (an + D/**über** + A) *find fault*		
(with) h w	angeln	1
kritzeln (an + A/**in** + A) *scribble*		
(on/in) h w	angeln	1
krönen (zu + D) *crown* A h w	machen	21
krümeln *crumble* h w	angeln	1
krümmen *bend* A h w	machen	21
sich krümmen *curve; writhe;*		
(**vor** + D) *double up (with)* h w	machen	21
kugeln *roll* A h (**sein** when intrans.)		
w	angeln	1

kühlen *cool;* (**an** + D) *vent (on)* A h w	machen	21
kulminieren in + D *culminate in* h w	informieren	15
kultivieren *cultivate* A h w	informieren	15
kümmern *concern* A h w	angeln	1
sich kümmern um + A *take care of; care about* h w	angeln	1
kund|geben *make known* A h st [i, a, e]	geben	9
kündigen *cancel;* (D) *give notice (to sb)* A h w	machen	21
kund|machen *proclaim* A h w	machen	21
kungeln (**mit** + D/**um** + A) *bargain (with/for)* h w	angeln	1
kupieren *crop; prune* A h w	informieren	15
kuppeln (**an** + A/**zu** + D) *couple (on to); link* A h w	angeln	1
kurbeln (**nach oben/nach unten**) *crank; wind (up/down)* A h w	angeln	1
küren (**zu** + D) *choose (as)* A h w	machen	21
kurieren (**von** + D) *cure (of)* A h w	informieren	15
kursieren *circulate* h/s w	informieren	15
kurven *circle (round)* s w	machen	21
kurz|arbeiten *work short time* h w	reden	24
kürzen *reduce;* (**um** + A) *shorten (by)* A h w	heizen	14
kurz|halten *keep short of money* A h st [ä, ie, a]	*schlafen	27
kurz|schließen *short-circuit* A h st [o, o]	schießen	26
kurz|treten *take things easy; retrench* h/s st [itt, a, e]	*geben	9
sich kuscheln (**an** + A/**in** + A) *snuggle up (to/in)* h w	angeln	1
kuschen *lie down;* (**vor** + D) *knuckle under (to)* h w	machen	21
küssen *kiss* A h w	heizen	14

kutschieren *drive in a carriage* A h
  (**sein** *when intrans.*) w | informieren | 15

lächeln (**über** + A) *smile (at)* h w | angeln | 1
lachen (**über** + A) *laugh (at)* h w | machen | 21
lackieren *varnish; paint* A h w | informieren | 15
laden *load (up with); summon* A h
  st [ä, u, a] | *tragen | 38
 laden aus + D *unload from* A h st
  [ä, u, a] | *tragen | 38
lädieren *damage* A h w | informieren | 15
lagern *store; be stored; camp* A h w | angeln | 1
lahmen *be lame* h w | machen | 21
lähmen (**an** + D) *paralyse (in)* A h w | machen | 21
lahm‖legen *bring to a standstill* A
  h w | machen | 21
laichen *spawn* h w | machen | 21
lallen *babble; mumble* A h w | machen | 21
lammen *lamb* h w | machen | 21
lancieren *spread; launch* A h w | informieren | 15
landen *land* A (**sein** *when intrans.*)
  h w | reden | 24
länden *recover* A h w | reden | 24
langen (**in** + A/**auf** + A/**bis zu** + D)
  reach (into/on to/up to) h w | machen | 21
längen *lengthen* A h w | machen | 21
lärmen *make a row* h w | machen | 21
lassen *let; have (done); leave* A h st
  [ä, ie, a] | *schlafen | 27
lasten (**auf** + D) *be a burden (on)*
  h w | reden | 24
lästern über + A *be malicious about*
  h w | angeln | 1
lauern *lurk;* (**auf** + A) *lie in wait*
  (for) h w | angeln | 1
laufen (**in** + A/**gegen** + A) *run (into);*
  walk (into); go s st [äu, ie, au] | laufen | 20
lauschen *listen; eavesdrop* h w | machen | 21

lausen *delouse* A h w	heizen	14
lauten *run; read* h w	reden	24
läuten *ring* h w	reden	24
leasen *rent* A h w	heizen	14
leben (von + D/**für** + A) *live (on/for)* A h w	machen	21
lecken (A/**an** + D) *lick (sth); leak* h w	machen	21
leeren *empty* A h w	machen	21
leer|laufen *run out/dry* s st [äu, ie, au]	laufen	20
legalisieren *legalize* A h w	informieren	15
legen (auf + A) *lay/lay down (on)* A h w	machen	21
legen an + A *lean up against* A h w	machen	21
sich legen *lie down; abate* h w	machen	21
legitimieren *legitimize; authorize* A h w	informieren	15
lehnen (an + A/**gegen** + A) *lean (on/against)* A h w	machen	21
lehren *teach* A h w	machen	21
leicht|fallen (D) *be easy (for sb)* s st [ä, iel, a]	*schlafen	27
leicht|machen (D) *make easy (for sb)* A h w	machen	21
leicht|nehmen *make light of* A h st [imm, a, omm]	*sprechen	33
leiden (an + D/**unter** + D) *suffer (from)* h st [itt, itt]	*streiten	37
leiden unter + D *suffer because of sb* h st [itt, itt]	*streiten	37
leihen (D) *lend (to)* A h st [ie, ie]	schreiben	28
leihen von + D/**bei** + D *borrow from* A h st [ie, ie]	schreiben	28
leimen (an + A) *glue (to)* A h w	machen	21
leisten *do; achieve* A h w	reden	24
leiten *lead; be in charge of; direct* A h w	reden	24

lenken *steer; control;* (**auf** + A)
  direct (to) A h w   machen   21
lernen (**aus** + D) *learn (from); study*
  A h w   machen   21
lesen *read; pick* A h st [ie, a, e]   *sehen   29
 lesen über + A/**aus** + D *read about/*
  from A h st [ie, a, e]   *sehen   29
 lesen in + D/**aus** + D *tell from* A h
  st [ie, a, e]   *sehen   29
leuchten *shine;* (D) *light the way*
  (for sb) h w   reden   24
leugnen *deny* A h w   atmen   2
liberalisieren *liberalize* A h w informieren 15
lichten *thin out* A h w   reden   24
 sich lichten *grow thin; dwindle;*
  clear h w   reden   24
liebäugeln mit + D *have one's eye*
  on; toy with h w   angeln   1
lieb|be'halten *go on loving* A h st
  [ä, ie, a]   *schlafen   27
lieben *love; like* A h w   machen   21
lieben|lernen *learn to love* A h w machen   21
lieb|ge'winnen *grow fond of* A h st
  [a, o]   sprechen   33
lieb|haben *love; be fond of* A h m
  [at, att, a]   *brennen   5
liefern (D/**an** + A) *deliver (to);*
  provide A h w   angeln   1
liegen *lie (down); be situated* h st
  [a, e]   sehen   29
 liegen (D) *suit; appeal to* h st
  [a, e]   sehen   29
 liegen an + D/**bei** + D *be sb's*
  responsibility h st [a, e]   sehen   29
liegen|bleiben *stay (lying); be left*
  undone s st [ie, ie]   schreiben   28
liegen|lassen *leave (behind); leave*
  undone A h st [ä, ie, a]   *schlafen   27

sich liieren mit + D *have an affair*		
with; form links with h w	informieren	15
lindern *alleviate* A h w	angeln	1
liquidieren *liquidate; eliminate* A h w	informieren	15
lispeln *lisp; whisper* A h w	angeln	1
lizenzieren *license* A h w	informieren	15
loben (für + A/**wegen** + G) *praise*		
(for) A h w	machen	21
lochen *punch* A h w	machen	21
locken (aus + D/**in** + A) *lure (out of/*		
into); tempt; curl A h w	machen	21
lockern *loosen; relax* A h w	angeln	1
löffeln (aus + D) *spoon up (from)*		
A h w	angeln	1
lohnen *be worth;* (D) *reward/repay*		
(sb) for A h w	machen	21
sich lohnen (für + A) *be worthwhile*		
(for) h w	machen	21
lokalisieren *locate; contain* A h w	informieren	15
los|be'kommen *get off/out/free* A h st		
[am, o]	kommen	17
los|binden *untie* A h st [a, u]	binden	4
los|brechen *break (out/off)* A h (**sein**		
when intrans.) st [i, a, o]	sprechen	33
löschen *put out; quench; erase* A h w	machen	21
losen um + A *draw lots for* h w	heizen	14
lösen (von + D) *remove (from);*		
release; cancel; buy A h w	heizen	14
lösen in + D *dissolve in* A h w	heizen	14
sich lösen (von + D) *come off (sth);*		
free oneself (from); be solved h w	heizen	14
los|fahren *set off;* (**auf** + A) *drive*		
(towards/at) s st [ä, u, a]	tragen	38
los|gehen (auf + A) *go (for sb);*		
set/start off s st [ing, ang]	*hängen	12
los|kaufen *buy (sb's) freedom* A h w	machen	21
los|lachen *burst out laughing* h w	machen	21
los|lassen *let go* A h st [ä, ie, a]	*schlafen	27

los|laufen *run off; start running* s st [äu, ie, au]	laufen	20
los|lösen *remove* A h w	heizen	14
los|rasen (auf + A) *race off (towards)* s w	heizen	14
los|reißen *tear/rip off* A h st [i, i]	beißen	3
sich los|sagen von + D *renounce; break with* h w	machen	21
los|schlagen *knock off/out;* **(auf** + A) *let fly (at)* h st [ä, u, a]	tragen	38
los|schnallen *unfasten* A h w	machen	21
los|sprechen von + D *absolve from* A h st [i, a, o]	sprechen	33
los|steuern auf + A *head for* s w	angeln	1
los|trennen *undo* A h w	machen	21
los|werden *get rid of* A s m [i, u, o]	werden	40
lotsen *pilot; guide* A h w	heizen	14
lüften *air; ventilate; raise; reveal* A h w	reden	24
lügen *lie; tell lies* h st [o, o]	kriechen	19
lullen (in + A) *lull (into)* A h w	machen	21
lutschen (A/an + D) *suck* h w	machen	21
lynchen *lynch* A h w	machen	21
machen (aus + D) *make (from); do; matter* A h w	machen	21
magnetisieren *magnetize* A h w	informieren	15
mähen *mow; bleat* A h w	machen	21
mahlen *grind* A h w (past part. **gemahlen**)	*machen	21
mahnen (zu + D) *urge (sth); urge on* A h w	machen	21
mahnen an + A *remind of* A h w	machen	21
mäkeln (an + D/**über** + A) *carp (at)* h w	angeln	1
malen *paint; colour* A h w	machen	21
mal|nehmen (mit + D) *multiply (by)* A h st [imm, a, omm]	*sprechen	33

malträtieren *ill-treat* A h w	informieren	15
managen *manage* A h w	machen	21
mangeln *be a lack of* (impers.: **es**		
mangelt mir an + D *I lack*) h w	angeln	1
manipulieren *manipulate; rig* A h w	informieren	15
manövrieren *manœuvre* A h w	informieren	15
markieren *mark* A h w	informieren	15
marschieren *march* s w	informieren	15
martern *torment* A h w	angeln	1
maskieren *mask; dress up* A h w	informieren	15
massakrieren *massacre* A h w	informieren	15
maß|halten *exercise moderation* h st		
[ä, ie, a]	*schlafen	27
massieren *mass; massage* A h w	informieren	15
mäßigen *moderate* A h w	machen	21
sich mäßigen bei + D *exercise*		
moderation in h w	machen	21
maßregeln *reprimand; discipline* A		
h w	angeln	1
mästen *fatten* A h w	reden	24
mauern *build* A h w	angeln	1
sich mausern *moult* h w	angeln	1
maximieren *maximize* A h w	informieren	15
mechanisieren *mechanize* A h w	informieren	15
meckern *bleat;* (**über** + A) *grumble*		
(about) h w	angeln	1
meditieren über + A *meditate on* h w	informieren	15
sich mehren *increase* h w	machen	21
meiden *avoid* A h st [ie, ie]	*schreiben	28
meinen *think; mean; say* A h w	machen	21
meiseln *chisel* A h w	angeln	1
meistern *master* A h w	angeln	1
melden (D) *report (to)* A h w	reden	24
sich melden (**zu** + D) *enrol (for);*		
answer h w	reden	24
melken *milk* A h w/st [o, o]	machen/	
	kriechen	21/19
menstruieren *menstruate* h w	informieren	15

merken (an + D) *notice (by)* A h w	machen	21
sich [D] **merken** *remember* A h w	machen	21
messen (nach + D) *measure (in)* A		
h st [i, a, e]	fressen	8
messen nach + D/**an** + D *judge by*		
A h st [i, a, e]	fressen	8
meutern (gegen + A) *mutiny*		
(against) h w	angeln	1
miauen *miaow* h w	machen	21
mieten *rent; hire* A h w	reden	24
mildern *moderate; alleviate* A h w	angeln	1
militarisieren *militarize* A h w	informieren	15
mimen *play; act* A h w	machen	21
mindern *reduce* A h w	angeln	1
mischen (in + A) *mix (into); blend;*		
shuffle A h w	machen	21
sich mischen mit + D/**in** + A/**unter**		
+ A *mix with; interfere in; mingle*		
with h w	machen	21
miß'achten *disregard; ignore* A h w	reden	24
miß'billigen *disapprove of* A h w	machen	21
miß'brauchen *abuse;* (**für** + A/**zu** + D)		
misuse (for) A h w	machen	21
miß'deuten *misinterpret* A h w	reden	24
miß'fallen *displease* (impers.: **es**		
mißfällt mir *I dislike it*) D h st		
[ä, iel, a]	*schlafen	27
miß'glücken (D) *fail (for sb)* s w	machen	21
miß'gönnen (D) *begrudge (sb)* A		
h w	machen	21
miß'handeln *maltreat* A h w	angeln	1
missionieren *do missionary work*		
h w	informieren	15
miß'lingen *fail; be a failure* s st [a,		
u]	klingen	16
miß'raten (D) *turn out badly (for sb)*		
s st [ä, ie, a]	*schlafen	27
miß'trauen *distrust* D h w	machen	21

miß'verstehen (miß stressed, but
insep. except in the inf. with **zu:**
mißzuverstehen) *misunderstand* A
h st [and, and] — stehen — 34
misten *manure* A h w — reden — 24
mit|arbeiten *collaborate;* (**in** + D)
participate (in) h w — reden — 24
mit|be'kommen *get; inherit; manage*
to see/hear A h st [am, o] — kommen — 17
mit|be'nutzen *share* A h w — heizen — 14
mit|be'stimmen *influence;* (**in** + D)
have a say (in) A h w — machen — 21
mit|bringen (D) *bring with one (for*
sb) A h m [ach, ach] — *brennen — 5
mit|denken *follow (an argument)* h
m [ach, ach] — *brennen — 5
mit|emp'finden mit + D *sympathize/*
empathize with h st [a, u] — binden — 4
mit|er'leben *witness; be involved in*
A h w — machen — 21
mit|essen *eat as well;* (**bei** + D) *eat*
(with) A h st [i, a, ge] — *fressen — 8
mit|fahren bei + D *travel with* s st
[ä, u, a] — tragen — 38
mit|fühlen mit + D *sympathize/*
empathize with h w — machen — 21
mit|führen *carry (with one); carry*
along A h w — machen — 21
mit|geben (D) *give (sb) to take along*
A h st [i, a, e] — geben — 9
mit|gehen (mit + D) *go along (with)*
s st [ing, ang] — *hängen — 12
mit|halten (bei + D/**mit** + D) *keep up*
(in/with) h st [ä, ie, a] — *schlafen — 27
mit|helfen (bei + D/**in** + D) *help*
(with) h st [i, a, o] — sprechen — 33
mit|hören *listen (to); overhear* A h w — machen — 21
mit|kämpfen *join in the fight* h w — machen — 21

mit|kommen *come too; keep up* s st
[am, o] kommen 17

mit|laufen (mit + D/bei + D) *run
(with/in)* s st [äu, ie, au] laufen 20

mit|lesen (mit + D) *read at the same
time (as)* A h st [ie, a, e] *sehen 29

mit|machen *join in;* **(bei + D)** *take
part (in)* A h w machen 21

mit|müssen *have to go along* h m
[u, u, u] müssen 23

mit|nehmen *take with one* A h st
[imm, a, omm] *sprechen 33

mit|rechnen *include in; work out at
the same time* A h w atmen 2

mit|reden *join in (the conversation)*
h w reden 24

mit|reisen mit + D *travel with* s w heizen 14

mit|reißen *sweep away; carry away*
A h st [i, i] beißen 3

mit|schicken *send along; enclose* A
h w machen 21

mit|schneiden *record (live)* A h st
[itt, itt] *streiten 37

mit|schreiben *take down* A h st [ie,
ie] schreiben 28

mit|singen *join in; sing along* A h st
[a, u] klingen 16

mit|spielen in + D *act/play in; join in*
h w machen 21

 mit|spielen bei + D *play a part in*
h w machen 21

mit|teilen (D) *inform (sb) of* A h w machen 21

mit|tragen *bear part of; share* A h st
[ä, u, a] tragen 38

mit|trinken mit + D *have a drink with*
h st [a, u] klingen 16

mit|ver'dienen *have a job as well*
h w machen 21

mit|wirken an + D/**bei** + D
collaborate on; be involved in
  h w | machine | 21

 mit|wirken in + D *act/play in* h w | machen | 21

mit|zählen *count (in); be valid* h w | machen | 21

mit|ziehen mit + D *go along with* s st
  [og, og] | *kriechen | 19

mixen (unter + A) *mix (into)* A h w | heizen | 14

mobilisieren *mobilize; summon up*
  A h w | informieren | 15

möblieren *furnish* A h w | informieren | 15

modellieren (nach + D) *model (on)*
  A h w | informieren | 15

moderieren *present (e.g. TV*
 programme) A h w | informieren | 15

modern *go mouldy; decay* h/s w | angeln | 1

modernisieren *modernize* A h w | informieren | 15

mögen *want to; like; may* A h m
  [a, och, och] | mögen | 22

monieren *criticize* A h w | informieren | 15

monopolisieren *monopolize* A h w | informieren | 15

montieren *assemble;* (**an** + A/D/**auf** +
  A/D) *fit (to/on)* A h w | informieren | 15

 montieren in + A *install in* A h w | informieren | 15

moppen *mop* A h w | machen | 21

morden *murder* A h w | reden | 24

motorisieren *motorize* A h w | informieren | 15

moussieren *sparkle* h w | informieren | 15

muhen *moo* h w | machen | 21

multiplizieren (mit + D) *multiply*
 (by) A h w | informieren | 15

mumifizieren *mummify* A h w | informieren | 15

münden in + A *flow into* s w | reden | 24

 münden in + A/D/**auf** + A/D *lead*
 into s w | reden | 24

münzen *coin* A h w | heizen | 14

murmeln *mutter; murmur; play*
 marbles A h w | angeln | 1

murren (über + A) *grumble (about)*		
h w	machen	21
musizieren *play/make music* h w	informieren	15
müssen *have to; must* h m [u, u, u]	müssen	23
mustern *eye; inspect* A h w	angeln	1
mutieren *mutate* h w	informieren	15
mutmaßen *conjecture* A h w	heizen	14
mystifizieren *shroud in mystery* A h w	informieren	15
nach|äffen *mimic* A h w	machen	21
nach|ahmen *imitate* A h w	machen	21
nach|arbeiten *make up (time);*		
retouch A h w	reden	24
nach|be'kommen *have more of* A h st		
[am, o]	kommen	17
nach|bessern *put right; repair* A h w	angeln	1
nach|be'stellen *reorder; order more*		
of A h w	machen	21
nach|bilden (D) *reproduce/copy*		
(from) A h w	reden	24
nach|datieren *backdate* A h w	informieren	15
nach|denken über + A *think about*		
h m [ach, ach]	*brennen	5
nach|drängen *crowd after; push*		
forwards s w	machen	21
nach|drucken *reprint* A h w	machen	21
nach|eifern *emulate* D h w	angeln	1
nach|eilen *hurry after* D s w	machen	21
nach|emp'finden *share; empathize*		
with; re-create A h st [a, u]	binden	4
nach|er'zählen *retell* A h w	machen	21
nach|fahren *follow on; (D) follow*		
(sb) s st [ä, u, a]	tragen	38
nach|fassen (an + D) *change one's*		
grip (on) h w	heizen	14
nach|feiern *have a belated celebration*		
(of) A h w	angeln	1
nach|folgen *follow; succeed* D s w	machen	21

nach|fordern *demand as a supplement*
A h w   angeln   1
nach|forschen *make enquiries;*
investigate h w   machen   21
nach|fragen *enquire;* (**bei** + D/**um** + A)
ask (sb/for) h w   machen   21
nach|fühlen *understand; show*
understanding of A h w   machen   21
nach|füllen *refill* A h w   machen   21
nach|geben (D) *give way/in (to sb);*
stretch; give more (to sb) A h st
[i, a, e]   geben   9
nach|gehen *follow; pursue; look into;*
(**um** + A) *be slow (by) (e.g. clock)*
D s st [ing, ang]   *hängen   12
nach|ge'raten *take after* D s st [ä, ie,
a]   *schlafen   27
nach|gießen (D) *top up (for sb)* A h
st [o, o]   schießen   26
nach|grübeln über + A *ponder over*
h w   angeln   1
nach|hallen *reverberate* h w   machen   21
nach|hängen *dwell on; stick to* D h st
[i, a]   hängen   12
nach|helfen *lend a hand to* D h st
[i, a, o]   sprechen   33
nach|holen *catch up on; fetch* A h w   machen   21
nach|jagen *chase after* D s w   machen   21
nach|klingen *go on sounding; linger* s
st [a, u]   klingen   16
nach|kommen *follow later; keep up;*
(D) *comply with (sth)* s st
[am, o]   kommen   17
nach|laden *reload* h st [ä, u, a]   *tragen   38
nach|lassen *decrease; get worse; let*
off A h st [ä, ie, a]   *schlafen   27
nach|laufen *chase after* D s st [äu, ie,
au]   laufen   20

nach|lesen *look up; check* A h st [ie, a, e]	*sehen	29
nach|liefern *supply later* A h w	angeln	1
nach|lösen *buy (e.g. ticket) on board; pay excess* A h w	heizen	14
nach|machen *copy; imitate* A h w	machen	21
nach|messen *check (the measurements of)* A h st [i, a, e]	fressen	8
nach|plappern *repeat (parrot-fashion)* A h w	angeln	1
nach|prägen *mint more; forge* A h w	machen	21
nach|prüfen *check; examine later* A h w	machen	21
nach|rechnen *check (figures)* A h w	atmen	2
nach|reden *repeat* A h w	reden	24
nach|reisen *travel/set off after* D s w	heizen	14
nach|rennen *chase after* D s m [a, a]	brennen	5
nach|rücken *move up;* (**auf** + A) *be promoted (to)* s w	machen	21
nach|rufen (D) *call after (sb)* A h st [ie, u]	rufen	25
nach|rühmen (D) *credit (sb) with* A h w	machen	21
nach|rüsten (**mit** + D) *upgrade (with)* A h w	reden	24
nach|sagen (D) *repeat (after sb); speak ill (of sb)* A h w	machen	21
nach|salzen (past part. **gesalzen** or **gesalzt**) *add salt to* A h w	*heizen	14
nach|schenken (D) *top up (sb's) glass with* A h w	machen	21
nach|schicken (D) *send on; send after (sb)* A h w	machen	21
nach|schlagen *look up* A h st [ä, u, a]	tragen	38
nach|schleichen *creep after* D s st [i, i]	gleichen	10
nach|sehen (D) *gaze after (sb); check; overlook* A h st [ie, a, e]	sehen	29

nach|senden *send on;* (D) *send after (sb)* A h w/m [a, a]	reden/senden	24/31
nach|sitzen *be in detention* h st [aß, ess]	*fressen	8
nach|spielen *mimic; re-enact* A h w	machen	21
nach|spionieren *spy on* D h w	informieren	15
nach|sprechen (D) *repeat (after sb)* A h st [i, a, o]	sprechen	33
nach|spülen *rinse* A h w	machen	21
nach|spüren *investigate; track down* D h w	machen	21
nach|stehen (an + D) *be inferior to (in)* D h st [and, and]	stehen	34
nach|stellen (D) *put after (sth); adjust; portray; put back (e.g. clock)* A h w	machen	21
nach|tanken *refuel* A h w	machen	21
nach|tragen (D) *hold against (sb); add; carry after (sb)* A h st [ä, u, a]	tragen	38
nach|trauern *pine for; lament the passing of* D h w	angeln	1
nachtwandeln *sleepwalk* h/s w	angeln	1
nach|voll'ziehen *reconstruct; comprehend* A h st [og, og]	*kriechen	19
nach|wachsen *grow again/back* s st [ä, u, a]	*tragen	38
nach|weinen *have regrets about* D h w	machen	21
nach|weisen (D) *prove (against sb); detect* A h st [ie, ie]	*schreiben	28
nach|werfen (D) *throw after (sb)* A h st [i, a, o]	sprechen	33
nach|winken *wave after* D h w	machen	21
nach|wirken (bei + D) *have a lasting effect (on)* h w	machen	21
nach|zahlen *pay in arrears; pay in addition* A h w	machen	21

nach|zählen *re-count; check* A h w	machen 21
nach|zeichnen *copy* A h w	atmen 2
nach|ziehen (D) *follow (sb); retrace; tighten up* A h (**sein** when intrans.) st [og, og]	*kriechen 19
nageln (**an** + A/**auf** + A) *nail (to/on)* A h w	angeln 1
nagen (**an** + D) *gnaw (at)* A h w	machen 21
nahe|kommen *get close to; approximate to* D s st [am, o]	kommen 17
nahe|legen (D) *suggest (to sb)* A h w	machen 21
nahe|liegen *arise* h st [a, e]	sehen 29
sich nahen *draw near* h w	machen 21
nähen (**an** + A/**auf** + A) *sew (on to)* A h w	machen 21
näher|bringen (D) *make more accessible (to sb)* A h m [ach, ach]	*brennen 5
näher|kommen *get on closer terms with* D h st [am, o]	kommen 17
näher|liegen *be more obvious* h st [a, e]	sehen 29
nähern (D) *bring closer (to sth)* A h w	angeln 1
sich nähern *approach* D h w	angeln 1
näher|stehen *be closer to* D h st [and, and]	stehen 34
nahe|stehen *be on close terms with* D h st [and, and]	stehen 34
nähren (**mit** + D) *feed (on); be nourishing* A h w	machen 21
sich nähren von + D *feed on* h w	machen 21
narkotisieren *anaesthetize* A h w	informieren 15
naschen *eat (sweet things);* (**von** + D) *have a nibble (at)* A h w	machen 21
näseln *talk through one's nose* h w	angeln 1

nasführen *lead up the garden path* A h w	machen	21
nationalisieren *nationalize* A h w	informieren	15
naturalisieren *naturalize* A h w	informieren	15
navigieren *navigate* A h w	informieren	15
nebeln *spray* A h w	angeln	1
nebeneinander|legen *place side by side* A h w	machen	21
nebeneinander|setzen *put next to each other* A h w	heizen	14
nebeneinander|sitzen *sit next to each other* h st [aß, ess]	*fressen	8
nebeneinander|stellen *place next to each other* A h w	machen	21
nebenher|fahren *drive alongside* s st [ä, u, a]	tragen	38
nebenher|gehen *walk alongside* s st [ing, ang]	*hängen	12
nebenher|laufen *run alongside/ concurrently* s st [äu, ie, au]	laufen	20
necken (**mit** + D) *tease (about)* A h w	machen	21
negieren *deny; reject* A h w	informieren	15
nehmen (**auf sich** [D]) *take (upon oneself); use; charge* A h st [imm, a, omm]	*sprechen	33
nehmen (D) *deprive (sb) of* A h st [imm, a, omm]	*sprechen	33
neigen *tilt;* (**zu** + D) *be prone (to); tend (towards)* A h w	machen	21
sich neigen *bend* h w	machen	21
nennen (+ two As) *call (sb/sth)* h m [a, a]	brennen	5
nennen nach + D *call after* A h m [a, a]	brennen	5
nennen *name;* (D) *give the name of (to sb)* A h m [a, a]	brennen	5
nesteln an + D *fumble with* h w	angeln	1

neutralisieren *neutralize* A h w	informieren	15
nicken *nod* h w	machen	21
nieder|brennen *burn down* A h (**sein** when intrans.) m [a, a]	brennen	5
nieder|donnern *thunder down* s w	angeln	1
nieder|drücken *press down; depress; oppress* A h w	machen	21
nieder|gehen *land; come down; go down* s st [ing, ang]	*hängen	12
nieder|halten *hold down; oppress* A h st [ä, ie, a]	*schlafen	27
nieder|holen *lower* A h w	machen	21
nieder|kämpfen *overcome; fight down* A h w	machen	21
sich nieder|knien *go down on one's knees* h w	*machen	21
nieder|lassen *lower* A h st [ä, ie, a]	*schlafen	27
sich nieder|lassen (als) *set oneself up in business (as)* h st [ä, ie, a]	*schlafen	27
nieder|legen *resign (from); discontinue* A h w	machen	21
nieder|prasseln *rain down* s w	angeln	1
nieder|reißen *pull down; knock over* A h st [i, i]	beißen	3
nieder|schießen *gun down; swoop down* A h (**sein** when intrans.) st [o, o]	schießen	26
nieder|schlagen *knock/turn/put down; lower* A h st [ä, u, a]	tragen	38
sich nieder|schlagen *condense;* (**in** + D) *be reflected (in)* h st [ä, u, a]	tragen	38
nieder|schmettern *send crashing down; devastate* A h w	angeln	1
nieder|schreiben *write (down)* A h st [ie, ie]	schreiben	28
nieder|setzen *put down* A h w	heizen	14
nieder|sinken *sink down* s st [a, u]	klingen	16
nieder|stimmen *vote down* A h w	machen	21

nieder|stoßen *swoop down; floor* h
(**sein** when intrans.) s st [ö, ie, o]   stoßen   36

sich nieder|strecken *lie down* h w   machen   21

nieder|treten *trample underfoot* A h
st [itt, a, e]   *geben   9

nieder|walzen *flatten* A h w   heizen   14

sich nieder|werfen vor + D *prostrate
oneself before* h st [i, a, o]   sprechen   33

nieseln *drizzle* (impers.: **es nieselt**)
h w   angeln   1

niesen *sneeze* h w   heizen   14

nieten *rivet* A h w   reden   24

nippen (**von** + D) *sip (at); nibble
(at)* h w   machen   21

nisten *nest* h w   reden   24

nivellieren *level out/down* A h w   informieren   15

nominieren *nominate* A h w   informieren   15

nörgeln an + D *grumble about* h w   angeln   1

normalisieren *normalize* A h w   informieren   15

normen/normieren *standardize* A h w   machen/
informieren 21/15

notieren (**mit** + D) *note down; be
quoted (at* + *price)* A h w   informieren   15

nötigen (**zu** + D) *compel (sth) of*
A h w   machen   21

not'landen (insep. but past part.
notgelandet and inf. with **zu**
notzulanden) *crash-land* A h (**sein**
when intrans.) w   reden   24

not'wassern (insep. but past part.
notgewassert and inf. with **zu**
notzuwassern) *ditch* A h (**sein**
when intrans.) w   angeln   1

nuancieren *give subtle nuances to* A
h w   informieren   15

numerieren *number* A h w   informieren   15

nutzen *use; exploit; take advantage
of* A h w   heizen   14

nützen (D) *be of use (to); use* A h w	heizen	14
objektivieren *objectify* A h w	informieren	15
observieren *observe; keep under observation* A h w	informieren	15
sich offen'baren als *reveal oneself to be* h w	machen	21
offen|bleiben *remain open/unsatisfied* s st [ie, ie]	schreiben	28
offen|halten *keep open* A h st [ä, ie, a]	*schlafen	27
offen|lassen *leave open* A h st [ä, ie, a]	*schlafen	27
offen|legen *reveal; disclose* A h w	machen	21
offen|stehen (D) *be open (to); hang open; be outstanding* h st [and, and]	stehen	34
offerieren *offer* A h w	informieren	15
öffnen *open* A h w	atmen	2
sich öffnen *open; (D/auf + A) open up (to/on to)* h w	atmen	2
ohrfeigen (A) *box (sb's) ears* h w	machen	21
okkupieren *occupy* A h w	informieren	15
operieren (A) *operate (on sb)* h w	informieren	15
opfern (D) *sacrifice (to)* A h w	angeln	1
opponieren gegen + A *oppose* h w	informieren	15
optimieren *optimize* A h w	informieren	15
orchestrieren *orchestrate* A h w	informieren	15
ordnen *arrange; regulate* A h w	atmen	2
sich ordnen *form up* h w	atmen	2
organisieren *organize* A h w	informieren	15
orientieren über + A *report on; inform about* A h w	informieren	15
sich orientieren an + D *get one's bearings by; be oriented towards* h w	informieren	15

sich orientieren über + A *inform*		
oneself about h w	informieren	15
oszillieren *oscillate* h w	informieren	15
paaren mit + D *combine/mate with*		
A h w	machen	21
sich paaren *mate* h w	machen	21
pachten *lease* A h w	reden	24
packen in + A/**aus** + D *pack in;*		
unpack from A h w	machen	21
packen (an + D) *seize (by); grip* A		
h w	machen	21
paddeln *paddle; canoe* h (**sein** when		
direction is given) w	angeln	1
paffen *puff at; puff out; puff away* A		
h w	machen	21
paginieren *paginate* A h w	informieren	15
paktieren mit + D *do deals with*		
h w	informieren	15
pappen (auf + A/**an** + A) *stick (on)*		
A h w	machen	21
pappen an + D *stick to* h w	machen	21
paradieren *parade* h w	informieren	15
paralysieren *paralyze* A h w	informieren	15
paraphieren *initial* A h w	informieren	15
paraphrasieren *paraphrase* A h w	informieren	15
parfümieren *perfume* A h w	informieren	15
parieren *parry* A h w	informieren	15
parken *park* A h w	machen	21
parodieren *parody* A h w	informieren	15
partizipieren an + D *participate in*		
h w	informieren	15
passen *suit;* (**in** + A/**zu** + D) *fit*		
(into/with) D h w	heizen	14
passen auf + A/**zu** + D *go with* h w	heizen	14
passieren *pass; cross; strain; happen*		
A h (**sein** when intrans.) w	informieren	15
pasteurisieren *pasteurize* A h w	informieren	15

patentieren (D) *patent; grant (sb) a*		
patent for A h w	informieren	15
patrouillieren *(be on) patrol* h/s w	informieren	15
pausen *trace* A h w	heizen	14
pausieren *pause; take a rest* h w	informieren	15
peilen *take one's bearings* h w	machen	21
peinigen *torment* A h w	machen	21
peitschen (**gegen** + A) *whip*		
(against); lash A h (**sein** when		
intrans.) w	machen	21
pellen *peel* A h w	machen	21
pendeln (**an** + D) (with **haben**) *swing*		
(by); (with **sein**) *commute* w	angeln	1
pensionieren *pension off* A h w	informieren	15
perfektionieren *perfect* A h w	informieren	15
perlen *sparkle;* (**auf** + D) *form*		
droplets (on) h/s w	machen	21
perlen von + D *trickle from* s w	machen	21
persiflieren *satirize* A h w	informieren	15
personalisieren *personalize* A h w	informieren	15
personifizieren *personify* A h w	informieren	15
pervertieren *corrupt;* (**zu** + D)		
become perverted (into) A h (**sein**		
when intrans.) w	informieren	15
pfänden *impound* A h w	reden	24
pfeffern *(season with) pepper* A h w	angeln	1
pfeifen (D/**nach** + D) *whistle (for);*		
pipe A h st [iff, iff]	greifen	11
pflanzen (**in** + A) *plant (in)* A h w	heizen	14
pflastern *surface; pave* A h w	angeln	1
pflegen *look after; care for* A h w	machen	21
pflegen (**etwas zu tun**) *be in the*		
habit of (doing sth) h w	machen	21
pflücken *pick* A h w	machen	21
pflügen *plough* A h w	machen	21
pfropfen (**auf** + A) *graft (on)* A h w	machen	21
phantasieren (**von** + D) *fantasize*		
(about) h w	informieren	15

philosophieren *philosophize* h w	informieren	15
phrasieren *phrase* A h w	informieren	15
picken (**nach** + D/**an** + A) *peck (at/ on)* A h w	machen	21
picknicken *picnic* h w	machen	21
piepen *bleep; chirp; squeak* h w	machen	21
pilgern *go on a pilgrimage* s w	angeln	1
pinseln *paint;* (**auf** + A) *apply, e.g. paint, (to)* A h w	angeln	1
plädieren (**für** + A/**auf** + A) *plead (for)* h w	informieren	15
plagen *torment; plague* A h w	machen	21
sich plagen *slave away;* (**mit** + D) *be troubled (by)* h w	machen	21
plakatieren *announce by poster; put up posters* A h w	informieren	15
planen *plan* A h w	machen	21
planieren *level* A h w	informieren	15
planschen *splash about; paddle* h w	machen	21
plärren *bawl; blare* A h w	machen	21
platschen (**an** + A/**gegen** + A) *splash (against)* h/s w	machen	21
plätschern *patter; burble; splash* h w	angeln	1
plätten *iron* A h w	reden	24
platzen *burst;* (**vor** + D) *be bursting (with)* s w	heizen	14
plaudern (**über** + A/**von** + D) *chat (about)* h w	angeln	1
plazieren *place; seat* A h w	informieren	15
sich plazieren (**auf** + A/D/**an** + A/D) *seat oneself (on); take up position (at)* h w	informieren	15
plissieren *pleat* A h w	informieren	15
plumpsen *fall with a bump; splash* s w	heizen	14
plündern *loot; plunder* A h w	angeln	1
plustern *ruffle (up)* A h w	angeln	1
pöbeln *make rude remarks* h w	angeln	1

pochen (an + A/gegen + A) *knock (at)* h w	machen	21
pökeln *salt* A h w	angeln	1
pokern *play poker;* (um + A) *bid (for)* h w	angeln	1
sich polarisieren *become polarized* h w	informieren	15
polieren *polish (up)* A h w	informieren	15
politisieren *talk politics; politicize* A h w	informieren	15
polstern *upholster* A h w	angeln	1
poltern (with **haben**) *crash about; rant;* (with **sein**) *clatter (along)* w	angeln	1
popularisieren *popularize* A h w	informieren	15
porträtieren *portray* A h w	informieren	15
posaunen *play the trombone; bawl* A h w (past part. **posaunt**)	machen	21
posieren *pose* h w	informieren	15
postieren *post; station* A h w	informieren	15
postulieren *demand; assert* A h w	informieren	15
potenzieren *increase* A h w	informieren	15
prädestinieren *predestine* A h w	informieren	15
prägen *emboss; coin; mould* A h w	machen	21
prahlen (mit + D) *boast (about)* h w	machen	21
praktizieren *practise* A h w	informieren	15
prallen (auf + A/gegen + A/an + A) (with **sein**) *crash (into); collide (with);* (with **haben**) *blaze* w	machen	21
prämi(i)eren *award a prize to* A h w	informieren	15
prangen *be on prominent display* h w	machen	21
präparieren *prepare* A h w	informieren	15
präsentieren *present; offer* A h w	informieren	15
präsidieren *preside* h w	informieren	15
prasseln *pelt down; rattle; crackle* h/s w	angeln	1
prassen (mit + D) *squander* h w	heizen	14
präzisieren *state more precisely* A h w	informieren	15

predigen (gegen + A) *preach (against)* A h w	machen	21
preisen *praise; acclaim* A h st [ie, ie]	*schreiben	28
preis|geben (D) *expose (to); relinquish; betray* A h st [i, a, e]	geben	9
prellen *bruise; bounce;* (**um** + A) *cheat (out of)* A h w	machen	21
preschen *dash* s w	machen	21
pressen (**in** + A) *press (into)* A h w	heizen	14
prickeln *tingle; sparkle* h w	angeln	1
privatisieren *privatize* A h w	informieren	15
privilegieren *grant privileges to* A h w	informieren	15
probieren *try (on); taste; sample* A h w	informieren	15
produzieren *produce* A h w	informieren	15
sich profilieren *make one's name* h w	informieren	15
profitieren (**von** + D/**bei** + D/**an** + D) *profit (by)* A h w	informieren	15
programmieren *program(me); schedule* A h w	informieren	15
projektieren *project; plan* A h w	informieren	15
proklamieren *proclaim* A h w	informieren	15
promovieren (**über** + A) *take/do one's doctorate (on)* h w	informieren	15
propagieren *propagate* A h w	informieren	15
prophezeien (past part. **prophezeit**) (D) *prophesy (for)* A h w	machen	21
sich prostituieren *prostitute oneself* h w	informieren	15
protestieren (**gegen** + A) *protest (against)* h w	informieren	15
protokollieren *take down; take the minutes* A h w	informieren	15
provozieren (**zu** + D) *provoke (into); cause* A h w	informieren	15
prozessieren (**mit** + D/**um** + A) *go to law (with/about)* h w	informieren	15

prüfen (in + D/auf + A) *test (in/for);* *check; scrutinize* A h w	machen	21
prügeln *beat* A h w	angeln	1
sich prügeln (mit + D/um + A) *fight* *(with/over)* h w	angeln	1
prunken *be resplendent;* **(mit + D)** *show off (with)* h w	machen	21
publizieren *publish* A h w	informieren	15
pudern *powder* A h w	angeln	1
pulsieren *pulsate; pulse* h w	informieren	15
pulverisieren *pulverize* A h w	informieren	15
pumpen *pump; lend* A h w	machen	21
punktieren *dot* A h w	informieren	15
purzeln (über + A) *tumble (over)* s w	angeln	1
putzen *polish; clean; decorate* A h w	heizen	14
quadrieren *square (a number)* A h w	informieren	15
quaken *quack; croak* A h w	machen	21
quäken *squawk; whine; bawl out* A h w	machen	21
quälen *torment; be cruel to* A h w	machen	21
sich quälen *suffer; struggle* h w	machen	21
qualifizieren *qualify* A h w	informieren	15
qualmen *belch smoke* (impers.: **es** **qualmt aus** + D *smoke is belching* *out from)* h w	machen	21
quantifizieren *quantify* A h w	informieren	15
quellen *gush; billow; bulge; swell* *(up)* s st [i, o, o]	dreschen	6
quetschen *crush;* **(an + A/in + A)** *squash (against/into)* A h w	machen	21
quieken *squeak;* **(vor + D)** *squeal* *(with)* h w	machen	21
quietschen *squeak; screech;* **(vor** **+ D)** *shriek (with)* h w	machen	21
quirlen *swirl (about)* A h w	machen	21

quittieren (mit + D) *greet (with);*
acknowledge; give a receipt for
A h w   informieren   15

rabattieren (mit + D) *give a discount*
(of . . .) on A h w   informieren   15
rächen *avenge;* **(an** + D) *take revenge*
for (on) A h w   machen   21
radebrechen *murder; mangle (a*
language) A h w   machen   21
rad|fahren (only inf. and past part.,
otherwise **ich fahre Rad**, etc.)
cycle s st [ä, u, a]   tragen   38
radieren *erase* A h w   informieren   15
radikalisieren *make more radical* A
h w   informieren   15
rad|schlagen (only inf. and past
part., otherwise **ich schlage Rad**,
etc.) *do cartwheels* h st [ä, u, a]   tragen   38
raffen *snatch; condense* A h w   machen   21
raffinieren *refine* A h w   informieren   15
ragen *tower up;* **(in** + A/**über** + A)
stick out (into/over) h w   machen   21
rahmen *frame* A h w   machen   21
rammen in + A *ram into* A h w   machen   21
  rammen gegen + A/**auf** + A *crash*
into s w   machen   21
randalieren *riot; rampage* h w   informieren   15
rangieren *shunt; be placed* A h w   informieren   15
sich ranken (an + D/**über** + A) *grow*
(up/over) h w   machen   21
  sich ranken um + A *(en)twine*
around h w   machen   21
rascheln (mit + D) *rustle (sth)* h w   angeln   1
rasen (with **sein**) *dash along;* **(gegen**
+ A) *crash (into);* (with **haben**)
rage w   heizen   14
sich rasieren *shave* h w   informieren   15

raspeln *rasp; grate* A h w	angeln	1
rasseln (**mit** + D) *rattle* h w	angeln	1
rasten *rest; take a break* h w	reden	24
raten (D = *sb*, A = *sth*) *advise; guess* h st [ä, ie, a]	*schlafen	27
ratifizieren *ratify* A h w	informieren	15
rationalisieren *rationalize* A h w	informieren	15
rationieren *ration* A h w	informieren	15
rätseln (**über** + A) *puzzle (over)* h w	angeln	1
rattern *rattle* h w	angeln	1
rauben (D) *steal (from sb); take away (from sb); kidnap* A h w	machen	21
rauchen *smoke* A h w	machen	21
räuchern *smoke (food)* A h w	angeln	1
sich raufen um + A/**wegen** + G *fight over* h w	machen	21
räumen *clear (away); vacate; clear up* A h w	machen	21
rauschen (with **haben**) *rustle; rush; roar;* (with **sein**) *sweep* w	machen	21
reagieren auf + A *react to* h w	informieren	15
reactivieren *bring back into service; brush up; recall* A h w	informieren	15
realisieren *realize* A h w	informieren	15
reanimieren *resuscitate* A h w	informieren	15
rebellieren (**gegen** + A) *rebel (against)* h w	informieren	15
rechnen *reckon; work out; calculate;* (**zu** + D) *count (among)* A h w	atmen	2
rechnen auf + A/**mit** + D *count on; reckon with* h w	atmen	2
rechtfertigen (**vor** + D) *justify (to)* A h w	machen	21
recken *stretch* A h w	machen	21
reden *say; speak;* (**mit** + D) *talk (to)* A h w	reden	24
reden von + D/**über** + A *talk about* h w	reden	24

redigieren *edit* A h w	informieren	15
reduzieren auf + A *reduce to* A h w	informieren	15
referieren (A/**über** + A) *give a report (on)* h w	informieren	15
reflektieren über + A *reflect upon* h w	informieren	15
reformieren *reform* A h w	informieren	15
regeln *settle; control* A h w	angeln	1
sich regen *move; stir* h w	machen	21
regenerieren *regenerate* A h w	informieren	15
regieren (**über** + A) *rule (over)* A h w	informieren	15
registrieren *register; note* A h w	informieren	15
reglementieren *regiment* A h w	informieren	15
regnen (with **haben**) *rain* (impers.: **es regnet** *it's raining*); (with **sein**) *rain down* w	atmen	2
regulieren *regulate; set* A h w	informieren	15
rehabilitieren *rehabilitate* A h w	informieren	15
reiben (**an** + D) *rub (against)* A h st [ie, ie]	schreiben	28
sich reiben an + D *come up against* h st [ie, ie]	schreiben	28
sich reiben mit + D *be at loggerheads with* h st [ie, ie]	schreiben	28
reichen (D) *be enough (for); serve; hand* A h w	machen	21
reichen bis zu + D *extend as far as* h w	machen	21
reifen *ripen;* (**zu** + D) *mature (into)* s w	machen	21
reihen *put into a line; string* A h w	machen	21
(sich) reimen (**auf** + A) *rhyme (with)* A h w	machen	21
reinigen *(dry-)clean; purify* A h w	machen	21
reisen *travel* s w	heizen	14
reißen *tear; drag;* (**an** + D) *pull (at)* A h st [i, i]	beißen	3

reiten (auf + D) *ride (on)* A h **(sein** when intrans.) st [itt, itt]	streiten	37
reizen *annoy; attract;* (**zu** + D) *provoke (to)* A h w	heizen	14
rekapitulieren *recapitulate* A h w	informieren	15
reklamieren *complain;* (**bei** + D) *complain about (to)* A h w	informieren	15
rekonstruieren *reconstruct* A h w	informieren	15
sich rekrutieren aus + D *be drawn from* h w	informieren	15
rennen *run;* (**an** + A/**gegen** + A) *bang (into)* s m [a, a]	brennen	5
renommieren mit + D *flaunt* h w	informieren	15
renovieren *renovate; redecorate* A h w	informieren	15
sich rentieren *be profitable; be worth while* h w	informieren	15
reorganisieren *reorganize* A h w	informieren	15
reparieren *repair* A h w	informieren	15
repräsentieren *represent; attend official functions* A h w	informieren	15
reproduzieren *reproduce* A h w	informieren	15
reservieren *reserve; book* A h w	informieren	15
residieren *reside* h w	informieren	15
resignieren *give up* h w	informieren	15
respektieren *respect* A h w	informieren	15
restaurieren *restore* A h w	informieren	15
resultieren aus + D *result from* h w	informieren	15
resümieren *summarize* A h w	informieren	15
retten (vor + D) *rescue (from)* A h w	reden	24
sich retten vor + D/**aus** + D *escape from* h w	reden	24
retuschieren *retouch; gloss over* A h w	informieren	15
reuen *fill with regret* (impers.: **es reut mich** *I regret*) A h w	machen	21

sich revanchieren (bei + D) *get one's*		
revenge (on) h w	informieren	15
sich revanchieren für + A *repay* h w	informieren	15
revidieren *revise; check* A h w	informieren	15
revoltieren gegen + A *rebel against*		
h w	informieren	15
revolutionieren *revolutionize* A h w	informieren	15
rezipieren *adopt; receive* A h w	informieren	15
rezitieren *recite* A h w	informieren	15
richten (auf + A) *direct (towards);*		
judge; condemn A h w	reden	24
richten an + A *address to* A h w	reden	24
sich richten nach + D *fit in with;*		
comply with; depend on h w	reden	24
riechen (A/**an** + D) *smell* h st [o, o]	kriechen	19
riechen nach + D *smell of* h st [o, o]	kriechen	19
rieseln (with **sein**) *trickle;* (impers.		
with **haben**) *drizzle* w	angeln	1
riffeln *ripple* A h w	angeln	1
ringeln *curl; coil* A h w	angeln	1
ringen *wrestle;* (**um** + A) *fight (for)*		
A h w	machen	21
rinnen *run; leak away* s st [a, o]	*sprechen	33
riskieren *risk* A h w	informieren	15
ritzen *scratch; engrave;* (**in** + A)		
carve (in) A h w	heizen	14
rivalisieren (mit + D/**um** + A)		
compete (with/for) h w	informieren	15
röcheln *give the death rattle* h w	angeln	1
rodeln *sledge; toboggan* s w	angeln	1
roden *clear; lift* A h w	reden	24
rollen *roll;* (**in** + A) *roll up (in)* A		
h w	machen	21
romantisieren *romanticize* A h w	informieren	15
röntgen *X-ray* A h w	atmen	2
rosten *rust* h/s w	reden	24
rösten *roast; toast; grill; fry* A h w	reden	24
röten *redden; make red* A h w	reden	24

rotieren *rotate* h w	informieren	15
rucken *jerk; jolt* A h w	machen	21
rücken *move;* (**an** + D) *pull at* A h (**sein** *when intrans.*) w	machen	21
rückwärts|gehen *go down; get worse* s st [ing, ang]	*hängen	12
rudern *row* A h (**sein** *when intrans.*) w	angeln	1
rufen (**nach** + D/**zu** + D) *call (for/to)* A h st [ie, u]	rufen	25
rügen (**wegen** + G) *reprimand (for)* A h w	machen	21
ruhen *rest; be at a standstill* h w	machen	21
ruhen|lassen (*past part.* **ruhenlassen**) *let rest* A h st [ä, ie, a]	*schlafen	27
ruhig|stellen *immobilize* A h w	machen	21
rühmen *praise* A h w	machen	21
sich rühmen (G) *boast (about)* h w	machen	21
rühren (**an** + A/**in** + A) *stir (into); move* A h w	machen	21
rühren an + A *touch on* h w	machen	21
ruinieren *ruin* A h w	informieren	15
rümpfen bei + D *wrinkle (nose) at* A h w	machen	21
runden *round (off)* A h w	reden	24
rund|gehen *be passed round; go the rounds* s st [ing, ang]	*hängen	12
runzeln *wrinkle (e.g. forehead)* A h w	angeln	1
rupfen *pluck; pull up* A h w	machen	21
rußen *smoke; give off/blacken with soot* A h w	heizen	14
rüsten (**zu** + D) *arm (for)* A h w	reden	24
rutschen *slide* s w	machen	21
rütteln (**an** + D) *shake (by); rattle (at)* A h w	angeln	1
sabotieren *sabotage* A h w	informieren	15

sacken *slump; sink* s w	machen	21
säen *sow* A h w	machen	21
sagen (D) (**über** + A/**von** + D) *say* *(to sb) (about); tell* A h w	machen	21
sagen (**zu** + D) *say (to sth); think* *(about sth)* A h w	machen	21
sägen *saw (up)* A h w	machen	21
salben *anoint; put ointment on* A h w	machen	21
saldieren *balance (the books)* A h w	informieren	15
salutieren vor + D *salute* h w	informieren	15
salzen *salt* A h w (past part. **gesalzen**)	*heizen	14
sammeln *collect; gather* A h w	angeln	1
sanieren *redevelop; renovate; heal* A h w	informieren	15
sanktionieren *sanction* A h w	informieren	15
satteln *saddle* A h w	angeln	1
sättigen *be filling; be full of; satisfy* A h w	machen	21
sauber|halten *keep clean;* (**von** + D) *keep clear (of)* A h st [ä, ie, a]	*schlafen	27
sauber|machen *clean;* (**bei** + D) *do the cleaning (for)* A h w	machen	21
säubern *clean* A h w	angeln	1
säuern *pickle; leaven* A h w	angeln	1
saufen *drink (of animals, or* *excessively)* A h st [äu, off, off]	*kriechen	19
saugen (A/**an** + D) *suck* h w/st [o, o]	machen/ kriechen	21/19
säugen *suckle* A h w	machen	21
säumen *hem; line* A h w	machen	21
säuseln *rustle; whisper* A h w	angeln	1
sausen (with **haben**) *roar; whirr;* (with **sein**) *rush along* w	heizen	14
schaben (**an** + D/**auf** + D) *scrape* *(against); plane* A h w	machen	21
schachern um + A *haggle over* h w	angeln	1

schaden *damage; harm* D h w	reden	24
schädigen *damage; cause loss to* A h w	machen	21
schaffen *create* A h st [uf, a]	*tragen	38
schaffen *manage; manage to do;* (**aus** + D/**in** + A) *get (out of/into)* A h w	machen	21
schälen *peel* A h w	machen	21
schallen *ring out* h w (st past tense **scholl** etc. is rare)	machen	21
schalten (**auf** + A) *switch (to); change gear* A h w	reden	24
sich schämen (G/**für** + A/**wegen** + G) *be ashamed (of)* h w	machen	21
schamponieren *shampoo* A h w	informieren	15
schänden *discredit; defile* A h w	reden	24
sich scharen *gather* h w	machen	21
schärfen *sharpen* A h w	machen	21
scharren *scrape;* (**an** + D) *scratch (at)* h w	machen	21
schattieren *shade* A h w	informieren	15
schätzen *guess; value* A h w	heizen	14
schätzen|lernen *come to appreciate* A h w	machen	21
schaudern (**bei** + D/**vor** + D) *shiver (at/with)* h w	angeln	1
schauen (**auf** + A/**nach** + D) *look (at/after)* h w	machen	21
schaufeln *shovel; dig* A h w	angeln	1
schaukeln *swing; sway; rock* A h w	angeln	1
schäumen *foam; lather;* (**vor** + D) *fume (with)* h w	machen	21
scheiden *divorce; separate;* (**von** + D) *part (from)* A h (**sein** when intrans.) st [ie, ie]	*schreiben	28
scheinen *shine;* (D) *seem (to sb)* h st [ie, ie]	schreiben	28
scheißen *shit* h st [i, i]	beißen	3

scheiteln *part (hair)* A h w	angeln	1
scheitern (**an** + D) *fail (because of);* *break down* s w	angeln	1
schellen (**an** + D/**nach** + D) *ring (at/* *for)* h w	machen	21
schelten *scold* A h st [i, a, o]	*sprechen	33
schematisieren *schematize; simplify* A h w	informieren	15
schenken (D) *give (to sb)* A h w	machen	21
scheren *shear; clip* A h w	machen	21
sich scheren (**um** + A/**in** + A) *not* *care (about); go off (to)* h w	machen	21
scherzen (**über** + A/ **mit** + D) *joke* *(about); trifle (with)* h w	heizen	14
scheuchen *shoo; drive; force* A h w	machen	21
scheuen *shun; shrink from;* (**vor** + D) *shy (at)* A h w	machen	21
scheuern *scour; rub* A h w	angeln	1
schichten *stack* A h w	reden	24
schicken (D/**an** + A) *send (to)* A h w	machen	21
schicken nach + D *send for* A h w	machen	21
sich schicken *befit;* (**in** + A) *resign* *oneself (to)* h w	machen	21
schieben *push;* (**auf** + A) *put off* *(until)* A h st [o, o]	kriechen	19
schief|gehen *go wrong* s st [ing, ang]	*hängen	12
schief|treten *wear down on one side* A h st [itt, a, e]	*geben	9
schielen *squint* h w	machen	21
schielen nach + D *steal a look at;* *have one's eye on* h w	machen	21
schießen (**auf** + A) *shoot (at);* (with **sein**) *shoot out* A h st [o, o]	schießen	26
schikanieren *harass* A h w	informieren	15
schildern *describe* A h w	angeln	1
schillern *shimmer* h w	angeln	1
schimmeln *go mouldy* h/s w	angeln	1
schimmern *shimmer; gleam* h w	angeln	1

schimpfen (A/mit + D) *tell (sb) off*		
h w	machen	21
schimpfen auf + A/**über** + A		
grumble about h w	machen	21
schinden *maltreat* A h w (past part.		
geschunden)	*reden	24
schlabbern *slobber; flap* h w	angeln	1
schlachten *kill; slaughter* A h w	reden	24
schlafen *sleep* h st [ä, ie, a]	schlafen	27
schlafwandeln *sleep-walk* h/s w	angeln	1
schlagen *hit; beat; strike;* (**in** + A)		
knock (into); wrap (in) A h		
(usually **sein** when intrans.) st		
[ä, u, a]	tragen	38
schlagen nach + D *hit out at* h st		
[ä, u, a]	tragen	38
sich schlagen (**mit** + D/**um** + A)		
fight (with/over) h st [ä, u, a]	tragen	38
sich schlängeln *wind one's/its way*		
h w	angeln	1
schlappen *lap* A h w	machen	21
schlecht|gehen *go badly* (impers.: **es**		
geht mir schlecht *things are going*		
badly for me; I'm ill) s st [ing,		
ang]	*hängen	12
schlecht|machen *disparage* A h w	machen	21
schleichen *creep* s st [i, i]	gleichen	10
schleifen *sharpen; grind* A h st [iff,		
iff]	greifen	11
schleifen *drag; raze* A h		
(sometimes **sein** when intrans.) w	machen	21
schleißen *strip; split* A h st [i, i; past		
often weak: **schleißte**]	beißen	3
schlemmen *feast (on)* A h w	machen	21
schlendern *stroll* s w	angeln	1
schlenkern *dangle; flap; swerve* A		
h w	angeln	1
schleppen *tow; drag* A h w	machen	21

schleudern *hurl; skid; spin-dry* A h **(sein** when intrans.) w	angeln	1
schleusen *pass through a lock;* **(in** + A) *smuggle (into)* A h w	heizen	14
schlichten *settle; smooth;* **(in** + D/ **zwischen** + D) *mediate (in/between)* A h w	reden	24
schließen *close;* **(an** + A) *connect (to)* A h st [o, o]	schießen	26
schließen A/**auf** + A **(aus** + D) *conclude (from)* h st [o, o]	schießen	26
schlingen *loop; wrap; bolt one's food;* **(um** + A) *tie (round)* A h st [a, u]	klingen	16
schlingern *roll; lurch* s w	angeln	1
schlittern *slide; skid* s w	angeln	1
schlitzen *slit (open)* A h w	heizen	14
schlottern (vor + D) *tremble (with); hang loose* h w	angeln	1
schluchzen *sob* h w	heizen	14
schlucken *swallow* A h w	machen	21
schlucksen *hiccup* h w	heizen	14
schlummern *slumber* h w	angeln	1
schlüpfen (in + A/**aus** + D) *slip (into/ out of)* s w	machen	21
schlurfen *shuffle (along)* s w	machen	21
schlürfen *drink noisily; savour* A h w	machen	21
schlußfolgern aus + D *conclude from* A h w	angeln	1
schmachten (nach + D) *pine (for)* h w	reden	24
schmälern *reduce; belittle* A h w	angeln	1
schmarotzen bei + D *freeload on; sponge on* h w	heizen	14
schmatzen *smack one's lips; squelch* h w	heizen	14
schmecken (nach + D) *taste (of); sample* A h w	machen	21

schmecken (D) *taste good (to)* h w	machen	21
schmeicheln *flatter* D h w	angeln	1
schmeißen (A/mit + D) **nach** + D *hurl (sth) at* h st [i, i]	beißen	3
schmelzen *melt (away)* A h (**sein** when intrans.) st [i, o, o]	*dreschen	6
schmerzen *hurt* A h w	heizen	14
schmettern (**an** + A/**gegen** + A) *hurl (at); blare out* A h (**sein** when intrans.) w	angeln	1
schmieden (**zu** + D/**aus** + D) *forge (into/from)* A h w	reden	24
sich schmiegen (**in** + A/**an** + A) *nestle (in/up to)* h w	machen	21
schmieren *grease; scrawl;* (**auf** + A) *spread (on)* A h w	machen	21
schminken *make up* A h w	machen	21
schmirgeln *rub down; sand* A h w	angeln	1
schmollen *sulk* h w	machen	21
schmorren *braise; stew* A h w	machen	21
schmücken *decorate* A h w	machen	21
schmuggeln (**in** + A/**aus** + D) *smuggle (into/out of)* A h w	angeln	1
schmunzeln (**vor sich** [A] **hin**/**über** + A) *smile quietly (to oneself/at)* h w	angeln	1
schmutzen *get dirty* h w	heizen	14
schnallen *buckle;* (**auf** + A) *strap (on to)* A h w	machen	21
schnalzen mit + D *click; snap* h w	heizen	14
schnappen (**nach** + D) *snap (at); gasp (for); snatch* A h w	machen	21
schnarchen *snore* h w	machen	21
schnarren *buzz* h w	machen	21
schnattern *cackle* h w	angeln	1
schnauben (**vor** + D) *snort (with)* h w	machen	21
schnaufen (**vor** + D) *pant (with)* h w	machen	21

schneiden (in + A) *cut (into)* A h st
[itt, itt]   *streiten   37
schneidern *make (clothes); tailor* A
h w   angeln   1
schneien (with **haben**) *snow* (impers.
es schneit *it's snowing*); (with **sein**)
fall like snow w   machen   21
schnellen (aus + D/**in** + A) *shoot*
(out of/into); send flying A h (**sein**
when intrans.) w   machen   21
sich [D] **schneuzen** *blow (one's nose)*
A h w   heizen   14
schniefen *sniffle* h w   machen   21
schnippen *snip; snap; flick* A h w   machen   21
schnitzeln *chop up; shred* A h w   angeln   1
schnitzen (an + D) *carve (at)* A
h w   heizen   14
schnüffeln (A/an + D) *sniff* h w   angeln   1
schnupfen *sniff* A h w   machen   21
schnuppern an + D *sniff at* h w   angeln   1
schnüren (auf + A) *tie (to); be too*
tight A h w   machen   21
schnurren *purr; hum* h w   machen   21
schockieren *shock* A h w   informieren   15
schonen *treat with care* A h w   machen   21
  sich schonen *take it easy* h w   machen   21
schönen *brighten; enhance* A h w   machen   21
schön|machen *sit up and beg (dog)*
h w   machen   21
  sich schön|machen *smarten oneself*
up h w   machen   21
schön|reden *flatter; sweet-talk* h w   reden   24
schön|schreiben *write out neatly* A h
st [ie, ie]   schreiben   28
schöpfen (aus + D) *draw (on); scoop*
up; ladle; coin A h w   machen   21
schrammen an + A *scratch; scrape*
(on) A h w   machen   21

schrauben (an + A/**auf** + A) *screw/*		
bolt (on to) A h w	machen	21
schrauben von + D *unscrew/unbolt*		
(from) A h w	machen	21
schrecken (aus + D) *startle (out of);*		
start up (from); give a start A	machen/	
h w [occasionally st: i, ak, o]	*sprechen	21/33
schreiben (D/**an** + A) *write (to)* A		
h st [ie, ie]	schreiben	28
schreiben über + A/**von** + D *write*		
about A h st [ie, ie]	schreiben	28
sich schreiben *be spelt* h st [ie, ie]	schreiben	28
schreien (nach + D) *cry (out for);*		
shout; scream A h st [ie, ie]	*schreiben	28
schreiten *stride; pace;* (**zu** + D)		
proceed (to) s st [itt, itt]	streiten	37
schrillen *shrill* h w	machen	21
schrubben *scrub* A h w	machen	21
schrumpfen *shrink; shrivel* s w	machen	21
schubsen *shove* A h w	heizen	14
schulden (D) *owe (to sb)* A h w	reden	24
schulen *train* A h w	machen	21
schulmeistern *lecture* h w	angeln	1
schultern *shoulder* A h w	angeln	1
sich schuppen *flake* h w	machen	21
schüren *poke; stir up* A h w	machen	21
schürfen *scrape; mine;* (**nach** + D)		
prospect (for) A h w	machen	21
schürzen *gather up; purse* A h w	heizen	14
schütteln A/**mit** + D *shake*		
h w	angeln	1
schütten *pour;* (**über** + A) *spill (on)*		
A h w	reden	24
schützen (vor + D/**gegen** + A) *protect*		
(from/against) A h w	heizen	14
schwächen *weaken* A h w	machen	21
schwadronieren *bluster* h w	informieren	15
schwängern *make pregnant* A h w	angeln	1

schwanken *sway; swing; shake; vary;*
waver h/s w — machen — 21

schwänzeln *wag its tail* A h w — angeln — 1

schwappen *splash;* (**über** + A/**auf** + A)
slosh (over/on to) A h w — machen — 21

schwärmen *swarm* h w — machen — 21

 schwärmen für + A *be mad about*
(sb) h w — machen — 21

 schwärmen von + D *go into raptures*
over (sth) h w — machen — 21

schwarz|arbeiten *work on the side;*
moonlight h w — reden — 24

schwärzen *blacken; black out* A h w — heizen — 14

schwarz|fahren *travel without a ticket*
s st [ä, u, a] — tragen — 38

schwarz|sehen *look on the black side;*
watch TV without a licence h st
[ie, a, e] — sehen — 29

schwarzweiß|malen *paint in black and*
white terms A h w — machen — 21

schwatzen (**über** + A) *chat (about)*
h w — heizen — 14

schweben *hover;* (**in** + D) *float (in);*
be pending h/s w — machen — 21

schweigen *stay/fall silent;* (**auf** + A/
zu + D) *say nothing (about)* h st
[ie, ie] — schreiben — 28

schweißen *weld* A h w — heizen — 14

schwelen *smoulder* h w — machen — 21

schwellen *swell* s st [i, o, o] — dreschen — 6

 schwellen *belly out; fill* A h w — machen — 21

schwemmen *wash* A h w — machen — 21

schwenken *swing; wave; rinse* A h
(**sein** when intrans.) w — machen — 21

schwer|fallen (D) *be difficult for (sb)*
s st [ä, iel, a] — *schlafen — 27

schwer|machen (D) *make difficult for*
(sb) A h w — machen — 21

schwer|nehmen *take seriously* A h st
[imm, a, omm] .... *sprechen 33

schwimmen *swim; float* usually **sein**
st [a, o] .... *sprechen 33

schwindeln *tell lies;* impers.: **mich/
mir schwindelt** *I feel dizzy* A/D
h w .... angeln 1

schwinden *fade; decline* s st [a, u] .... binden 4

schwingen *swing; vibrate; wave* A h
(usually **sein** when intrans.) st
[a, u] .... klingen 16

schwirren (**von** + D) *buzz (with);
whiz* h/s w .... machen 21

schwitzen *sweat* h w .... heizen 14

schwören (**auf** + A) *swear (on/by/to)*
A h st [o, o] .... *kriechen 19

segeln *sail* usually **sein** w .... angeln 1

segmentieren *segment* A h w .... informieren 15

segnen *bless* A h w .... atmen 2

sehen *see;* (**auf** + A) *look (at); be
concerned (about)* A h st [ie, a, e] .. sehen 29

 sehen nach + D *keep an eye on;
look for* h st [ie, a, e] .... sehen 29

sich sehnen nach + D *long for* h w ... machen 21

sein (**aus** + D) *be (from);* impers.:
mir ist *I feel* s st [ist, war, wes] .... sein 30

senden (**D/an** + A) *send (to sb)* A h
w/m [a, a] .... reden/senden 24/31

 senden *broadcast* A h w .... reden 24

sengen *singe; be scorching* A h w ...... machen 21

senken *lower* A h w .... machen 21

 sich senken *descend; subside* h w ... machen 21

sensibilisieren (**für** + A) *sensitize
(to)* A h w .... informieren 15

separieren *separate* A h w .... informieren 15

servieren *serve* A h w .... informieren 15

setzen *set;* (**auf** + A) *put (on to); bet
(on)* A h w .... heizen 14

sich setzen (auf + A/**in** + A/**zu** + D)		
sit down (on/in/with) h w	heizen	14
seufzen *sigh* h w	heizen	14
sezieren *dissect* A h w	informieren	15
shampoonieren *shampoo* A h w	informieren	15
sicher|gehen *play safe* s st [ing, ang]	*hängen	12
sichern *secure;* (**gegen** + A/**vor** + D)		
protect (against) A h w	angeln	1
sicher|stellen *impound; guarantee;*		
establish A h w	machen	21
sichten *sight; sift; examine* A h w	reden	24
sickern *seep; trickle (away)* s w	angeln	1
sieben *sieve; screen* A h w	machen	21
siedeln *settle* h w	angeln	1
sieden *boil; simmer* A h w/st [ott,	reden/	
ott]	*kriechen	24/19
siegen (mit + D) *win (by);* (**über** + A)		
win a victory (over) h w	machen	21
siezen *say 'Sie' to* A h w	heizen	14
signalisieren *indicate;* (D) *signal (to*		
sb) A h w	informieren	15
signieren *autograph* A h w	informieren	15
simplifizieren *over-simplify* A h w	informieren	15
simulieren *feign; sham* A h w	informieren	15
singen *sing* A h st [a, u]	klingen	16
sinken (in + A) *sink (into); go down;*		
fall s st [a, u]	klingen	16
sinnen *ponder;* (**auf** + A) *plot (sth)*		
h st [a, o]	sprechen	33
sinnieren über + A *ponder over* h w	informieren	15
sirren *buzz* h w	machen	21
sitzen *sit; fit; be based* h st [aß, ess]	*fressen	8
skalpieren *scalp* A h w	informieren	15
skandieren *chant; scan* A h w	informieren	15
skizzieren *sketch (out)* A h w	informieren	15
sohlen *sole* A h w	machen	21
sollen *be (supposed) to; should* h w	sollen	32
sondieren *sound out* A h w	informieren	15

sich sonnen *sun oneself;* (**in** + D)		
bask (in) h w	machen	21
sorgen für + A *look after; cause* h w	machen	21
sich sorgen um + A *worry about*		
h w	machen	21
sortieren (**nach** + D) *sort out (by)*		
A h w	informieren	15
soufflieren (D) *prompt (sb)* A h w	informieren	15
sozialisieren *socialize; nationalize*		
A h w	informieren	15
spachteln *stop; fill* A h w	angeln	1
spähen *peer* h w	machen	21
spalten *split* A h w (past part.		
usually **gespalten**)	*reden	24
spannen *tighten;* (**über** + A) *stretch*		
(over); (**in** + A) *insert (in)* A h w	machen	21
sparen (**für** + A/**auf** + A) *save (for)*		
A h w	machen	21
sparen an + D/**mit** + A *economize*		
on; be sparing with h w	machen	21
spaßen (**mit** + D) *joke (with)* h w	heizen	14
spazieren *stroll* s w	informieren	15
spazieren|fahren *go/take for a ride*		
A h (**sein** when intrans.) st [ä,		
u, a]	tragen	38
spazieren|gehen *go for a walk* s st		
[ing, ang]	*hängen	12
speicheln *salivate* h w	angeln	1
speichern *store* A h w	angeln	1
speien *spew out* A h st [ie, ie]	*schreiben	28
speisen *eat; feed;* (**mit** + D) *supply*		
(with) A h w	heizen	14
spekulieren *speculate;* (**auf** + D)		
count (on) h w	informieren	15
spenden (**für** + A) *donate (to); give*		
A h w	reden	24
spendieren (D) *stand (sb) . . .; buy*		
(for sb) A h w	informieren	15

sperren (für + A) *close (to); cut off*		
A h w	machen	21
sperren in + A *shut/lock in* A h w	machen	21
sich sperren gegen + A *balk at* h w	machen	21
sich spezialisieren auf + A *specialize*		
in h w	informieren	15
spezifieren *specify; itemize* A h w	informieren	15
spicken (mit + D) *lard (with)* A h w	machen	21
spiegeln *shine;* **(in** + D) *reflect (in)*		
A h w	angeln	1
spielen (mit + D/**um** + A/**auf** + D)		
play (with/for/on); act A h w	machen	21
spießen *spear;* **(in** + A) *stick (into)*		
A h w	heizen	14
spinnen *spin; think up; make up* A h		
st [a, o]	*sprechen	33
spionieren (gegen + A) *spy (against)*		
h w	informieren	15
spitzeln *act as an informer* h w	angeln	1
spitzen *sharpen; purse; prick up* A		
h w	heizen	14
spleißen *splice* A h w/st [i, i]	heizen/beißen	14/3
splittern *splinter; shatter* h/s w	angeln	1
sponsern *sponsor* A h w	angeln	1
spornen *spur* A h w	machen	21
spötteln (über + A) *poke fun (at)*		
h w	angeln	1
spotten (G/über + A) *mock (sb)* h w	reden	24
sprayen *spray* A h w	machen	21
sprechen (über + A/**von** + D) *speak*		
(about) A h st [i, a, o]	sprechen	33
sprechen für + A/**gegen** + A *speak*		
for/against h st [i, a, o]	sprechen	33
sprechen (A/mit + D) *speak (to sb)*		
h st [i, a, o]	sprechen	33
spreizen *spread* A h w	heizen	14
sprengen *blow up; break (open/up);*		
spray A h w	machen	21

sprenkeln *sprinkle* A h w	angeln	1
sprießen *shoot (up); sprout* s st [o, o]	schießen	26
springen (**auf** + A) *jump (to); bound;* *break* s st [a, u]	klingen	16
spritzen *spray; inject; dilute* A h w	heizen	14
sprudeln (**aus** + D) *bubble (out of)* h/s w	angeln	1
sprühen *spray;* (**vor** + D) *sparkle* *(with);* impers.: **es sprüht** *it's* *drizzling* A h/s w	machen	21
spucken *spit* A h w	machen	21
spuken *haunt* (impers.: **es spukt** *there are ghosts*) h w	machen	21
spulen *spool;* (**auf** + A) *wind (on to)* A h w	machen	21
spülen *rinse; wash up; flush* A h w	machen	21
spüren *feel* A h w	machen	21
spurten *spurt* s w	reden	24
stabilisieren *stabilize* A h w	informieren	15
stacheln *prick; prickle* h w	angeln	1
staffeln *stagger; grade* A h w	angeln	1
stagnieren *stagnate* h w	informieren	15
stählen *toughen* A h w	machen	21
staken *punt* A h (**sein** when intrans.) w	machen	21
stammeln *stammer* A h w	angeln	1
stammen von + D/**aus** + D *come* *from; date from* h w	machen	21
stampfen (**mit** + D) *stamp (feet* *etc.); pound* A h w	machen	21
stampfen *trudge; tramp* s w	machen	21
standardisieren *standardize* A h w	informieren	15
stand|halten *stand firm;* (D) *withstand (sth)* h st [ä, ie, a]	*schlafen	27
stanzen *stamp; punch* A h w	heizen	14
stapeln *pile up; accumulate* A h w	angeln	1
stapfen (**in** + A) *stamp (in); tramp* A h w	machen	21

stärken *strengthen; starch* A h w	machen	21
starren (in + A) *stare (into)* h w	machen	21
starren an + A/**auf** + A/**gegen** + A *stare at* h w	machen	21
starren vor + D/**von** + D *be covered in* h w	machen	21
starten *start; take off; launch;* (**bei** + D/**in** + D) *compete (in)* A h (**sein** when intrans.) w	reden	24
stationieren *deploy; station* A h w	informieren	15
statt|finden *take place; occur* h st [a, u]	binden	4
stauben *raise dust* h w	machen	21
stauchen *compress; jab* A h w	machen	21
stauen *dam (up)* A h w	machen	21
sich stauen *build up; form a tailback* h w	machen	21
staunen (über + A) *be amazed (at)* h w	machen	21
stechen *prick; sting; stab* A h st [i, a, o]	sprechen	33
stechen mit + D (**in** + A) *jab . . . (into)* h st [i, a, o]	sprechen	33
sich stechen an + D *prick oneself on* h st [i, a, o]	sprechen	33
stecken (in + A) *put (into); pin; plant; be* A h w	machen	21
stecken|bleiben (in + D) *get stuck (in)* s st [ie, ie]	schreiben	28
stehen *stand; be stationary;* (**auf** + D) *point (to);* h (sometimes **sein**) st [and, and]	stehen	34
stehen *suit* D h (sometimes **sein**) st [and, and]	stehen	34
stehen für + A *be a guarantee of* h (sometimes **sein**) st [and, and]	stehen	34
stehen|bleiben *stop; be left behind* s st [ie, ie]	schreiben	28

stehen|lassen *leave (standing)* A h st [ä, ie, a]	*schlafen	27
stehlen (D) *steal (from sb)* A h st [ie, a, o]	stehlen	35
sich stehlen *creep* h st [ie, a, o]	stehlen	35
steigen (A/**auf** + A) *climb; rise* s st [ie, ie]	schreiben	28
steigen aus + D/**in** + A *get out of/ into* s st [ie, ie]	schreiben	28
steigern (**auf** + A) *increase (to); intensify* A h w	angeln	1
steinigen *stone* A h w	machen	21
stellen *place; stand;* (**auf** + A) *put (on); set (for)* A h w	machen	21
sich stellen *place oneself; pretend; give oneself up* h w	machen	21
stelzen *strut* s w	heizen	14
stemmen *lift;* (**gegen** + A) *brace (against); chisel* A h w	machen	21
stempeln *stamp* A h w	angeln	1
stenographieren *do shorthand; take down in shorthand* A h w	informieren	15
sterben (**an** + D) *die (of)* s st [i, a, o]	*sprechen	33
sterben vor + A *be dying of (e.g. boredom)* s st [i, a, o]	*sprechen	33
sterilisieren *sterilize* A h w	informieren	15
steuern *steer; fly; control* A h w	angeln	1
sticheln *sew;* (**gegen** + A) *make snide remarks (about)* h w	angeln	1
sticken *embroider* A h w	machen	21
stieben *fly up* s w/st [o, o]	machen/ kriechen	21/19
stiften *found; cause;* (**für** + A) *donate (to)* A h w	reden	24
stigmatisieren *stigmatize* A h w	informieren	15
stilisieren *stylize* A h w	informieren	15
stillegen (separable, splits **still-legen**) *shut down* A h w	machen	21

stillen *satisfy; stanch; breast-feed*
A h w | machen | 21

still|halten *keep still/quiet* h st [ä, ie, a] | *schlafen | 27

still|sitzen *sit still* h st [aß, ess] | *fressen | 8

still|stehen *stop; be at a standstill; stand to attention* h st [and, and] | stehen | 34

stimmen *be right; vote; tune; make . . . feel* A h w | machen | 21

stimulieren *stimulate* A h w | informieren | 15

stinken (**nach** + D) *stink (of)* h st [a, u] | klingen | 16

stipulieren *stipulate* A h w | informieren | 15

stochern in + D *poke* h w | angeln | 1

stocken *be held up; halt; falter* h w | machen | 21

stöhnen *moan; groan* h w | machen | 21

stolpern *stumble;* (**über** + A) *trip (over)* s w | angeln | 1

stolzieren *strut* s w | informieren | 15

stopfen *darn;* (**in** + A) *stuff (into)* A h w | machen | 21

stoppen *stop; clock time/speed at* A h w | machen | 21

stören (**in** + D/**an** + D) *disturb (in/ about)* A h w | machen | 21

sich stören an + D *take exception to* h w | machen | 21

stornieren *cancel* A h w | informieren | 15

stoßen *punch; kick; thrust;* (**gegen** + A) *bump (into)* A h (**sein** when intrans.) st [ö, ie, o] | stoßen | 36

stoßen auf + A *come across; lead into* s st [ö, ie, o] | stoßen | 36

stoßen an + A *be next to* s st [ö, ie, o] | stoßen | 36

sich stoßen an + D *take exception to* h st [ö, ie, o] | stoßen | 36

stottern *stammer* A h w | angeln | 1

strafen (mit + D) *punish (with)* A h w	machen	21
straffen *tighten; straighten* A h w	machen	21
strahlen *shine;* (**vor** + D) *beam (with)* h w	machen	21
stramm|stehen *stand to attention* h st [and, and]	stehen	34
strampeln *kick (about)* h w	angeln	1
stranden *run aground* s w	reden	24
strangulieren *strangle* A h w	informieren	15
strapazieren *be a strain on; tax* A h w	informieren	15
sich sträuben *bristle; resist* h w	machen	21
streben *go briskly;* (**nach** + D) *strive (for)* h w	machen	21
strecken *stretch* A h w	machen	21
streicheln *stroke* A h w	angeln	1
streichen *stroke; paint; spread; cross out* A h st [i, i]	gleichen	10
streichen (D) **über** + A *stroke (sb's) . . .* h st [i, i]	gleichen	10
streifen *graze; slip;* (**an** + D) *brush (against)* A h w	machen	21
streiken (um + A) *strike (for)* h w	machen	21
streiten *fight* h st [itt, itt]	streiten	37
sich streiten (um + A/**über** + A) *quarrel (over/about)* h st [itt, itt]	streiten	37
stressen *put under stress; be stressful* A h w	heizen	14
streuen *spread; sprinkle* A h w	machen	21
streunen *stray; roam about* s w	machen	21
stricheln *hatch (in)* A h w	angeln	1
stricken (A/**an** + D) *knit* h w	machen	21
striegeln *groom* A h w	angeln	1
strolchen *wander about* s w	machen	21
strömen *stream; pour* s w	machen	21
strotzen von + D/**vor** + D *be bursting with* h w	heizen	14

strudeln *eddy* h w	angeln	1
strukturieren *structure* A h w	informieren	15
stückeln *cut in pieces; patch* A h w	angeln	1
studieren *study; be at university* A h w	informieren	15
stufen *terrace; grade* A h w	machen	21
stülpen auf + A/**über** + A *pull on to/ over* A h w	machen	21
stümpern *bungle* h w	angeln	1
stürmen *rush; storm* (impers.: **es stürmt** *it's blowing a gale*) A h w	machen	21
stürzen (**aus** + D/**von** + D) *fall (from); dash; hurl; overturn* A h (**sein** when intrans.) w	heizen	14
sich stürzen (**auf** + A) *pounce (on); (**in** + A) plunge (into)* h w	heizen	14
stutzen *stop short; be puzzled; trim* A h w	heizen	14
stützen (**auf** + A) *support (on)* A h w	heizen	14
sublimieren *sublimate* A h w	informieren	15
subtrahieren *subtract* A h w	informieren	15
subventionieren *subsidize* A h w	informieren	15
suchen *seek;* (**nach** + D) *search (for)* A h w	machen	21
sich suhlen (**in** + D) *wallow (in)* h w	machen	21
sühnen *punish;* (**für** + A) *atone (for)* A h w	machen	21
summen *hum; buzz* A h w	machen	21
sich summieren auf + A *add up to; grow to* h w	informieren	15
sündigen (**gegen** + A) *sin (against); indulge oneself* h w	machen	21
surfen *surf* h w	machen	21
surren *hum; whirr* h/s w	machen	21
süßen *sweeten* A h w	heizen	14
swingen *swing (e.g. music)* h w	machen	21
symbolisieren *symbolize* A h w	informieren	15

sympathisieren mit + D *sympathize
  with* h w | informieren | 15
synchronisieren *dub; synchronize* A
  h w | informieren | 15
synkopieren *syncopate* A h w | informieren | 15
systematisieren *systematize* A h w | informieren | 15

tadeln (für + A/**wegen** + G) *rebuke
  (for)* A h w | angeln | 1
täfeln *panel* A h w | angeln | 1
tagen *meet;* (**über** + A) *confer
  (about)* h w | machen | 21
tändeln *flirt* h w | angeln | 1
tanken *fill up (with)* A h w | machen | 21
tänzeln *prance; skip* s w | angeln | 1
tanzen *dance* A h (**sein** *when intrans.
  and direction indicated*) w | heizen | 14
tapezieren *(wall)paper* A h w | informieren | 15
tappen (nach + D) *grope (for)* h/s w | machen | 21
tarnen *camouflage* A h w | machen | 21
tasten (nach + D) *feel (for); key in*
  A h w | reden | 24
tätigen *effect* A h w | machen | 21
tätowieren *tattoo* A h w | informieren | 15
tätscheln *pat* A h w | angeln | 1
tauchen (nach + D) *dive (for)* h/s w | machen | 21
tauchen *dip* A h w | machen | 21
tauchen aus + D *emerge from* s w | machen | 21
tauen *melt;* impers. (with **haben**): **es
  taut** *it's thawing* A h (**sein** *when
  intrans.*) w | machen | 21
taufen *baptize* A h w | machen | 21
taugen (zu + D/**für** + A) *be suitable/
  good (for)* h w | machen | 21
taumeln *stagger;* (**vor** + D) *reel
  (with)* h w | angeln | 1
tauschen (gegen + A) *exchange (for)*
  A h w | machen | 21

täuschen *deceive; be deceptive* A h w   machen   21
  sich täuschen in + D/**über** + A *be*
  mistaken in/about h w   machen   21
taxieren auf + A *value at* A h w   informieren   15
teilen (durch + A/**unter** + D) *divide*
  (by/among); share A h w   machen   21
teil|haben an + D *share in* h m [at,
  att, a]   *brennen   5
teil|nehmen an + D *take part in;*
  attend h st [imm, a, omm]   *sprechen   33
telefonieren (mit + D) *telephone (sb)*
  h w   informieren   15
telegrafieren (D) *send a telegram (to*
  sb) h w   informieren   15
telexen *telex* A h w   heizen   14
temperieren *bring to the right*
  temperature A h w   informieren   15
tendieren (zu + D) *tend (towards)*
  h w   informieren   15
terminieren auf + A *set a time/*
  time-limit for h w   informieren   15
terrorisieren *terrorize* A h w   informieren   15
testen auf + A *test for* A h w   reden   24
texten *write (the words of)* A h w   reden   24
thronen *sit enthroned; tower* h w   machen   21
ticken *tick* h w   machen   21
tief|stapeln *understate the case* h w   angeln   1
tilgen *erase; efface* A h w   machen   21
timen *time* A h w   machen   21
tippen *type; tap;* (**auf** + A) *bet (on)*
  A h w   machen   21
tirilieren *trill* h w   informieren   15
tischlern *make (in wood)* A h w   angeln   1
titulieren *call* A h w   informieren   15
toasten *toast* A h w   reden   24
toben *rage;* (**vor** + D) *go wild (with)*
  h/s w   machen   21
tolerieren *tolerate* A h w   informieren   15

tollen *romp (about)* h/s w	machen	21
tönen *tint; resound* A h w	machen	21
töpfern *make (in pottery)* A h w	angeln	1
torpedieren *torpedo* A h w	informieren	15
tosen *roar; rage* h (**sein** when direction indicated) w	heizen	14
töten *kill* A h w	reden	24
tot|fahren *run over and kill* A h st [ä, u, a]	tragen	38
tot|sagen *declare dead* A h w	machen	21
tot|schießen *shoot dead* A h st [o, o]	schießen	26
tot|schlagen *beat to death* A h st [ä, u, a]	tragen	38
tot|schweigen *hush up* A h st [ie, ie]	schreiben	28
sich tot|stellen *play dead* h w	machen	21
tot|treten *trample to death* A h st [itt, a, e]	*geben	9
traben *trot* s w	machen	21
trachten nach + D *strive for* h w	reden	24
tragen *carry; wear; bear* A h st [ä, u, a]	tragen	38
trainieren *train* A h w	informieren	15
traktieren (**mit** + D) *set about (with)* A h w	informieren	15
trällern *warble* A h w	angeln	1
trampeln (**auf** + A) *trample (on)* A h (**sein** when intrans.) w	angeln	1
trampen *hitch-hike* s w	machen	21
tranchieren *carve* A h w	informieren	15
tränen *water* h w	machen	21
tränken *soak* A h w	machen	21
transferieren (**auf** + A/**zu** + D) *transfer (to)* A h w	informieren	15
transformieren (**in** + A/**auf** + A) *transform (into/to)* A h w	informieren	15
transkribieren *transcribe* A h w	informieren	15
transpirieren *perspire* h w	informieren	15
transplantieren *transplant* A h w	informieren	15

transportieren *transport; convey* A h w	informieren	15
trappeln *patter (along)* s w	angeln	1
trauen *marry (as vicar)* A h w	machen	21
trauen *trust* D h w	machen	21
sich [A, occasionally D] **trauen** *dare* h w	machen	21
trauern um + A *mourn for* h w	angeln	1
träufeln (in + A) *trickle (into); drip* A h w	angeln	1
träumen (von + D) *dream (about)* A h w	machen	21
treffen *hit; meet; hurt; make* A h st [i, af, o]	*sprechen	33
treffen auf + A *come up against* s st [i, af, o]	*sprechen	33
treiben (in + A/**durch** + A) *drive (into/ through); force; go in for; drift* A h (**sein** *when intrans.*) st [ie, ie]	schreiben	28
trennen (von + D) *separate (from); divide* A h w	machen	21
sich trennen *part; draw;* (**von** + D) *split up (from)* h w	machen	21
treten (in + A/**auf** + A) *step (into/on to)* s st [itt, a, e]	*geben	9
treten A/**gegen** + A *kick* h st [itt, a, e]	*geben	9
triefen (von + D/**vor** + D) *drip (with)* h/s w/st [off, off]	machen/ *kriechen	21/19
trillern *trill* A h w	angeln	1
trimmen *trim; keep fit* A h w	machen	21
trinken (auf + A) *drink (to)* A h st [a, u]	klingen	16
trippeln *trip; mince* s w	angeln	1
triumphieren *exult;* (**über** + A) *triumph (over)* h w	informieren	15
trocken|legen *change (baby); drain* A h w	machen	21

trocken|reiben *rub/wipe dry* A h st [ie, ie]	schreiben	28
trocken|schleudern *spin-dry* A h w	angeln	1
trocknen *dry* A h (**sein** when intrans.) w	angeln	1
trommeln (**auf** + A/**an** + A) *drum (on/against); beat out* A h w	angeln	1
trompeten *(play the) trumpet; proclaim* A h w (past part. **trompetet**)	reden	24
tröpfeln (**auf** + A) *drip (on to)* A h (**sein** when intrans.) w	angeln	1
tropfen (**auf** + A) *drip (on to);* impers.: **es tropft** *it's spitting with rain* A h (**sein** when intrans.) w	machen	21
trösten *comfort* A h w	reden	24
trotten *trot (along)* s w	reden	24
trotzen *defy; brave* D h w	heizen	14
trüben *cloud; cast a cloud over* A h w	machen	21
trudeln *roll; wobble; spin* s w	angeln	1
trügen *deceive; be deceptive* A h st [o, o]	kriechen	19
trumpfen *trump* A h w	machen	21
tuckern *chug* h/s w	angeln	1
sich tummeln *romp about* h w	angeln	1
tun (D) *do (to sb); pretend to be* A h st [at, a]	tun	39
tünchen *distemper; whitewash* A h w	machen	21
tüpfeln (**mit** + D) *stipple (with); speckle* A h w	angeln	1
tupfen (**auf** + A) *dab (on to)* A h w	machen	21
türmen *pile up* A h w	machen	21
turnen *do gymnastics* h w	machen	21
turteln *bill and coo* h w	angeln	1
tuscheln *whisper* A h w	angeln	1
tuschen *ink in; paint (with water-colours)* A h w	machen	21

tuten *hoot* h w		reden	24
tyrannisieren *tyrannize* A h w		informieren	15
übel|nehmen (D) *hold against (sb);* *take offence at* A h st [imm, a, omm]		*sprechen	33
übel|wollen (D) *wish (sb) ill* h m [i, o, o]		*sollen	32
üben *practise; exercise* A h w		machen	21
über'anstrengen *overtax* A h w		machen	21
sich über'arbeiten *overwork* h w		reden	24
überbeanspruchen¹ *overstrain* A h w		machen	21
überbelasten¹ *overload* A h w		reden	24
überbelichten¹ *over-expose* A h w		reden	24
überbetonen¹ *overstress* A h w		machen	21
überbewerten¹ *overrate* A h w		reden	24
überbezahlen¹ *overpay* A h w		machen	21
über'bieten um + A *outbid by; outdo by* A h st [o, o]		*kriechen	19
über'bringen *deliver; convey* A h m [ach, ach]		*brennen	5
über'brücken *bridge* A h w		machen	21
über'dachen *roof over* A h w		machen	21
über'dauern *survive* A h w		angeln	1
über'decken (**mit** + D) *cover (with)* A h w		machen	21
über'dehnen *overstretch* A h w		machen	21
über'denken *think over* A h m [ach, ach]		*brennen	5
über'drehen *overwind; overtighten* A h w		machen	21
über'drucken *overprint* A h w		machen	21
über'eignen (D) *make over (to sb)* A h w		atmen	2
über'eilen *rush* A h w		machen	21

---

¹ Insep. except in the inf. with **zu**, e.g. **überbelasten: ich überbelaste**, but **überzubelasten**.

übereinander|legen *lay one on top of the other* A h w	machen	21
übereinander|liegen *lie/be situated one over the other* h st [a, e]	sehen	29
übereinander|stehen *stand one on top of the other* h st [and, and]	stehen	34
übereinander|stellen *put one on top of the other* A h w	machen	21
überein|kommen über + A *agree upon* s st [am, o]	kommen	17
überein|stimmen *match;* (**mit** + D/ **in** + D) *agree (with/on)* h w	machen	21
sich über'essen an + D *eat too much of* h st [i, a, ge]	*fressen	8
über|fahren *ferry over; cross over* A h (**sein** *when intrans.*) st [ä, u, a]	tragen	38
über'fahren *run over; go over* A h st [ä, u, a]	tragen	38
über'fallen *attack; hold up; come over* A h st [ä, ie, a]	schlafen	27
über'fliegen *fly over; skim through* A h st [o, o]	kriechen	19
über'fluten *flood* A h w	reden	24
über'fordern (**mit** + D) *overtax (with)* A h w	angeln	1
über'frachten *overload; overcharge* A h w	reden	24
sich über'fressen *overeat (of animals)* h st [i, a, e]	fressen	8
über'frieren *freeze over* s st [o, o]	kriechen	19
über|führen *transfer; convert* A h w	machen	21
über'führen *transfer;* (G) *convict (of)* A h w	machen	21
über'füttern *overfeed* A h w	angeln	1
über'geben (D/**an** + D) *hand over (to)* A h st [i, a, e]	geben	9
sich über'geben *vomit* h st [i, a, e]	geben	9

über|gehen *pass;* (**in** + A) *turn (into);* (**zu** + D) *go over (to)* s st [ing, ang] · **hängen* · 12

 über'gehen *ignore; pass over* A h st [ing, ang] · **hängen* · 12

über|gießen (D) *pour over (sb)* A h st [o, o] · schießen · 26

 über'gießen (**mit** + D) *pour (sth) over* A h st [o, o] · schießen · 26

über'golden *gild* A h w · reden · 24

über'greifen auf + A *spread to; encroach on* h st [iff, iff] · greifen · 11

überhand|nehmen *get out of hand* h st [imm, a, omm] · **sprechen* · 33

über'hängen *overhang* h st [i, a] · hängen · 12

 sich [D] **über|hängen** *sling over one's shoulder* A h st [i, a] · hängen · 12

über'häufen mit + D *heap on; shower with* A h w · machen · 21

sich über'heben *be arrogant* h st [o, o] · kriechen · 19

über'heizen/über'hitzen *overheat* A h w · heizen · 14

über|holen *ferry across* A h w · machen · 21

 über'holen *overtake; outstrip* A h w · machen · 21

über'hören *not hear* A h w · machen · 21

über|kippen *tip over* s w · machen · 21

über|kleben *paste over* A h w · machen · 21

über|klettern *climb over* A h w · angeln · 1

über|kochen *boil over* s w · machen · 21

über'kommen *overcome; come over* A h st [am, o] · kommen · 17

überkompensieren (insep., but inf. with **zu: überzukompensieren**) *over-compensate for* A h w · informieren · 15

sich über'kreuzen *cross; intersect* h w · heizen · 14

über'krusten *encrust* A h w · reden · 24

über'laden *overload* A h st [ä, u, a] · **tragen* · 38

über'lagern *overlie; be superimposed*		
on A h w	angeln	1
über'lappen *overlap* A h w	machen	21
über'lassen (D) *let (sb) have; leave*		
(to sb) A h st [ä, ie, a]	*schlafen	27
sich über'lassen *abandon oneself to*		
D h st [ä, ie, a]	*schlafen	27
über'lasten *overburden* A h w	reden	24
über|laufen *overflow;* (**zu** + D) *defect*		
(to) s st [äu, ie, au]	laufen	20
über'laufen *seize; come over; run*		
past A h st [äu, ie, au]	laufen	20
über'leben *survive; outlive* A h w	machen	21
über|legen (D) *put . . . over (sb)* A		
h w	machen	21
über'legen *consider; reflect* A h w	machen	21
sich [D] **über'legen** *change one's*		
mind (about) A h w	machen	21
über'leiten zu + D *move on to;*		
in + A *lead into* h w	reden	24
über'lesen *overlook; miss* A h st		
[ie, a, e]	*sehen	29
über'liefern *hand down* A h w	angeln	1
über'listen *outwit* A h w	reden	24
über'malen *overpaint* A h w	machen	21
über'mannen *overcome* A h w	machen	21
über'mitteln *send; pass on* A h w	angeln	1
über'müden *overtire* A h w	reden	24
über'nachten (**bei** + D) *spend the*		
night (at sb's) h w	reden	24
über'nehmen (**von** + D) *receive (from);*		
take on/over (from) A h st [imm,		
a, omm]	*sprechen	33
sich über'nehmen *overdo things;*		
(**mit** + D) *take on too much (with)*		
h st [imm, a, omm]	*sprechen	33
über|ordnen (D) *give precedence*		
(over sth/sb) A h w	atmen	2

über'prüfen (auf + A) *check (for);*
  consider A h w   machen   21
über'quellen *spill over;* **(von + D)** *be*
  brimming (with) s st [i, o, o]   dreschen   6
über'queren *cross* A h w   machen   21
über|ragen *jut out* h w   machen   21
 über'ragen *tower over;* **(an + D)**
  outstrip (in) A h w   machen   21
über'raschen *surprise* A h w   machen   21
über'reden (zu + D) *persuade (into)*
  A h w   reden   24
über'reichen (D) *present (to sb)*
  A h w   machen   21
über'reizen *overtax* A h w   heizen   14
über'rennen *overrun* A h m [a, a]   brennen   5
über'rollen *overwhelm; sweep through*
  A h w   machen   21
über'rumpeln (mit + D) *take by*
  surprise (with) A h w   angeln   1
über'sättigen *satiate* A h w   machen   21
über'schatten *overshadow* A h w   reden   24
über'schätzen *overestimate* A h w   heizen   14
über'schlagen *cross; break (as wave)*
  A h **(sein** when intrans.**)** st [ä, u,
  a]   tragen   38
sich über'schneiden *intersect; overlap*
  h st [itt, itt]   *streiten   37
über'schreiben (auf + A) *transfer*
  (to); entitle A h st [ie, ie]   schreiben   28
über'schreiten *cross; exceed* A h st
  [itt, itt]   streiten   37
über'schütten mit + D *cover with* A
  h w   reden   24
über|schwappen *slop over* s w   machen   21
über'schwemmen mit + D *flood with*
  A h w   machen   21
über'sehen *survey; assess; overlook*
  A h st [ie, a, e]   sehen   29

über'senden *send; remit* A h w/m
[a, a] — reden/senden 24/31

über|setzen *ferry over* A h w — heizen 14

über'setzen (in + A/aus + D)
translate (into/from) A h w — heizen 14

über|siedeln/über'siedeln (nach + D)
move (to) s w — angeln 1

über'spannen *over-tighten; span;*
cover A h w — machen 21

über'spielen *cover up;* **(auf + A)**
transfer (to) A h w — machen 21

über'spitzen *go too far with* A h w — heizen 14

über'sprechen *talk over* A h st [i, a,
o] — sprechen 33

über|springen *jump across;* **(auf + A)**
be communicated (to); switch
abruptly to s s st [a, u] — klingen 16

über'springen *jump; miss out; skip*
A h st [a, u] — klingen 16

über|sprudeln (von + D) *bubble over*
(with) s w — angeln 1

über'spülen *wash over* A h w — machen 21

über'stehen *come through; survive*
A h st [and, and] — stehen 34

über'steigen *climb over; exceed* A h
st [ie, ie] — schreiben 28

über'steigern *push up too far* A
h w — angeln 1

über'stellen an + A *hand over to* A
h w — machen 21

über'stimmen *outvote* A h w — machen 21

über'strahlen *illuminate; outshine* A
h w — machen 21

überstrapazieren (insep., but inf. with
zu: überzustrapazieren) *overtax* A
h w — informieren 15

sich [D] über|streifen *slip . . . on* A
h w — machen 21

über|strömen *overflow;* (**von** + D) *be bursting (with)* s w	machen	21
über'strömen *flood (over)* A h w	machen	21
über'stürzen *rush* A h w	heizen	14
über'tönen *drown out* A h w	machen	21
über'tragen (**auf** + A) *transfer (to);* (**in** + A) *translate (into); broadcast* A h st [ä, u, a]	tragen	38
über'treffen (**an** + D/**in** + D) *surpass (in/at)* A h st [i, af, o]	*sprechen	33
über'treiben *exaggerate; overdo* A h st [ie, ie]	schreiben	28
über|treten *change sides;* (**zu** + D) *go over (to)* s st [itt, a, e]	*geben	9
über'treten *contravene; break* A h st [itt, a, e]	*geben	9
über'trumpfen *trump; outdo* A h w	machen	21
über'tünchen *whitewash* A h w	machen	21
über'wachen *watch; monitor* A h w	machen	21
über'wältigen *overpower; overcome* A h w	machen	21
über'wälzen auf + A *shift on to* A h w	heizen	14
über'wechseln auf + A *cross/change over to* s w	angeln	1
über'weisen (**an** + A/**auf** + A) *transfer (to);* (**an** + A) *refer (to)* A h st [ie, ie]	*schreiben	28
sich über'werfen mit + D *fall out with* h st [i, a, o]	sprechen	33
über'wiegen *outweigh; predominate* A h st [o, o]	kriechen	19
über'winden *overcome* A h st [a, u]	binden	4
sich über'winden zu + D *bring oneself to* h st [a, u]	binden	4
über'wintern *overwinter* h w	angeln	1
über'wölben *arch over* A h w	machen	21

über'zeugen (von + D) *convince (of)* A h w	machen	21
über|ziehen *pull on* A h st [og, og]	*kriechen	19
über'ziehen *overdo;* **(mit** + D) *cover (with);* **(um** + A) *overdraw/overrun (by)* A h st [og, og]	*kriechen	19
übrig|be'halten *have left over* A h st [ä, ie, a]	*schlafen	27
übrig|bleiben *remain; be left over* s st [ie, ie]	schreiben	28
übrig|lassen *leave (over)* A h st [ä, ie, a]	*schlafen	27
ulken *clown around;* **(über** + A) *make fun (of)* h w	machen	21
um|adressieren *redirect* A h w	informieren	15
um|ändern *change* A h w	angeln	1
um|arbeiten *rework; alter* A h w	reden	24
um'armen *embrace* A h w	machen	21
um|bauen *rebuild;* **(zu** + D) *convert (into)* A h w	machen	21
um|be'nennen (in + A) *change the name of (to)* A h m [a, a]	brennen	5
um|be'setzen *recast* A h w	heizen	14
um|be'stellen *change one's order* h w	machen	21
um|biegen *bend* A h (**sein** when intrans.) st [o, o]	kriechen	19
um|bilden *reorganize* A h w	reden	24
um|binden *put on; tie on* A h st [a, u]	binden	4
um|blättern *turn over; turn the pages* A h w	angeln	1
sich um|blicken *look around;* **(nach** + D) *look back (at)* h w	machen	21
um|brechen *break up; fall down* A h (**sein** when intrans.) st [i, a, o]	sprechen	33
um|bringen *kill* A h m [ach, ach]	*brennen	5
um|buchen auf + A *change (one's booking) to* A h w	machen	21
um|denken *rethink* h m [ach, ach]	*brennen	5

um|deuten *reinterpret* A h w	reden	24
um|disponieren *make new arrangements* h w	informieren	15
um|drängen *crowd round* A h w	machen	21
um|drehen *turn (round/inside out)* A h w	machen	21
sich um|drehen nach + D *turn to look at* h w	machen	21
um|er'ziehen *re-educate* A h st [og, og]	*kriechen	19
um|fahren *knock down* A h st [ä, u, a]	tragen	38
um'fahren *go round; bypass* A h st [ä, u, a]	tragen	38
um|fallen *fall over; collapse* s st [ä, iel, a]	*schlafen	27
um'fangen *envelop* A h st [ä, i, a]	*hängen	12
um'fassen *embrace; include* A h w	heizen	14
um'fliegen *fly round* A h st [o, o]	kriechen	19
um'fließen *flow round* A h st [o, o]	schießen	26
um|formen *remodel* A h w	machen	21
um|füllen (**in** + A) *transfer (into)* A h w	machen	21
um|funktionieren *change the function of;* (**zu** + D) *turn (into)* A h w	informieren	15
um'garnen *beguile* A h w	machen	21
um'geben mit + D *surround with* A h st [i, a, e]	geben	9
um|gehen *go round* s st [ing, ang]	*hängen	12
um|gehen mit + D *treat; handle* s st [ing, ang]	*hängen	12
um'gehen *go/get round; avoid* A h st [ing, ang]	*hängen	12
um|ge'stalten *reshape;* (**zu** + D) *turn (into)* A h w	reden	24
um|gießen *recast;* (**in** + A) *pour (into)* A h st [o, o]	schießen	26
um|graben *dig over* A h st [ä, u, a]	tragen	38
um'grenzen *enclose; delimit* A h w	heizen	14

um|gruppieren *rearrange* A h w	informieren 15
um|haben *have . . . on* A h m [at, att, a]	*brennen 5
um'halsen *embrace* A h w	heizen 14
sich [D] um|hängen *hang round one's neck/shoulders* A h w	machen 21
um|hauen *fell* A h st [ieb, au]	*laufen 20
umhin|können: ich kann nicht umhin, zu + inf. *I can't help . . . ing* h m [a, o, o]	können 18
sich um|hören (nach + D) *keep one's ears open (for); ask around (about)* h w	machen 21
um'hüllen mit + D *wrap/shroud in* A h w	machen 21
um'jubeln *cheer* A h w	angeln 1
um'kämpfen *fight over; contest* A h w	machen 21
um|kehren *turn back/upside down/ inside out* A h (**sein** when intrans.) w	machen 21
um|kippen *overturn; knock over* A h (**sein** when intrans.) w	machen 21
um'klammern *clutch* A h w	angeln 1
um|klappen *fold down* A h w	machen 21
sich um|kleiden *change one's clothes* h w	reden 24
um'kleiden *cover* A h w	reden 24
um|knicken *bend/fold over* A h (**sein** when intrans.) w	machen 21
um|kommen (vor + D) *die (of)* s st [am, o]	kommen 17
um'kränzen *garland; encircle* A h w	heizen 14
um'kreisen *circle* A h w	heizen 14
um|krempeln *roll up* A h w	angeln 1
um|laden *transfer; reload* A h st [ä, u, a]	*tragen 38
um'lagern *besiege* A h w	angeln 1

um|laufen *knock over; rotate* A h **(sein** *when intrans.)* st [äu, ie, au]	laufen	20
um'laufen *run around; orbit* A h st [äu, ie, au]	laufen	20
um|legen (D) *put . . . on (sb); flatten; turn over* A h w	machen	21
um|legen auf + A *transfer to; share between* A h w	machen	21
um|leiten *divert* A h w	reden	24
um|lernen (auf + A) *retrain (as)* h w	machen	21
um'mauern *surround with a wall* A h w	angeln	1
sich um|melden *report a change of address* h w	reden	24
um|münzen in + A *convert into* A h w	heizen	14
um'nebeln *cloud; befog* A h w	angeln	1
um|organisieren *reorganize* A h w	informieren	15
um|packen (in + A) *repack (into)* A h w	machen	21
um|pflanzen *transplant* A h w	heizen	14
um|pflügen *plough up* A h w	machen	21
um|quartieren (in + A) *reaccommodate (in)* A h w	informieren	15
um'rahmen *frame* A h w	machen	21
um'randen *ring;* (**mit** + D) *border (with)* A h w	reden	24
um|räumen *rearrange* A h w	machen	21
um|rechnen in + A *convert into* A h w	atmen	2
um|reißen *tear down* A h st [i, i]	beißen	3
um'reißen *outline; summarize* A h st [i, i]	beißen	3
um|rennen *knock down* A h m [a, a]	brennen	5
um'ringen *surround* A h w	machen	21
um|rühren *stir* A h w	machen	21
um'runden *go round; orbit* A h w	reden	24
um|rüsten (auf + A) *re-equip with* A h w	reden	24

um|rüsten (auf + A/zu + D) *convert (to/into)* A h w	reden	24
um|säumen *hem* A h w	machen	21
um'säumen *surround* A h w	machen	21
um|schalten (auf + A/in + A) *switch (to/into)* A h w	reden	24
um|schichten *restack; restructure* A h w	reden	24
um|schlagen *turn up/over/round;* **(in + A)** *change (into)* A h (**sein** when intrans.) st [ä, u, a]	tragen	38
um'schließen *surround; embrace* A h st [o, o]	schießen	26
um'schlingen *embrace; twine round* A h st [a, u]	klingen	16
um|schnallen *buckle on;* **(D)** *buckle (on to)* A h w	machen	21
um|schreiben *rewrite;* **(auf + A)** *transfer (to)* A h st [ie, ie]	schreiben	28
um|schulden *reschedule (debts)* A h w	reden	24
um|schulen *transfer (to a different school);* **(auf + A/zu + D)** *retrain (as)* A h w	machen	21
um|schütten *decant; spill* A h w	reden	24
um'schwärmen *swarm around* A h w	machen	21
um'schwenken *swing round; veer* s w	machen	21
um'schwirren *buzz around* A h w	machen	21
um'segeln *circumnavigate* A h w	angeln	1
sich um|sehen *look round;* **(nach + D)** *look out (for)* h st [ie, a, e]	sehen	29
um|setzen (auf + A/in + A) *move (to); implement* A h w	heizen	14
sich um|setzen *change seats/tables; transform itself* h w	heizen	14
um|siedeln *resettle;* **(in + A/nach + D)** *move to* A h (**sein** when intrans.) w	angeln	1

um|sinken *sink to the ground* s st [a, u]	klingen	16
um'sorgen *care for; look after* A h w	machen	21
um'spannen *clasp; encompass* A h w	machen	21
um|spielen *play about; swirl around* A h w	machen	21
um|springen *change;* (**auf** + A) *veer round (to)* s st [a, u]	klingen	16
um|spulen *rewind* A h w	machen	21
um'spülen *wash round* A h w	machen	21
um'stehen *stand round; surround* A h st [and, and]	stehen	34
um|steigen (**in** + D/**in** + A) *change (in/on to)* s st [ie, ie]	schreiben	28
um|steigen nach + D/**auf** + A *change for/to* s st [ie, ie]	schreiben	28
um|stellen *rearrange; reset;* (**auf** + A) *change (to)* A h w	machen	21
um'stellen *surround* A h w	machen	21
um|stimmen *win round* A h w	machen	21
um|stoßen *knock over; upset; change* A h st [ö, ie, o]	stoßen	36
um|strukturieren *restructure* A h w	informieren	15
um|stülpen *turn out/inside out/upside down* A h w	machen	21
um|stürzen *overturn; knock over* A h w	heizen	14
um|taufen *rename;* (**auf** + A) *change the name of . . . (to)* A h w	machen	21
um|tauschen (**gegen** + A/**in** + A) *change (for/into)* A h w	machen	21
um|topfen *repot* A h w	machen	21
um|ver'teilen *redistribute* A h w	machen	21
um|wälzen *roll over; circulate* A h w	heizen	14
um|wandeln (**in** + A) *convert (into); alter* A h w	angeln	1
um|wechseln in + A *change into* A h w	angeln	1

um|wenden *turn over/round/inside out*		
A h w/m [a, a]	reden/senden	24/31
um'werben *court; woo* A h st [i, a, o]	sprechen	33
um|werfen *knock over; put around*		
the shoulders A h st [i, a, o]	sprechen	33
um'wickeln (mit + D) *bind up (with);*		
bandage A h w	angeln	1
um|widmen (in + A/zu + D)		
redesignate (as) A h w	atmen	2
um'wölken *shroud; veil* A h w	machen	21
um|wühlen *churn up* A h w	machen	21
um'zäunen *fence off* A h w	machen	21
um|ziehen (an + A/in + A/nach + D)		
move (to) s st [og, og]	*kriechen	19
sich um|ziehen *change; get changed*		
h st [og, og]	*kriechen	19
um'zingeln *encircle* A h w	angeln	1
uniformieren *uniform* A h w	informieren	15
unterbelichten¹ *underexpose* A h w	reden	24
unterbewerten¹ *undervalue* A h w	reden	24
unterbezahlen¹ *underpay* A h w	machen	21
unter'bieten (um + A) *undercut (by);*		
beat A h st [o, o]	*kriechen	19
unter'binden *stop* A h st [a, u]	binden	4
unter'bleiben *not occur* s st [ie, ie]	schreiben	28
unter'brechen *interrupt* A h st [i, a, o]	sprechen	33
unter'bringen *put; fit; put up* A h m [ach, ach]	*brennen	5
unter'drücken *suppress; oppress* A h w	machen	21
untereinander|liegen *lie one below the other* h st [a, e]	sehen	29
unter'fahren *drive under* A h st [ä, u, a]	tragen	38

---

¹ Insep. except in the inf. with **zu**, e.g. **unterbelichten: ich unterbelichte**, but **unterzubelichten**.

unter'fordern (A) **mit** + D *demand*
  too little (of sb) with h w   angeln   1
unter'führen *put ditto marks for* A
  h w   machen   21
unter'füttern *line* A h w   angeln   1
unter|gehen *go down;* (**in** + D) *be lost*
  (in) s st [ing, ang]   *hängen   12
unter'gliedern *subdivide* A h w   angeln   1
unter'graben *undermine* A h st [ä, u,
  a]   tragen   38
  unter|graben *dig in* A h st [ä, u, a]   tragen   38
unter'halten *maintain; run; entertain*
  A h st [ä, ie, a]   *schlafen   27
  sich unter'halten (**mit** + D/**über** + A)
  talk (to/about); enjoy oneself h st
  [ä, ie, a]   *schlafen   27
unter'handeln (**über** + A) *negotiate*
  (on) h w   angeln   1
unter'höhlen *hollow out; undermine;*
  erode A h w   machen   21
unter'jochen *subjugate* A h w   machen   21
unter|kommen *find accommodation* s
  st [am, o]   kommen   17
unter'lassen *refrain from; omit* A h
  st [ä, ie, a]   *schlafen   27
unter'laufen *occur; happen; evade* h
  (**sein** *when intrans.*) st [äu, ie, au]   laufen   20
unter|legen (D) *put underneath*
  (sb/sth) A h w   machen   21
  unter'legen (**mit** + D) *underlay*
  (with); (D) *put (to)* A h w   machen   21
unter'liegen (**in** + D) *be beaten (in)*
  s st [a, e]   sehen   29
unter'malen mit + D *accompany with*
  A h w   machen   21
unter'mauern *underpin; support* A
  h w   angeln   1
unter|mengen *mix in* A h w   machen   21

unter'minieren *undermine* A h w	informieren	15
unter|mischen *mix in* A h w	machen	21
unter'nehmen *undertake* A h st [imm, a, omm]	*sprechen	33
unter|ordnen (D) *subordinate (to)* A h w	atmen	2
unter|pflügen *plough in* A h w	machen	21
unter'queren *cross under* A h w	machen	21
unter'richten *teach;* (**über** + A) *inform (of)* A h w	reden	24
unter|rühren *stir in* A h w	machen	21
unter'sagen (D) *forbid (sb)* A h w	machen	21
unter'schätzen *underestimate; underrate* A h w	heizen	14
unter'scheiden (**von** + D/**zwischen** + D) *distinguish (from/between)* A h st [ie, ie]	*schreiben	28
sich unter'scheiden (**von** + D/ **durch** + A) *differ (from/in)* h st [ie, ie]	*schreiben	28
unter|schieben *push under* A h st [o, o]	kriechen	19
unter'schieben (D) *foist on (sb); falsely attribute to (sb)* A h st [o, o]	kriechen	19
unter|schlagen *cross (legs); fold (arms)* A h st [ä, u, a]	tragen	38
unter'schlagen *suppress; embezzle* A h st [ä, u, a]	tragen	38
unter|schlüpfen vor + D *take shelter from* s w	machen	21
unter'schreiben *sign; put one's name to* A h st [ie, ie]	schreiben	28
unter'schreiten *fall/keep below* A h st [itt, itt]	streiten	37
unter|setzen *put underneath* A h w	heizen	14
unter|sinken *sink* s st [a, u]	klingen	16

unter'stehen *take shelter;* (D) *be*		
subordinate (to); be the		
responsibility (of) h st [and, and]	stehen	34
sich unter'stehen *dare* h st [and,		
and]	stehen	34
unter|stellen *store; put underneath*		
A h w	machen	21
unter'stellen *assume;* (D) *accuse*		
(sb) of; put (sb) in charge of		
A h w	machen	21
unter'steuern *understeer* h w	angeln	1
unter'streichen *underline; emphasize*		
A h st [i, i]	gleichen	10
unter'suchen *investigate;* (**auf** + A)		
examine (for) A h w	machen	21
unter'suchen nach + D/**auf** + A		
search for A h w	machen	21
unter|tauchen *duck; dive; disappear*		
A h (**sein** when intrans.) w	machen	21
unter'teilen *(sub)divide* A h w	machen	21
unter'treiben *play things down* h st		
[ie, ie]	schreiben	28
unter'tunneln *tunnel through* A h w	angeln	1
unter|ver'mieten *sublet* A h w	reden	24
unter|ver'sichern *under-insure* A h w	angeln	1
unter'wandern *infiltrate* A h w	angeln	1
unter'werfen *subjugate;* (D) *subject*		
(to) A h st [i, a, o]	sprechen	33
sich unter'werfen (D) *submit (to)* h		
st [i, a, o]	sprechen	33
unter'zeichnen *sign* A h w	atmen	2
unter|ziehen *put on underneath* A h		
st [og, og]	*kriechen	19
sich unter'ziehen *undertake; undergo*		
D h st [og, og]	*kriechen	19
urbanisieren *urbanize* A h w	informieren	15
urinieren (**an** + A) *urinate (against)*		
h w	informieren	15

urteilen (über + A) *judge* h w	machen	21
urteilen nach + D *judge by* h w	machen	21
usurpieren *usurp* A h w	informieren	15
variieren *vary* A h w	informieren	15
vegetieren *vegetate* h w	informieren	15
ver'abreden *arrange* A h w	reden	24
sich ver'abreden (mit + D) *arrange*		
to meet (sb) h w	reden	24
ver'abreichen *administer* A h w	machen	21
ver'abscheuen *detest* A h w	machen	21
ver'abschieden *retire; adopt; say*		
goodbye to A h w	reden	24
sich ver'abschieden von + D *say*		
goodbye to h w	reden	24
ver'absolutieren *make absolute* A h w	informieren	15
ver'achten *despise* A h w	reden	24
ver'albern *make fun of; mock* A h w	angeln	1
ver'allgemeinern *generalize* A h w	angeln	1
ver'alten *become obsolete* s w	reden	24
ver'ändern *change* A h w	angeln	1
ver'ängstigen *frighten* A h w	machen	21
ver'ankern *anchor; fix; embody* A		
h w	angeln	1
ver'anlassen *cause; see to;* (**zu** + D)		
lead (to sth) A h st [ä, ie, a]	*schlafen	27
ver'anschaulichen *illustrate* A h w	machen	21
ver'anschlagen mit + D *estimate at*		
A h w	machen	21
ver'anstalten *organize; hold* A h w	reden	24
ver'antworten *take responsibility for*		
A h w	reden	24
sich ver'antworten (für + A/**vor** + D)		
answer (for/to) h w	reden	24
ver'arbeiten *use; digest;* (**zu** + D)		
make (into sth) A h w	reden	24
ver'ärgern *annoy* A h w	angeln	1
ver'armen *become poor* s w	machen	21

sich ver'ästeln *branch out* h w	angeln	1
ver'ätzen *corrode* A h w	heizen	14
sich ver'ausgaben *wear oneself out* h w	machen	21
ver'bannen *banish* A h w	machen	21
ver'barrikadieren *barricade* A h w	informieren	15
ver'bauen *block* A h w	machen	21
ver'beißen *suppress* A h st [i, i]	beißen	3
sich ver'beißen in + A *bite into* h st [i, i]	beißen	3
ver'bergen (D/**vor** + D) *hide (from)* A h st [i, a, o]	sprechen	33
ver'bessern *improve; correct* A h w	angeln	1
sich ver'beugen vor + D *bow to* h w	machen	21
ver'beulen *dent* A h w	machen	21
ver'biegen *bend* A h st [o, o]	kriechen	19
ver'bieten (D) *forbid (sb)* A h st [o, o]	*kriechen	19
ver'bilden *bring up badly* A h w	reden	24
ver'billigen *reduce the cost of* A h w	machen	21
ver'binden *bandage;* (D/**durch** + A) *link (to/by)* A h st [a, u]	binden	4
ver'binden mit + D *associate with; put through to* A h st [a, u]	binden	4
sich [D] ver'bitten *refuse to tolerate* h st [at, et]	*geben	9
ver'bittern *embitter* A h w	angeln	1
ver'blassen *fade* s w	heizen	14
ver'bleiben *leave the matter;* (D) *remain (for sb)* s st [ie, ie]	schreiben	28
ver'bleichen *fade; grow pale* s w/st [i, i]	machen/ gleichen	21/10
ver'bleien *add lead to* A h w	machen	21
ver'blenden *blind;* (**mit** + D) *face (with)* A h w	reden	24
ver'blüffen *astonish* A h w	machen	21
ver'blühen *fade* s w	machen	21
ver'bluten *bleed to death* s w	reden	24

ver'brämen *dress up;* (**mit** + D) *trim*		
(with) A h w	machen	21
ver'brauchen *use; consume; wear out*		
A h w	machen	21
ver'breiten *spread* A h w	reden	24
sich ver'breiten *spread;* (**über** + A)		
go on (about) h w	reden	24
ver'breitern *widen* A h w	angeln	1
ver'brennen *burn; destroy by burning;*		
cremate A h (**sein** *when intrans.*)		
m [a, a]	brennen	5
ver'briefen *attest* A h w	machen	21
ver'bringen *spend (time)* A h m		
[ach, ach]	*brennen	5
sich ver'brüdern mit + D *fraternize*		
with; ally oneself with h w	angeln	1
ver'brühen *scald* A h w	machen	21
ver'buchen *enter; notch up* A h w	machen	21
sich ver'bünden *form an alliance*		
h w	reden	24
verbürgen *guarantee* A h w	machen	21
sich verbürgen für + A *vouch for*		
h w	machen	21
ver'büßen *serve (out)* A h w	heizen	14
ver'dächtigen (G) *suspect (of sth)*		
A h w	machen	21
ver'dammen *damn;* (**zu** + D)		
condemn (to) A h w	machen	21
ver'dämmern *fade; drowse away* A h		
(**sein** *when intrans.*) w	angeln	1
ver'dampfen *evaporate; abate* A h		
(**sein** *when intrans.*) w	machen	21
ver'danken (D) *owe (to sb); have*		
(sb) to thank for A h w	machen	21
ver'dauen *digest* A h w	machen	21
ver'decken *hide; cover* A h w	machen	21
ver'denken (D) *blame (sb) for* A h		
m [ach, ach]	*brennen	5

ver'derben *spoil* A h (**sein** when
  intrans.) st [i, a, o]   *sprechen   33
ver'deutschen *Germanize* A h w   machen   21
ver'dichten (**zu** + D) *condense (into)*
  A h w   reden   24
  sich ver'dichten *thicken; intensify*
  h w   reden   24
sich ver'dicken *swell; thicken* h w   machen   21
ver'dienen *earn; deserve* A h w   machen   21
ver'doppeln *double; redouble* A h w   angeln   1
ver'dorren *wither* s w   machen   21
ver'drängen (**aus** + D) *drive out*
  (from); displace A h w   machen   21
ver'drehen *twist* A h w   machen   21
ver'dreifachen *treble* A h w   machen   21
ver'drießen *annoy* A h st [o, o]   schießen   26
ver'dummen *dull (sb's) mind; become*
  dulled A h (**sein** when intrans.) w   machen   21
ver'dunkeln *darken* A h w   angeln   1
ver'dünnen *dilute; taper off* A h w   machen   21
ver'dunsten *evaporate* A h (**sein** when
  intrans.) w   reden   24
ver'dursten *die of thirst* s w   reden   24
ver'düstern *darken* A h w   angeln   1
ver'edeln *refine* A h w   angeln   1
ver'ehren *venerate; adore* A h w   machen   21
ver'eidigen *swear in;* (**auf** + A) *make*
  . . . swear (to sth) A h w   machen   21
ver'einbaren *agree;* (**mit** + D)
  reconcile (with) A h w   machen   21
ver'einen *unite; reconcile;* (**zu** + D)
  merge (into) A h w   machen   21
ver'einfachen *simplify* A h w   machen   21
ver'einigen *unite* A h w   machen   21
  sich ver'einigen *merge;* (**zu** + D)
  assemble (for) h w   machen   21
ver'eisen *freeze over; ice up* s w   heizen   14
ver'eiteln *thwart* A h w   angeln   1

ver'eitern *go septic* s w	angeln	1
ver'ekeln (D) *put (sb) off* A h w	angeln	1
ver'enden *perish; die* s w	reden	24
ver'engen *narrow* A h w	machen	21
ver'erben (D/**an** + A) *bequeath (to)* A h w	machen	21
sich ver'erben auf + A *be transmitted to* h w	machen	21
ver'ewigen *immortalize; perpetuate* A h w	machen	21
ver'fahren *spend; proceed;* (**mit** + D) *deal (with)* A h (**sein** when intrans.) st [ä, u, a]	tragen	38
sich ver'fahren *lose one's way* h st [ä, u, a]	tragen	38
ver'fallen *deteriorate; expire;* (D) *fall victim (to)* s st [ä, iel, a]	*schlafen	27
ver'fallen auf + A *think of; hit upon* s st [ä, iel, a]	*schlafen	27
ver'fallen in + A *drop (back) into* s st [ä, iel, a]	*schlafen	27
ver'fälschen *falsify; distort; adulterate* A h w	machen	21
ver'fangen bei + D *be effective with* h st [ä, i, a]	*hängen	12
sich ver'fangen in + D *get caught up in* h st [ä, i, a]	*hängen	12
sich ver'färben *change/lose colour; turn* h w	machen	21
ver'fassen *write; draw up* A h w	heizen	14
ver'faulen *rot; decay* s w	machen	21
ver'fechten *champion* A h w	reden	24
ver'fehlen *miss* A h w	machen	21
sich ver'feinden mit + D *make an enemy of* h w	reden	24
ver'feinern *refine* A h w	angeln	1
ver'fertigen *produce* A h w	machen	21
ver'festigen *strengthen* A h w	machen	21

sich ver'festigen zu + D *become*		
established as h w	machen	21
ver'fetten *become fat* s w	reden	24
ver'feuern *burn up; fire off* A h w	angeln	1
ver'filmen *film* A h w	machen	21
ver'finstern *obscure* A h w	angeln	1
ver'flachen *flatten (out); become*		
shallow/superficial A h (**sein** when		
intrans.) w	machen	21
ver'flechten *intertwine; involve* A h st		
[i, o, o]	dreschen	6
ver'fliegen *disperse; evaporate* s st		
[o, o]	kriechen	19
sich ver'fliegen *fly off course* h st		
[o, o]	kriechen	19
ver'fließen *merge; run* s st [o, o]	schießen	26
ver'fluchen *curse* A h w	machen	21
sich ver'flüchtigen *disperse* h w	machen	21
ver'folgen *pursue; persecute;*		
prosecute A h w	machen	21
ver'formen *distort* A h w	machen	21
ver'frachten *transport* A h w	reden	24
ver'fremden (D) *make unfamiliar*		
(to sb) A h w	reden	24
sich ver'frühen *arrive too early*		
h w	machen	21
ver'fügen *decree* A h w	machen	21
ver'fügen über + A *have at one's*		
disposal/command h w	machen	21
ver'führen *seduce; (zu + D) tempt*		
(to) A h w	machen	21
ver'gällen *spoil; sour* A h w	machen	21
ver'gären (**zu** + D) *ferment (into)* A	machen/	
h (**sein** when intrans.) w/st [o, o]	kriechen	21/19
ver'gasen *gas* A h w	heizen	14
ver'gattern *enjoin; reprimand* A h w	angeln	1
ver'geben (D) *forgive (sb) for; waste*		
A h st [i, a, e]	geben	9

ver'geben an + A *award (to)* A h st [i, a, e]	geben	9
sich [D] **ver'gegenwärtigen** *imagine* A h w	machen	21
ver'gehen *pass;* (**vor** + D) *die (of)* s st [ing, ang]	*hängen	12
sich ver'gehen gegen + A/**an** + D *violate* h st [ing, ang]	*hängen	12
ver'gelten (D) *repay (sb) for* A h st [i, a, o]	*sprechen	33
ver'gelten durch + A *repay with* A h st [i, a, o]	*sprechen	33
ver'gesellschaften *socialize* A h w	reden	24
ver'gessen *forget* A h st [i, a, e]	fressen	8
ver'geuden *waste* A h w	reden	24
ver'gewaltigen *rape* A h w	machen	21
sich ver'gewissern *make sure of* G h w	angeln	1
ver'gießen *spill; shed* A h st [o, o]	schießen	26
ver'giften *poison* A h w	reden	24
ver'gittern *bar* A h w	angeln	1
ver'glasen *glaze* A h w	heizen	14
ver'glimmen *go out* s w/st [o, o]	machen/ kriechen	21/19
ver'glühen *burn out; fade* s w	machen	21
ver'gnügen *amuse* A h w	machen	21
sich ver'gnügen *amuse oneself; have a good time* h w	machen	21
ver'golden *gild* A h w	reden	24
ver'gönnen (D) *grant (to sb)* A h w	machen	21
ver'göttern *idolize* A h w	angeln	1
ver'göttlichen *worship; deify* A h w	machen	21
ver'graben (**in** + A or D) *bury (in)* A h st [ä, u, a]	tragen	38
ver'grämen *antagonize* A h w	machen	21
sich ver'greifen an + D *misappropriate; assault* h st [iff, iff]	greifen	11

sich ver'greifen in + D *choose the wrong . . .* h st [iff, iff]	greifen	11
ver'greisen *go senile; age* s w	heizen	14
ver'gröbern *coarsen* A h w	angeln	1
ver'größern *increase; enlarge* A h w	angeln	1
ver'güten (D) *reimburse (sb) for* A h w	reden	24
ver'haften *arrest* A h w	reden	24
ver'haken (in + D) *hook (in); hook up* A h w	machen	21
ver'hallen *die away* s w	machen	21
sich ver'halten *behave; react; be* h st [ä, ie, a]	*schlafen	27
ver'handeln (A/über + A) *negotiate (about); try a case* h w	angeln	1
ver'harmlosen *play down* A h w	heizen	14
ver'härten *harden* A h w	reden	24
ver'heeren *devastate* A h w	machen	21
ver'heilen *heal* s w	machen	21
ver'heimlichen (D) *conceal (from sb)* A h w	machen	21
sich ver'heiraten mit + D *get married to* h w	reden	24
ver'heißen (D) *predict (for sb)* A h st [ie, ei]	heißen	13
ver'heizen *burn (out)* A h w	heizen	14
ver'helfen (D) **zu** + D *help (sb) achieve . . .* h st [i, a, o]	sprechen	33
ver'herrlichen *glorify* A h w	machen	21
ver'hetzen *incite* A h w	heizen	14
ver'hexen *bewitch;* (**in** + A) *turn (into)* A h w	heizen	14
ver'hindern *prevent* A h w	angeln	1
ver'höhnen *mock* A h w	machen	21
ver'hören *interrogate* A h w	machen	21
sich ver'hören *mishear* h w	machen	21
ver'hüllen *disguise; enshroud* A h w	machen	21
ver'hungern *starve to death* s w	angeln	1

ver'hüten *prevent* A h w	reden	24
ver'hütten *smelt* A h w	reden	24
verifizieren *verify* A h w	informieren	15
sich ver'irren *lose one's way;* (**in** + A/ **an** + A) *stray (into)* h w	machen	21
ver'jagen *chase away* A h w	machen	21
ver'jazzen *jazz up* A h w	heizen	14
ver'jüngen *rejuvenate* A h w	machen	21
ver'kabeln *connect up* A h w	angeln	1
ver'kalken *fur up; calcify* s w	machen	21
sich ver'kalkulieren *miscalculate* h w	informieren	15
ver'kaufen (**D/an** + A) *sell (to)* A h w	machen	21
ver'kehren *run* h (sometimes **sein**) w	machen	21
ver'kehren mit + D *associate with* h w	machen	21
ver'kehren in + D/**bei** + D *frequent* h w	machen	21
ver'kehren *reverse;* (**in** + A) *turn (into)* A h w	machen	21
ver'keilen in + A *wedge into* A h w	machen	21
ver'kennen *misjudge* A h m [a, a]	brennen	5
sich ver'ketten *become interlinked* h w	reden	24
ver'klagen *sue* A h w	machen	21
ver'klären *transfigure* A h w	machen	21
ver'klausulieren *hedge round with qualifications* A h w	informieren	15
ver'kleben *stick together/down* A h w	machen	21
ver'kleiden *disguise; dress up; cover* A h w	reden	24
ver'kleinern *reduce* A h w	angeln	1
sich ver'klemmen *jam; stick* h w	machen	21
ver'klingen *fade away* s st [a, u]	klingen	16
ver'klumpen *go lumpy* s w	machen	21
ver'knappen *cut back (on)* A h w	machen	21
ver'knittern *crumple* A h w	angeln	1

ver'knoten *knot;* (**an** + A) *tie (to)*		
A h w	reden	24
ver'knüpfen *tie;* (**mit** + D) *link (with)*		
A h w	machen	21
ver'kochen *boil away* s w	machen	21
ver'kohlen *char* A h w	machen	21
ver'kommen *go to ruin;* (**zu** + D)		
degenerate (into) s st [am, o]	kommen	17
ver'komplizieren *complicate* A h w	informieren	15
ver'koppeln *couple; link up* A h w	angeln	1
ver'korken *cork up* A h w	machen	21
ver'körpern *embody; personify* A h w	angeln	1
sich ver'körpern in + D *be embodied*		
in h w	angeln	1
ver'kosten *taste* A h w	reden	24
ver'köstigen *feed* A h w	machen	21
ver'kraften *cope with* A h w	reden	24
sich ver'krallen in + A *dig one's*		
fingers into h w	machen	21
sich ver'krallen in + D/A *cling to*		
h w	machen	21
sich ver'krampfen *tense up* h w	machen	21
ver'kratzen *scratch* A h w	heizen	14
sich ver'kriechen (**in** + A/D) *hide*		
oneself away (in) h st [o, o]	kriechen	19
ver'krümmen *bend* A h w	machen	21
ver'krüppeln *cripple; become stunted*		
A h (**sein** when intrans.) w	angeln	1
sich ver'kühlen *catch a chill* h w	machen	21
ver'kümmern *waste away; decline* s w	angeln	1
ver'künden *announce; proclaim* A h w	reden	24
ver'kuppeln mit + D *pair off with* A		
h w	angeln	1
ver'kürzen (**auf** + A) *reduce (to)* A		
h w	heizen	14
ver'lachen *laugh at; ridicule* A h w	machen	21
ver'laden *load* A h st [ä, u, a]	*tragen	38
ver'lagern *shift* A h w	angeln	1

ver'landen *silt up* s w	reden	24
ver'langen *demand; ask for* A h w	machen	21
ver'langen nach + D *crave for* h w	machen	21
ver'längern (**um** + A) *lengthen (by); renew* A h w	angeln	1
ver'langsamen *slow; slacken* A h w	machen	21
ver'lassen *leave* A h st [ä, ie, a]	*schlafen	27
sich ver'lassen auf + A *rely on* h st [ä, ie, a]	*schlafen	27
ver'lästern *malign* A h w	angeln	1
ver'laufen *run; go; melt;* (**in** + D) *disappear (in)* s st [äu, ie, au]	laufen	20
sich ver'laufen *lose one's way; disperse* h st [äu, ie, au]	laufen	20
ver'lautbaren *announce; become known* A h (**sein** when intrans.) w	machen	21
ver'lauten *announce; be reported* A h (**sein** when intrans.) w	reden	24
ver'leben *spend* A h w	machen	21
ver'lebendigen *make . . . come alive* A h w	machen	21
ver'legen *mislay; lay; move; block; publish* A h w	machen	21
ver'legen auf + A *postpone until; bring forward to* A h w	machen	21
sich ver'legen auf + A *take up; resort to* h w	machen	21
ver'leiden (D) *spoil (for sb)* A h w	reden	24
ver'leihen *rent out;* (D) *confer (on sb)* A h st [ie, ie]	schreiben	28
ver'leiten zu + D *lead into* A h w	reden	24
ver'lernen *forget* A h w	machen	21
sich ver'lesen *make a mistake reading* h st [ie, a, e]	*sehen	29
ver'letzen *hurt; infringe* A h w	heizen	14
ver'leugnen *deny; disown* A h w	atmen	2
ver'leumden *slander; libel* A h w	reden	24

sich ver'lieben in + A *fall in love with*		
h w	machen	21
ver'lieren (an + D) *lose (some of)* A		
h st [o, o]	kriechen	19
ver'lieren bei + D *become less highly*		
regarded by h st [o, o]	kriechen	19
sich ver'lieren *lose one's way; vanish*		
h st [o, o]	kriechen	19
sich ver'loben (mit + D) *get engaged*		
(to) h w	machen	21
verloren|gehen *get/be lost* s st [ing,		
ang]	*hängen	12
ver'löschen *go out* s st [i, o, o]	dreschen	6
ver'losen *raffle* A h w	heizen	14
ver'lottern *become run-down* s w	angeln	1
ver'machen (D) *bequeath (to sb);*		
give (to sb) A h w	machen	21
sich ver'mählen (D/**mit** + D) *wed*		
(sb) h w	machen	21
ver'markten *market* A h w	reden	24
ver'mauern *wall up* A h w	angeln	1
ver'mehren um + A *increase by* A		
h w	machen	21
ver'meiden *avoid* A h st [ie, ie]	*schreiben	28
ver'melden *report* A h w	reden	24
ver'mengen (mit + D) *mix (with)*		
A h w	machen	21
ver'merken *note; make a note of*		
A h w	machen	21
ver'messen *measure; survey* A h st		
[i, a, e]	fressen	8
ver'mieten (an + A) *rent out (to);*		
hire (to) A h w	reden	24
ver'mindern *reduce* A h w	angeln	1
ver'mischen (mit + D) *mix (with)*		
A h w	machen	21
ver'missen *miss; not have*		
A h w	heizen	14

ver'mitteln (D) *arrange (for sb);*		
pass on (to sb) A h w	angeln	1
ver'mitteln in + D *mediate in* h w	angeln	1
ver'modern *decay* s w	angeln	1
ver'mögen *be able* A h m [a, och,		
och]	mögen	22
ver'mummen *wrap up; disguise*		
A h w	machen	21
ver'muten *suspect* A h w	reden	24
ver'nageln *nail up* A h w	angeln	1
ver'nähen *sew up* A h w	machen	21
ver'narben *heal* s w	machen	21
sich ver'narren in + A *become*		
infatuated with h w	machen	21
ver'nebeln *obscure* A h w	angeln	1
ver'nehmen *examine; hear* A h st		
[imm, a, omm]	*sprechen	33
ver'neinen *reject; say no to* A h w	machen	21
ver'nichten *destroy* A h w	reden	24
ver'niedlichen *trivialize* A h w	machen	21
ver'öden *become deserted/barren* s w	reden	24
ver'öffentlichen *publish* A h w	machen	21
ver'ordnen (D) *prescribe (for sb)*		
A h w	atmen	2
ver'pachten *lease* A h w	reden	24
ver'packen *wrap up* A h w	machen	21
ver'passen *miss* A h w	heizen	14
ver'pesten *pollute* A h w	reden	24
ver'pfänden *pawn; mortgage* A h w	reden	24
ver'pflanzen *transplant* A h w	heizen	14
ver'pflegen *cater for* A h w	machen	21
ver'pflichten *oblige; take on;* (**zu** + D)		
swear (to) A h w	reden	24
sich ver'pflichten *undertake;* (**zu**		
+ D) *commit oneself (to)* h w	reden	24
ver'planen *book up* A h w	machen	21
ver'prassen *squander* A h w	heizen	14
ver'prellen *alienate* A h w	machen	21

ver'prügeln *beat up* A h w	angeln	1
ver'puffen *fall flat* s w	machen	21
ver'putzen *plaster* A h w	heizen	14
ver'rammeln *barricade* A h w	angeln	1
ver'raten (an + A) *betray (to)* A h st [ä, ie, a]	*schlafen	27
ver'rauchen *clear; subside* s w	machen	21
ver'räuchern *fill with smoke* A h w	angeln	1
ver'rechnen *include* A h w	atmen	2
sich ver'rechnen *make a mistake;* (**um + A**) *miscalculate (by)* h w	atmen	2
ver'reiben *rub in* A h st [ie, ie]	schreiben	28
ver'reisen *go away* s w	heizen	14
ver'renken *dislocate* A h w	machen	21
sich ver'rennen *get off course;* (**in + A**) *become obsessed (with)* h m [a, a]	brennen	5
ver'richten *perform* A h w	reden	24
ver'riegeln *bolt* A h w	angeln	1
ver'ringern *reduce* A h w	angeln	1
ver'rinnen *seep away* s st [a, o]	*sprechen	33
ver'rohen *brutalize; become brutal* A h (**sein** when intrans.) w	machen	21
ver'rosten *rust* s w	reden	24
ver'rotten *rot* s w	reden	24
ver'rücken *shift* A h w	machen	21
ver'rühren *stir together* A h w	machen	21
ver'rutschen *slip (to one side)* s w	machen	21
ver'sagen *fail; break down;* (D) *deny . . . (to sb)* A h w	machen	21
ver'salzen *over-salt* A h w	heizen	14
ver'sammeln *assemble* A h w	angeln	1
ver'sanden *silt up* s w	reden	24
ver'säumen *miss; neglect* A h w	machen	21
ver'schachern *sell off* A h w	angeln	1
ver'schaffen (D) *provide (sb) with* A h w	machen	21

sich [D] **ver'schaffen** *get hold of;* *gain* A h w	machen	21
sich **ver'schanzen in** + D *take refuge in* h w	heizen	14
ver'schärfen *intensify; aggravate* A h w	machen	21
ver'scharren *bury* A h w	machen	21
ver'schätzen *misjudge* A h w	heizen	14
sich **ver'schätzen in** + D *misjudge* h w	heizen	14
ver'schenken (an + A) *give away (to sb)* A h w	machen	21
sich [D] **ver'scherzen** *forfeit* A h w	heizen	14
ver'scheuchen *scare away* A h w	machen	21
ver'schicken *send away* A h w	machen	21
ver'schieben *move;* **(auf** + A/**um** + A) *postpone (until/by)* A h st [o, o]	kriechen	19
ver'schießen *fire; fade* A h (**sein** when intrans.) st [o, o]	schießen	26
ver'schiffen *ship* A h w	machen	21
ver'schimmeln *go mouldy* s w	angeln	1
ver'schlafen *oversleep; sleep through* A h st [ä, ie, a]	schlafen	27
ver'schlagen (D) *take away (from sb)* A h st [ä, u, a]	tragen	38
ver'schlagen an + A/**nach** + D *drive to* A h st [ä, u, a]	tragen	38
ver'schlammen *become muddy* s w	machen	21
ver'schlechtern *make worse* A h w	angeln	1
ver'schleiern *veil; hide* A h w	angeln	1
ver'schleifen *smooth* A h st [iff, iff]	greifen	11
ver'schleißen *wear out* A h (**sein** when intrans.) st [i, i]	beißen	3
ver'schleppen *carry (off); delay* A h w	machen	21
ver'schleudern *sell at a loss* A h w	angeln	1
ver'schließen *close; lock;* (**in** + D or A) *lock away (in)* A h st [o, o]	schießen	26

ver'schlimmern *make worse* A h w	angeln	1
ver'schlingen (zu + D) *twine (into);* *devour* A h st [a, u]	klingen	16
ver'schlucken *swallow; absorb* A h w	machen	21
sich ver'schlucken *choke* h w	machen	21
ver'schlüsseln *encode* A h w	angeln	1
ver'schmälern (um + A) *narrow (by)* A h w	angeln	1
ver'schmelzen *fuse;* **(zu + D)** *merge* *(into)* A h (**sein** when intrans.) w	heizen	14
ver'schmerzen *get over* A h w	heizen	14
ver'schmieren *smear; smudge; mess* *up* A h w	machen	21
ver'schmutzen *dirty; become polluted* A h (**sein** when intrans.) w	heizen	14
ver'schneiden *blend; castrate* A h st [itt, itt]	*streiten	37
ver'schnüren *tie up* A h w	machen	21
ver'schonen (mit + D) *spare (from* *sth)* A h w	machen	21
ver'schönen/ver'schönern *brighten up* A h w	machen/ angeln	21/1
ver'schränken *fold (arms); cross* *(legs)* A h w	machen	21
ver'schrecken *scare (off)* A h w	machen	21
ver'schreiben (D) *prescribe (for sb)* A h st [ie, ie]	schreiben	28
sich ver'schreiben *make a slip of the* *pen;* **(D)** *devote oneself (to sth)* h st [ie, ie]	schreiben	28
ver'schrotten *scrap* A h w	reden	24
ver'schüchtern *intimidate* A h w	angeln	1
ver'schulden *be to blame for* A h w	reden	24
sich ver'schulden *get into debt* h w	reden	24
ver'schütten *spill; bury; submerge* A h w	reden	24
ver'schweigen (D) *conceal (from sb)* A h st [ie, ie]	schreiben	28

ver'schweißen (mit + D) *weld (to)*
A h w   heizen   14
ver'schwenden an + A *waste on* A
h w   reden   24
ver'schwimmen *become blurred* s st
[a, o]   sprechen   33
ver'schwinden (in + D or A)
disappear (into) s st [a, u]   binden   4
sich ver'schwören *devote oneself to*
D h st [o, o]   kriechen   19
 sich ver'schwören gegen + A
conspire against h st [o, o]   kriechen   19
ver'sehen (mit + D) *provide (with);*
hold A h st [ie, a, e]   sehen   29
 sich ver'sehen *make a slip* h st
[ie, a, e]   sehen   29
sich ver'selbständigen *become*
independent h w   machen   21
ver'senden *send out* A h w/m [a, a]   reden/senden 24/31
ver'sengen *scorch* A h w   machen   21
ver'senken (in + A) *sink (into);*
lower A h w   machen   21
ver'setzen (in + A) *transfer (to); put*
(into); pawn A h w   heizen   14
 ver'setzen (D) *let (sb) have; retort*
(to sb) A h w   heizen   14
ver'seuchen *contaminate* A h w   machen   21
ver'sichern *affirm; (D) assure (sb)*
of A h w   angeln   1
 ver'sichern (mit + D/bei + D) *insure*
(for/with) A h w   angeln   1
ver'sickern *drain away* s w   angeln   1
ver'siegeln *seal* A h w   angeln   1
ver'siegen *run out* s w   machen   21
ver'silbern *silver; plate* A h w   angeln   1
ver'sinken in + D *sink into* s st [a, u] klingen   16
 ver'sinken in + A *become wrapped*
up in s st [a, u]   klingen   16

ver'sinnbildlichen *symbolize* A h w	machen	21
ver'sklaven *enslave* A h w	machen	21
ver'söhnen (mit + D) *reconcile (with sth/to sb)* A h w	machen	21
ver'sorgen *provide for; see to;* (mit + D) *supply (with)* A h w	machen	21
sich ver'spannen *tense up* h w	machen	21
sich ver'späten *be late* h w	reden	24
sich ver'spekulieren *make a bad bet* h w	informieren	15
ver'sperren *block* A h w	machen	21
ver'spielen *gamble away* A h w	machen	21
sich ver'spielen *play a wrong note* h w	machen	21
ver'spinnen (zu + D) *spin (into)* A h st [a, o]	*sprechen	33
ver'spotten *ridicule* A h w	reden	24
ver'sprechen (D) *promise (sb)* A h st [i, a, o]	sprechen	33
sich [D] ver'sprechen (von + D) *hope for (from sb/sth); make a slip of the tongue* A h st [i, a, o]	sprechen	33
ver'sprengen *sprinkle; scatter* A h w	machen	21
ver'spritzen *spray* A h w	heizen	14
ver'sprühen *spray* A h w	machen	21
ver'spüren (zu + D) *feel (for)* A h w	machen	21
ver'staatlichen *nationalize* A h w	machen	21
ver'ständigen (von + D/über + A) *notify (of)* A h w	machen	21
sich ver'ständigen mit + D *communicate with;* (über + A/auf + A) *reach agreement with (about sth)* h w	machen	21
ver'stärken *strengthen;* (um + A) *augment (by)* A h w	machen	21
ver'stauben *get dusty* s w	machen	21
ver'stäuben *spray* A h w	machen	21
ver'stauchen *sprain* A h w	machen	21

ver'stauen (in + D or A) *stow away (in)* A h w	machen	21
ver'stecken (vor + D) *hide (from)* A h w	machen	21
ver'stehen (unter + D) *understand (by)* A h st [and, and]	stehen	34
sich ver'stehen *be understood;* **(mit** + D) *get on (with)* h st [and, and]	stehen	34
sich ver'stehen auf + A *know all about* h st [and, and]	stehen	34
ver'steifen *stiffen; shore up* A h (**sein** when intrans.) w	machen	21
ver'steigern *auction* A h w	angeln	1
ver'steinern *fossilize; go rigid* s w	angeln	1
ver'stellen *misplace; adjust; disguise; obstruct* A h w	machen	21
sich ver'stellen *pretend; alter* h w	machen	21
ver'sterben *pass away* s st [i, a, o]	sprechen	33
ver'steuern *pay tax on* A h w	angeln	1
ver'stimmen *annoy; put into a bad mood* A h w	machen	21
ver'stopfen (von + D/**durch** + A) *block (with)* A h w	machen	21
ver'stören *distress* A h w	machen	21
ver'stoßen *disown* A h st [ö, ie, o]	stoßen	36
ver'stoßen gegen + A *infringe* h st [ö, ie, o]	stoßen	36
ver'strahlen *radiate; contaminate* A h w	machen	21
ver'streichen *apply; go by* A h (**sein** when intrans.) st [i, i]	gleichen	10
ver'streuen *scatter; spill* A h w	machen	21
ver'stricken in + A *involve in* A h w	machen	21
ver'strömen *exude* A h w	machen	21
ver'stümmeln *mutilate* A h w	angeln	1
ver'stummen *become silent* s w	machen	21
ver'suchen *try; tempt* A h w	machen	21

sich ver'suchen in + D/**an** + D *try*		
one's hand at h w	machen	21
ver'sumpfen *become marshy* s w	machen	21
sich ver'sündigen an + D *sin against*		
h w	machen	21
ver'süßen (D) *make more pleasant*		
(for sb) A h w	heizen	14
ver'tagen (auf + A) *adjourn (until)*		
A h w	machen	21
ver'tauschen (mit + D/**gegen** + A)		
exchange (for) A h w	machen	21
ver'teidigen *defend* A h w	machen	21
ver'teilen (an + A/**unter** + A/**auf** + A)		
distribute (to/among/over) A h w	machen	21
sich ver'teuern *become more*		
expensive h w	angeln	1
ver'teufeln *denigrate* A h w	angeln	1
ver'tiefen (um + A) *deepen (by)* A		
h w	machen	21
sich ver'tiefen in + A *become*		
absorbed in h w	machen	21
ver'tilgen *exterminate; kill off* A h w	machen	21
ver'tippen *mistype* A h w	machen	21
ver'tragen *endure; take* A h st [ä, u,		
a]	tragen	38
sich ver'tragen mit + D *get along*		
with; go with h st [ä, u, a]	tragen	38
ver'trauen (auf + A) *trust (in)* D h w	machen	21
ver'träumen *dream away* A h w	machen	21
ver'treiben (aus + D) *drive out (of)*		
A h st [ie, ie]	schreiben	28
ver'treten *deputize for; represent;*		
support A h st [itt, a, e]	*geben	9
ver'trocknen *dry up* s w	atmen	2
ver'trösten (auf + A) *put off (until)*		
A h w	reden	24
ver'tun *waste* A h st [at, a]	tun	39
ver'tuschen *hush up* A h w	machen	21

ver'übeln *take amiss;* (D) *blame (sb)*		
for A h w	angeln	1
ver'üben *commit* A h w	machen	21
ver'unglücken *have an accident; go*		
wrong s w	machen	21
ver'unreinigen *pollute* A h w	machen	21
ver'unstalten *disfigure* A h w	reden	24
ver'untreuen *embezzle* A h w	machen	21
ver'unzieren *spoil the look of* A h w	machen	21
ver'ursachen (D) *cause (sb)* A h w	machen	21
ver'urteilen (zu + D/wegen + G)		
sentence (to/for) A h w	machen	21
ver'vielfachen *multiply; redouble* A		
h w	machen	21
ver'vielfältigen *duplicate* A h w	machen	21
ver'vollkommnen *perfect* A h w	atmen	2
ver'vollständigen *complete* A h w	machen	21
ver'wachsen *heal up;* (mit + D) *grow*		
together (with) s st [ä, u, a]	*tragen	38
ver'wachsen zu + D *grow into* s st		
[ä, u, a]	*tragen	38
sich ver'wählen *misdial* h w	machen	21
ver'wahren *keep safe; detain* A h w	machen	21
ver'wahrlosen *fall into disrepair* s w	heizen	14
ver'waisen *become orphaned* s w	heizen	14
ver'walten *administer* A h w	reden	24
ver'wandeln (in + A/zu + D)		
transform (into) A h w	angeln	1
ver'warnen (wegen + G) *caution (for/*		
about) A h w	machen	21
ver'wässern *water down* A h w	angeln	1
ver'weben (in + A) *weave (into);*		
interweave A h w	machen	21
ver'wechseln *confuse;* (mit + D)		
mistake (for) A h w	angeln	1
ver'wehen *cover (over); blow away*		
A h w	machen	21
ver'wehren (D) *refuse (sb)* A h w	machen	21

ver'weichlichen *grow/make soft* A h		
(**sein** when intrans.) w	machen	21
ver'weigern (D) *refuse (sb)* A h w	angeln	1
sich ver'weigern *refuse to accept* D		
h w	angeln	1
ver'weisen an + A/**auf** + A *refer to* A		
h st [ie, ie]	*schreiben	28
ver'weisen von + D/**aus** + D *expel*		
from A h st [ie, ie]	*schreiben	28
ver'welken *wilt; fade* s w	machen	21
ver'wenden (**für** + A/**zu** + D) *use*		
(for) A h w/m [a, a]	reden/senden	24/31
ver'wenden auf + A *spend on* A h		
w/m [a, a]	reden/senden	24/31
ver'werfen *reject* A h st [i, a, o]	sprechen	33
ver'werten (**zu** + D) *utilize (for)* A h		
w	reden	24
ver'wesen *decompose* s w	heizen	14
ver'wickeln in + A *entangle in* A h w	angeln	1
sich ver'wickeln in + A or D *get*		
caught up in h w	angeln	1
ver'wildern *go wild* s w	angeln	1
ver'wirklichen *realize* A h w	machen	21
ver'wirren *entangle; confuse* A h w	machen	21
ver'wischen *smudge; blur* A h w	machen	21
ver'wittern *weather* s w	angeln	1
ver'wohnen *ruin* A h w	machen	21
ver'wöhnen *spoil* A h w	machen	21
ver'wunden *wound* A h w	reden	24
ver'wundern *surprise* A h w	angeln	1
sich ver'wundern über + A *be*		
surprised at/by h w	angeln	1
ver'wünschen *curse* A h w	machen	21
ver'wüsten *devastate* A h w	reden	24
ver'zagen *despair* s/h w	machen	21
sich ver'zählen *miscount* h w	machen	21
ver'zahnen mit + D *connect up to* A		
h w	machen	21

ver'zärteln *mollycoddle* A h w	angeln	1
ver'zaubern *bewitch;* (**in** + A)		
transform (into) A h w	angeln	1
ver'zehren *consume* A h w	machen	21
ver'zeichnen *record* A h w	atmen	2
ver'zeihen (D) *forgive (sb)* A h st		
[ie, ie]	schreiben	28
ver'zerren (**zu** + D) *contort (into);*		
distort; strain A h w	machen	21
ver'zetteln *dissipate* A h w	angeln	1
ver'zichten auf + A *do without;*		
renounce A h w	reden	24
ver'ziehen *screw up; spoil; move*		
away A h (**sein** when intrans.) st		
[og, og]	*kriechen	19
sich ver'ziehen *become distorted;*		
disperse h st [og, og]	*kriechen	19
ver'zieren *decorate* A h w	machen	21
ver'zinsen (**mit** + D) *pay interest*		
(at . . .) on A h w	heizen	14
ver'zögern *slow down;* (**um** + A)		
delay (by) A h w	angeln	1
ver'zollen *pay duty on* A h w	machen	21
ver'zweifeln (**über** + A/**an** + D)		
despair (at/of) h/s w	angeln	1
sich ver'zweigen *branch (out)* h w	machen	21
vibrieren *vibrate* h w	informieren	15
vierteln *quarter* A h w	angeln	1
visieren *take aim* h w	informieren	15
vivisezieren *vivisect* A h w	informieren	15
volladen (separable: **ich lade voll,**		
vollzuladen, etc.) *load up* A h st		
[ä, u, a]	*tragen	38
vollaufen (separable: **es läuft voll,**		
vollzulaufen, etc.) *fill up* s st [äu,		
ie, au]	laufen	20
voll'bringen *accomplish* A h m [ach,		
ach]	*brennen	5

voll'enden *complete* A h w	reden	24
voll'führen *perform* A h w	machen	21
voll|füllen *fill up* A h w	machen	21
voll|gießen *fill (up)* A h st [o, o]	schießen	26
voll|machen *complete* A h w	machen	21
voll|packen *pack full* A h w	machen	21
voll|pfropfen *cram full* A h w	machen	21
voll|pumpen *pump up* A h w	machen	21
voll|schreiben *fill with writing* A h st [ie, ie]	schreiben	28
voll|spritzen (mit + D) *spray (sth) all over* A h w	heizen	14
voll'strecken *enforce; execute;* **(an + D)** *carry out (on)* A h w	machen	21
voll|tanken *fill up* A h w	machen	21
voll'ziehen (an + D) *carry out (on)* A h st [og, og]	*kriechen	19
sich voll'ziehen *take place; occur* h st [og, og]	*kriechen	19
volontieren bei + D *work as a trainee with* h w	informieren	15
voran|bringen *make progress with* A h m [ach, ach]	*brennen	5
voran|gehen *go first; make progress;* (D) *go ahead (of sb);* s st [ing, ang]	*hängen	12
voran|kommen *make progress* s st [am, o]	kommen	17
voran|stellen (D) *place first (in)* A h w	machen	21
sich vor|arbeiten auf + A *work one's way forward to* h w	reden	24
voraus|ahnen *have a presentiment of* A h w	machen	21
voraus|be'rechnen *calculate in advance* A h w	atmen	2
voraus|be'stimmen *predetermine; determine in advance* A h w	machen	21

voraus|be'eilen (D) *hurry on ahead (of sb)* s w	machen	21
voraus|gehen (D) *go on ahead (of sb); precede (sth)* s st [ing, ang]	*hängen	12
voraus|haben (D) *have (over sb/sth)* A h m [at, att, a]	*brennen	5
voraus|laufen *run on ahead* s st [äu, ie, au]	laufen	20
voraus|planen *plan in advance* A h w	machen	21
voraus|sagen *predict* A h w	machen	21
voraus|schauen *look ahead* h w	machen	21
voraus|schicken *send ahead; say first* A h w	machen	21
voraus|sehen *foresee* A h st [ie, a, e]	sehen	29
voraus|setzen *assume; presuppose* A h w	heizen	14
vor|bauen *make provision* h w	machen	21
vor|be'halten (D) *reserve (for)* A h st [ä, ie, a]	*schlafen	27
vorbei|fahren (an + D) *drive past (sb)* s st [ä, u, a]	tragen	38
vorbei|führen an + D *run past sth* h w	machen	21
vorbei|gehen an + D *miss; go past; pass* s st [ing, ang]	*hängen	12
vorbei|kommen an + D *pass; get past* s st [am, o]	kommen	17
vorbei|können an + D *be able to get past* h m [a, o, o]	können	18
vorbei|marschieren an + D *march past* s w	informieren	15
vorbei|reden (an + D) *miss the point of (sth)* h w	reden	24
vorbei|reden aneinander *talk at cross purposes* h w	reden	24
vorbei|schießen an + D (with **haben**) *miss;* (with **sein**) *shoot past* st [o, o]	schießen	26

vorbei|ziehen an + D *pass by;*
overtake s st [og, og] — *kriechen — 19

vor|be'reiten (auf + A/**für** + A)
prepare (for) A h w — reden — 24

vor|be'stellen *order in advance* A h w — machen — 21

vor|beugen *bend forward;* (D/**gegen**
+ A) *prevent (sth)* A h w — machen — 21

vor|bringen *produce; bring forward* A
h m [ach, ach] — *brennen — 5

sich vor|drängen (bis an + A/**an** + D)
push one's way forward (to) h w — machen — 21

vor|dringen *advance;* (**bis zu** + D) *get*
(as far as) s st [a, u] — klingen — 16

vor|ent'halten (sometimes: **ich**
vorenthalte) (D) *withhold (from)*
A h st [ä, ie, a] — *schlafen — 27

vor|fahren (vor + D) *drive up*
(outside); move forward s st [ä, u,
a] — tragen — 38

vor|fallen *occur; fall forward* s st [ä,
iel, a] — *schlafen — 27

vor|finden *find* A h st [a, u] — binden — 4

vor|fühlen bei + D *sound out* h w — machen — 21

vor|führen (D) *bring forward*
(before); show (to); demonstrate
(to) A h w — machen — 21

vor|gaukeln (D) *lead (sb) to believe*
in A h w — angeln — 1

vor|geben *pretend; predetermine* A h
st [i, a, e] — geben — 9

vor|gehen *go on; go on ahead; be*
fast; (**gegen** + A) *take action*
(against) s st [ing, ang] — *hängen — 12

vor|greifen (bei + D/**in** + D)
anticipate (in) D st [iff, iff] — greifen — 11

  vor|greifen mit + D *anticipate with*
D st [iff, iff] — greifen — 11

vor|haben *intend* A h m [at, att, a] — *brennen — 5

vor|halten *hold up; (D) reproach (sb) for* A h st [ä, ie, a]   *schlafen   27

vor|heizen *pre-heat* A h w   heizen   14

vorher|be'stimmen *predetermine* A h w   machen   21

vor|herrschen *predominate* h w   machen   21

vorher|sagen *forecast* A h w   machen   21

vor|heucheln *(D) feign (to sb)* A h w   angeln   1

vor|kommen *occur; (D) happen (to); seem (to)* s st [am, o]   kommen   17

vor|kommen (hinter + D/unter + D) *come out (from behind/from under)* s st [am, o]   kommen   17

vorlieb|nehmen mit + D *put up with* h st [imm, a, omm]   *sprechen   33

vor|liegen *be available; exist; (D) be (with/before)* h st [a, e]   sehen   29

vor|merken für + A *put down for* A h w   machen   21

vor|nehmen *carry out; perform* A h st [imm, a, omm]   *sprechen   33

sich [D] vor|nehmen *plan* A h st [imm, a, omm]   *sprechen   33

sich vor|neigen *lean forward* h w   machen   21

vornüber|fallen *fall forwards* s st [ä, iel, a]   *schlafen   27

vor|preschen *rush ahead* s w   machen   21

vor|programmieren *pre-programme* A h w   informieren   15

vor|ragen *jut out* h w   machen   21

vor|rechnen *(D) work out (for sb)* A h w   atmen   2

vor|reiten *ride ahead* s st [itt, itt]   streiten   37

vor|rücken *advance* A h w   machen   21

vor|sagen *recite* A h w   machen   21

vor|schieben *push forward; use as an excuse* A h st [o, o]   kriechen   19

vor|schlagen (D/für + A/**als**) *suggest (to/for/as)* A h st [ä, u, a]   tragen   38

vor|schreiben *stipulate;* (D) *dictate (to)* A h st [ie, ie]   schreiben   28

vor|schützen *feign; plead as excuse* A h w   heizen   14

vor|sehen *plan;* (**für** + A/**als**) *intend (for/as)* A h st [ie, a, e]   sehen   29

  sich vor|sehen vor + D *be careful of* h st [ie, a, e]   sehen   29

vor|setzen *move forward;* (D) *serve (sb)* A h w   heizen   14

vor|singen (D) *sing (to sb); audition* A h st [a, u]   klingen   16

vor|sitzen *chair; preside over* D h st [aß, ess]   *fressen   8

vor|sorgen für + A *provide for* h w   machen   21

vor|spiegeln (D) *delude (sb) into believing* A h w   angeln   1

vor|spielen (D) *perform (to sb); feign (to sb)* A h w   machen   21

vor|sprechen *recite;* (**bei** + D) *call (on sb)* h st [i, a, o]   sprechen   33

vor|stehen *jut out* h st [and, and]   stehen   34

vor|stellen *put forward;* (D) *introduce (to); represent* A h w   machen   21

  sich [D] **vor|stellen** *imagine;* (**unter** + D) *understand (by)* A h w   machen   21

vor|stoßen (**in** + A) *advance (into)* s st [ö, ie, o]   stoßen   36

vor|strecken *stick out; advance* A h w   machen   21

vor|stürmen *rush forward* s w   machen   21

sich vor|tasten *feel one's way forward* h w   reden   24

vor|täuschen *feign; fake* A h w   machen   21

vor|tragen *perform; present* A h st [ä, u, a]   tragen   38

vor|treten *step forward* s st [itt, a, e]   *geben   9

vorüber|gehen an + D *go past; ignore*
s st [ing, ang]   *hängen   12
vor|ver'legen (auf + A/**um** + A) *bring*
forward (to/by) A h w   machen   21
sich vor|wagen *venture forward* h w   machen   21
vor|wärmen *pre-heat* A h w   machen   21
vor|warnen *forewarn* A h w   machen   21
vorwärts|bringen *advance* A h m
[ach, ach]   *brennen   5
vorwärts|gehen *make progress* s st
[ing, ang]   *hängen   12
vorwärts|kommen *get ahead* s st [am,
o]   kommen   17
vorweg|nehmen *anticipate* A h st
[imm, a, omm]   *sprechen   33
vor|weisen *produce* A h st [ie, ie]   *schreiben   28
vor|werfen (D) *reproach (sb) with;*
accuse (sb) of A h st [i, a, o]   sprechen   33
vor|wiegen *predominate* h st [o, o]   kriechen   19
sich vor|wölben *bulge; billow out* h w   machen   21
vor|zeichnen *prescribe; set out* A h w   atmen   2
vor|zeigen *show; produce* A h w   machen   21
vor|ziehen (D) *prefer (to); give*
preference (to) A h st [og, og]   *kriechen   19
vor|ziehen (um + A) *bring forward*
(by); draw A h st [og, og]   *kriechen   19

wachen (über + A) *watch (over)* h w   machen   21
wach|rufen *arouse; evoke* A h st [ie,
u]   rufen   25
wach|rütteln *rouse; stir* A h w   angeln   1
wachsen *grow* s st [ä, u, a]   *tragen   38
wackeln *wobble; wag; be loose* h w   angeln   1
wagen *risk; dare* A h w   machen   21
sich wagen an + A *dare to tackle* h
w   machen   21
wägen *weigh (up)* A h w/st [o, o]   machen/
kriechen   21/19

wählen (zu + D) *choose (as); dial; vote for* A h w	machen	21
wahr|nehmen *discern; exploit; carry out* A h st [imm, a, omm]	*sprechen	33
wahrsagen/wahr|sagen *predict; tell fortunes* A h w	machen	21
wallen *boil; bubble* h w	machen	21
walten *prevail* h w	reden	24
walzen *roll* A h w	heizen	14
wälzen *roll;* **(auf + A)** *burden (sb) with* A h w	heizen	14
wandeln *change* A h w	angeln	1
sich wandeln in + A *change into* h w	angeln	1
wandern *hike; move; travel* s w	angeln	1
wanken *sway; stagger* (usually **sein**) w	machen	21
wärmen *warm; be warm* A h w	machen	21
warm|laufen *warm up* s st [äu, ie, au]	laufen	20
warnen vor + D *warn of* A h w	machen	21
warten (auf + A) *wait (for); service* A h w	reden	24
waschen *wash* A h st [ä, u, a]	tragen	38
wassern *splash down; come down on water* s w	angeln	1
wässern *water; soak* A h w	angeln	1
waten *wade* s w	reden	24
watscheln *waddle* s w	angeln	1
weben *weave* A h w/st [o, o]	machen/ kriechen	21/19
wechseln *exchange;* **(in + A)** *change (into)* A h w	angeln	1
wecken *wake; arouse* A h w	machen	21
wedeln A/**mit** + D *wag; wave* h w	angeln	1
weg|blasen *blow away* A h st [ä, ie, a]	*schlafen	27
weg|bleiben *stay away* s st [ie, ie]	schreiben	28

weg|bringen *take away* A h m [ach, ach] | *brennen | 5

sich [D] **weg|denken** *imagine . . . not to be there* A h m [ach, ach] | *brennen | 5

weg|dürfen *be allowed to go out/away* h m [a, u, u] | dürfen | 7

weg|essen *eat up* A h st [i, a, ge] | *fressen | 8

weg|fahren *drive off* s st [ä, u, a] | tragen | 38

weg|fahren in + D *leave (e.g. town)* s st [ä, u, a] | tragen | 38

weg|fallen *be omitted; no longer apply* s st [ä, iel, a] | *schlafen | 27

weg|fegen *sweep away* A h w | machen | 21

weg|fliegen *fly away* s st [o, o] | kriechen | 19

weg|führen *lead away* A h w | machen | 21

weg|geben *give away; send out* A h st [i, a, e] | geben | 9

weg|gehen (**von** + D) *leave (sb)* s st [ing, ang] | *hängen | 12

weg|gießen *pour away* A h st [o, o] | schießen | 26

weg|hören *not listen; stop listening* h w | machen | 21

weg|jagen *chase away* A h w | machen | 21

weg|kommen *get away; go missing* s st [am, o] | kommen | 17

weg|können *be able to get away/to be thrown away* h m [a, o, o] | können | 18

weg|kriegen *get rid of;* (**von** + D) *get away (from)* A h w | machen | 21

weg|lassen *leave out; let out* A h st [ä, ie, a] | *schlafen | 27

weg|laufen (**von** + D/**vor** + D) *run away (from)* s st [äu, ie, au] | laufen | 20

weg|legen *put away* A h w | machen | 21

weg|müssen *have to leave; have to be removed* h m [u, u, u] | müssen | 23

weg|nehmen (D) *take away (from); remove* A h st [imm, a, omm] | *sprechen | 33

weg|packen *put away* A h w	machen	21
weg|putzen *clean off* A h w	heizen	14
weg|räumen *clear away* A h w	machen	21
weg|schaffen *get rid of* A h w	machen	21
weg|schicken *send off; send away* A h w	machen	21
weg|schieben *push away* A h st [o, o]	kriechen	19
weg|schleichen *creep away* s st [i, i]	gleichen	10
weg|schleppen *tow away; carry off* A h w	machen	21
weg|schließen *lock away* A h st [o, o]	schießen	26
weg|schütten *pour away* A h w	reden	24
weg|sehen *look away* h st [ie, a, e]	sehen	29
weg|sollen *be to go* (**es soll weg** *it is to be removed*) h w	sollen	32
weg|spülen *wash away* A h w	machen	21
weg|stecken *put away* A h w	machen	21
weg|stellen *put away; move out of the way* A h w	machen	21
weg|stoßen *shove away* A h st [ö, ie, o]	stoßen	36
weg|tragen *carry away* A h st [ä, u, a]	tragen	38
weg|treten *step away; kick away* A h (**sein** when intrans.) st [itt, a, e]	*geben	9
weg|werfen *throw away* A h st [i, a, o]	sprechen	33
weg|wischen *wipe away; dispel* A h w	machen	21
weg|wollen *want to go (away)* h m [i, o, o]	*sollen	32
weg|zaubern *spirit away* A h w	angeln	1
weg|zerren *drag away* A h w	machen	21
weg|ziehen *pull away/off; move away* A h (**sein** when intrans.) st [og, og]	*kriechen	19
wehen *blow* A h w	machen	21

sich wehren *defend oneself; resist;*
  (**gegen** + A) *fight (against)* h w   machen   21
weichen *soak* A h (**sein** *when*
  intrans.) w   machen   21
 weichen *move; subside;* (D/**vor** + D)
  give way (to) s st [i, i]   gleichen   10
weiden *graze* h w   reden   24
 sich weiden an + D *revel in* h w   reden   24
sich weigern *refuse* h w   angeln   1
weihen *consecrate; ordain;* (D)
  dedicate (to) A h w   machen   21
weinen *shed (tears);* (**um** + A/**über**
  + A/**vor** + D) *cry (for/over/with)*
  A h w   machen   21
weisen *send;* (**aus** + D) *expel (from)*
  A h st [ie, ie]   *schreiben   28
 weisen auf + A *point to* h st [ie, ie]   *schreiben   28
weissagen *foretell* A h w   machen   21
weißen *whitewash* A h w   heizen   14
weiten *widen* A h w   reden   24
weiter|arbeiten *carry on working* h
  w   reden   24
weiter|be'stehen *continue to exist* h
  st [and, and]   stehen   34
weiter|bringen *take (any) further* A
  h m [ach, ach]   *brennen   5
weiter|drehen *wind on; continue*
  filming A h w   machen   21
weiter|emp'fehlen *recommend (to*
  one's friends) A h st [ie, a, o]   stehlen   35
sich weiter|ent'wickeln *develop*
  further; mature h w   angeln   1
weiter|er'zählen *pass on; continue*
  telling A h w   machen   21
weiter|fahren *travel on; continue* s st
  [ä, u, a]   tragen   38
weiter|führen *continue; get (any)*
  further A h w   machen   21

weiter|geben an + A *pass (on) to* A
  h st [i, a, e]   geben   9
weiter|gehen *go on; move along* s st
  [ing, ang]   *hängen   12
weiter|helfen mit + D *help (along)*
  with D h st [i, a, o]   sprechen   33
weiter|kämpfen *fight on* h w   machen   21
weiter|klingen *resound* h st [a, u]   klingen   16
weiter|kommen *make progress; get*
  further s st [am, o]   kommen   17
weiter|laufen *walk on; continue* s st
  [äu, ie, au]   laufen   20
weiter|leben *live on* h w   machen   21
weiter|leiten *pass on; forward* A h w   reden   24
weiter|machen *carry on with* A h w   machen   21
weiter|reden *go on talking* h w   reden   24
weiter|reichen *pass on* A h w   machen   21
weiter|reisen *travel on* s w   heizen   14
weiter|rücken *move along/up* s w   machen   21
weiter|sagen *pass on* A h w   machen   21
weiter|schicken *forward; send on* A h
  w   machen   21
sich weiter|schleppen *trudge on* h w   machen   21
weiter|senden *forward; send on* A h
  w/m [a, a]   reden/senden 24/31
  weiter|senden *continue broadcasting*
  A h w   reden   24
weiter|spielen *play on* A h w   machen   21
weiter|sprechen *carry on talking* h st
  [i, a, o]   sprechen   33
weiter|ver'arbeiten *process* A h w   reden   24
weiter|ver'breiten *spread; propagate*
  A h w   reden   24
weiter|ver'folgen *follow up* A h w   machen   21
weiter|ver'kaufen *resell* A h w   machen   21
weiter|ver'mieten *sublet* A h w   reden   24
weiter|zahlen *go on paying* A h w   machen   21
weiter|ziehen *move on* s st [og, og]   *kriechen   19

welken *wilt; fade* s w	machen	21
sich wellen *undulate; be wavy* h w	machen	21
wenden *turn* A h w/m [a, a]	reden/senden	24/31
sich wenden an + A *turn to* h w/m [a, a]	reden/senden	24/31
wenden *turn over; turn inside out; turn round* A h w	reden	24
werben (für + A) *advertise (for); recruit* A h st [i, a, o]	*sprechen	33
werben um + A *court* h st [i, a, o]	*sprechen	33
werden (N/zu + D) *become: be; will* s st [i, u, o]	werden	40
werden aus + D *become of* s st [i, u, o]	werden	40
werfen (A/mit + D) *throw* h st [i, a, o]	*sprechen	33
werfen in + A/**nach** + D *throw in/at* A h st [i, a, o]	*sprechen	33
werken *work; busy about* h w	machen	21
werten *judge* A h w	reden	24
wetteifern mit + D/**um** + A *compete with/for* h w	angeln	1
wetten (auf + A) *bet (on)* A h w	reden	24
wetten (mit + D) **um** + A *bet (sb) sth* h w	reden	24
wetterleuchten *flash with summer lightning* h w	reden	24
wetzen *sharpen* A h w	heizen	14
wickeln (zu + D/**auf** + A) *wind (into/ on to); change (baby); bandage* A h w	angeln	1
wickeln in + A/**aus** + D *wrap in/ unwrap from* A h w	angeln	1
wider'fahren (D) *happen (to sb)* s st [ä, u, a]	tragen	38
wider|hallen von + D *resound with/ from* h w	machen	21

wider'legen *disprove; prove wrong* A
  h w   machen   21
wider'rufen *retract; repeal* A h st [ie,
  u]   rufen   25
sich wider'setzen *oppose* D h w   heizen   14
wider|spiegeln/wider'spiegeln *reflect*
  A h w   angeln   1
wider'sprechen *contradict; oppose* D
  h st [i, a, o]   sprechen   33
wider'stehen *resist; withstand* D h st
  [and, and]   stehen   34
wider'streben (D) *be distasteful (to*
  sb); go against (sth) h w   machen   21
widmen (D) *dedicate (to); devote*
  (to) A h w   atmen   2
wiederauf|bauen[1] *reconstruct* A h w   machen   21
wiederauf|be'reiten[1] *recycle* A h w   reden   24
wiederauf|führen[1] *revive* A h w   machen   21
wiederauf|nehmen[1] *resume;*
  re-establish A h st [imm, a, omm]   *sprechen   33
wiederauf|tauchen[1] *turn up again* s
  w   machen   21
wieder|be'kommen *get back* A h st
  [am, o]   kommen   17
wieder|be'leben *revive* A h w   machen   21
wieder|bringen *bring back* A h m
  [ach, ach]   *brennen   5
wieder|ent'decken *rediscover* A h w   machen   21
wieder|er'kennen *recognize (again)*
  A h m [a, a]   brennen   5
wieder|er'obern *recapture* A h w   angeln   1
wieder|er'wecken *reawaken; revive* A
  h w   machen   21

---

[1] **Wieder** prefixed to a verb that already has a separable
prefix: the **wieder** separates from the prefix when the prefix
stands separate from the verb. So **wiederaufgebaut**, but **ich
baue wieder auf**.

wieder|finden *regain; find again* A h st [a, u]	binden	4
wieder|geben *give back; report; repeat; reproduce* A h st [i, a, e]	geben	9
wieder|ge'winnen *recover; regain* A h st [a, o]	*sprechen	33
wiedergut|machen[1] *put right; make good* A h w	machen	21
wieder|haben *have back* A h m [at, att, a]	*brennen	5
wiederher|stellen[1] *restore* A h w	machen	21
wieder'holen *repeat* A h w	machen	21
wieder|holen *get back* A h w	machen	21
wieder|käuen *ruminate; rehash* A h w	machen	21
wieder|kehren *return; recur* s w	machen	21
wieder|kommen *come back; come again* s st [am, o]	kommen	17
wieder|sehen *see again* A h st [ie, a, e]	sehen	29
wieder|tun *do again* A h st [at, a]	tun	39
wieder|ver'einigen *reunify* A h w	machen	21
wieder|ver'wenden *reuse* A h w/m [a, a]	reden/senden	24/31
wieder|wählen *re-elect* A h w	machen	21
wiegen *weigh* A h st [o, o]	kriechen	19
wiegen *rock; sway* A h w	machen	21
wiehern *whinny* h w	angeln	1
wieseln *scurry* s w	angeln	1
wildern *poach* A h w	angeln	1
wimmeln von + D *be swarming with* h w	angeln	1
wimmern *whimper* h w	angeln	1

---

[1] **Wieder** prefixed to a verb that already has a separable prefix: the **wieder** separates from the prefix when the prefix stands separate from the verb. So **wiederaufgebaut**, but **ich baue wieder auf**.

winden *winch; bind* A h st [a, u]	binden	4
sich winden (**um** + A) *coil (round); writhe; wind its way* h st [a, u]	binden	4
winken (D/A) *beckon (to sb); signal (to sb)* h w	machen	21
winken (D) **mit** + D *wave (to sb)* h w	machen	21
winseln *whine;* (**um** + A) *plead (for)* h w	angeln	1
wippen *bob about; see-saw* h w	machen	21
wirbeln *whirl* A h (**sein** when intrans.) w	angeln	1
wirken (**bei** + D/**auf** + A) *have an effect (on sb); appear* h w	machen	21
wirtschaften *manage; run* A h w	reden	24
wischen (A/**über** + A) *wipe* h w	machen	21
wischen *scurry* s w	machen	21
wissen (**um** + A/**von** + D) *know (about)* A h m [ei, u, u]	wissen	41
wittern *get wind of; sniff the air* A h w	angeln	1
witzeln über + A *joke about* h w	angeln	1
wogen *surge* h w	machen	21
wohl|tun (D) *do (sb) good* h st [at, a]	tun	39
wohl|wollen (D) *wish (sb) well* h m [i, o, o]	*sollen	32
wohnen *live; stay* h w	machen	21
wölben *curve; arch* A h w	machen	21
wollen *want; be about to* A h m [i, o, o]	*sollen	32
wringen *wring* A h st [a, u]	klingen	16
wuchern *run wild;* (**mit** + D) *profiteer (on)* h/s w	angeln	1
wühlen *dig;* (**gegen** + A) *agitate (against)* h w	machen	21
wühlen in + D/**nach** + D *rummage around in/for* h w	machen	21
wummern *hum* h w	angeln	1

wundern *surprise* (impers.: **es**
   wundert mich *I'm surprised*) A h w   angeln   1
  sich wundern über + A *be surprised*
   at h w   angeln   1
wünschen (D) *wish (sb)* A h w   machen   21
würdigen *recognize; appreciate; (G)*
  deem worthy (of) A h w   machen   21
würfeln (**um** + A) *throw/play dice*
  (for); dice up A h w   angeln   1
würgen *strangle;* (**an** + D) *almost*
  choke (on) A h w   machen   21
wurzeln in + D *take root in; be*
  rooted in h w   angeln   1
würzen *spice; season* A h w   heizen   14
wuscheln A/**in** + D *tousle* h w   angeln   1
wüsten mit + D *squander* h w   reden   24
wüten *rage* h w   reden   24

zacken *serrate* A h w   machen   21
zahlen (**an** + A) *pay (to)* A h w   machen   21
zählen (**bis** + D) *count (to)* A h w   machen   21
  zählen zu + D *number among* A h
  w   machen   21
  zählen auf + A *count on* h w   machen   21
zähmen *tame* A h w   machen   21
zahnen *be teething* h w   machen   21
sich zanken um + A/**über** + A
  squabble about h w   machen   21
zapfen *tap; draw* A h w   machen   21
zappeln *wriggle* h w   angeln   1
zaubern *do magic; conjure up* A h w   angeln   1
zaudern *procrastinate* h w   angeln   1
zausen *ruffle* A h w   heizen   14
zehren von + D *live off* h w   machen   21
  zehren an + D *wear down; sap* h w   machen   21
zeichnen *draw; mark;* (**für** + A) *sign*
  (for) A h w   atmen   2
zeigen (D) *show (sb)* A h w   machen   21

zeigen (mit + D) **auf** + A *point (sth)*		
at h w	machen	21
zelebrieren *celebrate; make a ritual*		
of A h w	informieren	15
zelten *camp* h w	reden	24
zementieren *cement; make permanent*		
A h w	informieren	15
zensieren *mark; censor* A h w	informieren	15
zentralisieren *centralize* A h w	informieren	15
zentrieren um + A *centre on* A h w	informieren	15
zer'beißen *bite all over; bite in two*		
A h st [i, i]	beißen	3
zer'bersten *burst apart* s st [i, a, o]	*sprechen	33
zer'bomben *bomb to pieces* A h w	machen	21
zer'brechen *smash; break up* A h		
(**sein** when intrans.) st [i, a, o]	sprechen	33
zer'bröckeln *crumble (away)* A h		
(**sein** when intrans.) w	angeln	1
zer'dehnen *stretch out of shape* A h		
w	machen	21
zer'drücken *mash; crush* A h w	machen	21
zer'fallen in + A/**zu** + D *disintegrate*		
into s st [ä, iel, a]	*schlafen	27
zer'fasern *fray* s w	angeln	1
zer'fetzen (**in** + A) *tear up (into);*		
tear to shreds A h w	heizen	14
zer'fleischen *tear limb from limb* A h		
w	machen	21
zer'fließen *run; melt away* s st [o, o]	schießen	26
zer'fransen *fray* A h w	heizen	14
zer'fressen *eat away; corrode* A h st		
[i, a, e]	fressen	8
zer'gehen *melt; dissolve* s st [ing,*		
ang]	*hängen	12
zer'gliedern *dissect; analyse* A h w	angeln	1
zer'hacken (**zu** + D) *chop up (into)*		
A h w	machen	21
zer'kauen *chew up* A h w	machen	21

zer'kleinern *chop up; crush* A h w	angeln	1
zer'knallen *burst with a bang* A h w	machen	21
zer'knicken *snap* A h w	machen	21
zer'knittern *crease; crumple* A h w	angeln	1
zer'kochen *overcook* A h w	machen	21
zer'kratzen *scratch* A h w	heizen	14
zer'krümeln *crumble up* A h w	angeln	1
zer'lassen *melt* A h st [ä, ie, a]	*schlafen	27
zer'legen *dismantle;* (**in** + A) *split up (into)* A h w	machen	21
zer'mahlen *grind* A h w (past part. **zermahlen**)	*machen	21
zer'malmen *crush* A h w	machen	21
zer'mürben *wear down* A h w	machen	21
zer'nagen *gnaw away* A h w	machen	21
zer'pflücken *pick apart; pull to pieces* A h w	machen	21
zer'platzen (**vor** + D) *explode (with)* s w	heizen	14
zer'quetschen *crush; mash* A h w	machen	21
zer'raufen *tousle* A h w	machen	21
zer'reiben *crush; wipe out* A h st [ie, ie]	schreiben	28
zer'reißen (**an** + D) *tear (on); tear up; dismember* A h (**sein** when intrans.) st [i, i]	beißen	3
zerren *drag;* (**an** + D) *tug (at)* A h w	machen	21
zer'rinnen *melt; vanish* s st [a, o]	*sprechen	33
zer'rupfen *tear to bits* A h w	machen	21
zer'rütten *ruin; shatter* A h w	reden	24
zer'sägen *saw up* A h w	machen	21
zer'schlagen *smash (up)* A h st [ä, u, a]	tragen	38
zer'schmelzen *melt* s st [i, o, o]	*dreschen	6
zer'schmettern *smash; shatter* A h w	angeln	1
zer'schneiden *carve; cut (in two)* A h st [itt, itt]	*streiten	37

zer'setzen *subvert; corrode* A h w	heizen	14
zer'siedeln *overdevelop* A h w	angeln	1
zer'spalten (in + A) *split up (into)* A h w (past part. **zerspaltet** or **zerspalten**)	*reden	24
zer'splittern *splinter; shatter* A h (**sein** when intrans.) w	angeln	1
zer'sprengen *blow up* A h w	machen	21
zer'springen *shatter;* (**vor** + D) *burst (with)* s st [a, u]	klingen	16
zer'stampfen *pound; trample down* A h w	machen	21
zer'stäuben *spray* A h w	machen	21
zer'stechen *jab holes in; puncture* A h st [i, a, o]	sprechen	33
zer'stören *destroy; wreck* A h w	machen	21
sich zer'streiten mit + D *fall out with* h st [itt, itt]	streiten	37
zer'streuen *scatter; dispel;* (**mit** + D) *entertain (with)* A h w	machen	21
zer'stückeln *break into bits; dismember* A h w	angeln	1
zer'trampeln *trample underfoot* A h w	angeln	1
zer'treten *stamp on; stamp out* A h st [itt, a, e]	*geben	9
zer'trümmern *wreck; reduce to ruins* A h w	angeln	1
zer'zausen *ruffle; tousle* A h w	heizen	14
zeugen *procreate; engender* A h w	machen	21
zeugen (**von** + D) *testify (to)* h w	machen	21
zeugen für + A/**gegen** + A *give evidence for/against* h w	machen	21
ziehen (**an** + D) *pull (on); draw* (impers.: **es zieht** *it's draughty*) A h st [og, og]	*kriechen	19
ziehen *move* s st [og, og]	*kriechen	19
zielen (**auf** + A/**nach** + D) *aim (at)* h w	machen	21

sich zieren *be coy* h w	machen	21
zimmern *carpenter* A h w	angeln	1
zirkeln *lay out precisely* A h w	angeln	1
zirkulieren *circulate* h/s w	informieren	15
zirpen *chirp* h w	machen	21
zischeln *whisper angrily* A h w	angeln	1
zischen *hiss; sizzle* A h w	machen	21
ziselieren *engrave* A h w	informieren	15
zitieren (aus + D/**nach** + D) *quote (from); summon* A h w	informieren	15
zittern (vor + D) *tremble (with); be terrified (of)* h w	angeln	1
zittern um + A/**für** + A *be very worried about* h w	angeln	1
zivilisieren *civilize* A h w	informieren	15
zögern *hesitate* h w	angeln	1
zu|bauen *build on* A h w	machen	21
zu|be'kommen *get shut; manage to repair* A h st [am, o]	kommen	17
zu|be'reiten *prepare; cook* A h w	reden	24
zu|betonieren *concrete over* A h w	informieren	15
zu|be'wegen auf + D *move . . . towards* A h w	machen	21
zu|billigen (D) *grant (sb)* A h w	machen	21
zu|binden *tie up* A h st [a, u]	binden	4
zu|blinzeln *wink at* D h w	angeln	1
zu|bringen *spend* A h m [ach, ach]	*brennen	5
züchten *breed; cultivate* A h w	reden	24
zucken *twitch; start; flicker* h (**sein** when direction indicated) w	machen	21
zücken *draw; take out* A h w	machen	21
zuckern *sugar* A h w	angeln	1
zu|decken *cover up* A h w	machen	21
zu|drehen *turn (off)* A h w	machen	21
zu|drücken *push/press shut* A h w	machen	21
zu|eignen (D) *dedicate (to)* A h w	atmen	2
zu|eilen auf + A *rush towards* s w	machen	21

zueinander|finden *come together* h st
[a, u]   binden   4

zueinander|halten *stick together* h st
[ä, ie, a]   *schlafen   27

zueinander|kommen *get together* s st
[am, o]   kommen   17

zueinander|stehen *stand by one
another* h st [and, and]   stehen   34

zu|er'kennen (D) *grant (to sb)* A h
m [a, a]   brennen   5

zu|fahren auf + A *head towards; drive
at* s st [ä, u, a]   tragen   38

zu|fallen *slam shut; close;* (D) *fall
(to sb)* s st [ä, iel, a]   *schlafen   27

zu|fliegen auf + A *fly towards* s st [o,
o]   kriechen   19

zu|fließen *flow towards; go to* D s st
[o, o]   schießen   26

zu|flüstern (D) *whisper (to sb)* A h
w   angeln   1

sich zufrieden|geben (mit + D) *be
satisfied (with)* h st [i, a, e]   geben   9

zufrieden|lassen *leave alone* A h st
[ä, ie, a]   *schlafen   27

zufrieden|stellen *satisfy* A h w   machen   21

zu|frieren *freeze over* s st [o, o]   kriechen   19

zu|fügen (D) *inflict (on sb); add (to
sth)* A h w   machen   21

zu|führen (D) *supply (to sth)* A h w   machen   21

 zu|führen auf + A *lead towards* h w   machen   21

zu|geben (D) *admit (to sb); give (sb)
as an extra; add (to)* A h st [i, a,
e]   geben   9

zu|gehen auf + A *approach* (impers.:
es geht . . . zu *things are. . .)* s st
[ing, ang]   *hängen   12

zügeln *rein in; curb* A h w   angeln   1

sich zu|ge'sellen *join* D h w   machen   21

zu|ge'stehen *grant (to sb); admit (to sb)* A h st [and, and]	stehen	34
zu|gießen (D) *add (to); top (sb) up* A h st [o, o]	schießen	26
zu|greifen *grasp; help oneself; take action* h st [iff, iff]	greifen	11
zu|halten *keep closed;* (**auf** + A) *head (for)* A h st [ä, ie, a]	*schlafen	27
zu|hören (D) *listen (to)* h w	machen	21
zu|jubeln (D) *cheer (sb) on* h w	angeln	1
zu|kehren (D) *turn (towards)* A h w	machen	21
zu|klappen *shut; fold/slam shut* A h w	machen	21
zu|kleben *seal (up)* A h w	machen	21
zu|knallen *slam* A h w	machen	21
zu|kneifen *shut tightly* A h st [iff, iff]	greifen	11
zu|knöpfen *button up* A h w	machen	21
zu|knoten *knot; tie up* A h w	reden	24
zu|kommen *be due to; befit; be up to* D s st [am, o]	kommen	17
zu|kommen auf + A *approach; come towards* s st [am, o]	kommen	17
zu|korken *cork up* A h w	machen	21
zu|lächeln *smile at* D h w	angeln	1
zu|lachen (D) *give (sb) a friendly laugh* h w	machen	21
zu|lassen *allow; leave closed;* (**zu** + D/**bei** + D) *admit (to)* A h st [ä, ie, a]	*schlafen	27
zu|laufen (**auf** + A) *run (towards); run in* s st [äu, ie, au]	laufen	20
zu|legen *increase* h w	machen	21
sich [D] **zu|legen** *get oneself* A h w	machen	21
zu|leiten *supply; forward* A h w	reden	24
zu|liefern *supply* A h w	angeln	1
zu|machen *close* A h w	machen	21
zu|mauern *wall up* A h w	angeln	1
zu|muten (D) *expect (of sb)* A h w	reden	24

sich [D] **zu|muten** *take on* A h w	reden	24
zu|nageln *nail up* A h w	angeln	1
zünden *light; fire* A h w	reden	24
zu|nehmen (an + D) *increase (in);* *put on weight* h st [imm, a, omm]	*sprechen	33
zu|neigen (D) *incline (towards)* h w	machen	21
sich zu|neigen (D) *be attracted (to);* *lean (towards)* h w	machen	21
züngeln *dart; flicker* s w	angeln	1
zu|nicken (D) *nod (to sb)* h w	machen	21
zu|ordnen (D) *relate (to); assign (to)* A h w	atmen	2
zu|packen *grab it/them; knuckle down* *to it* h w	machen	21
zupfen an + D/**aus** + D *pluck at/from* A h w	machen	21
zu|pressen *press shut* A h w	heizen	14
zu|prosten *drink to* D h w	reden	24
zu|raten (D) *advise (sb) to do so* h st [ä, ie, a]	*schlafen	27
zu|rechnen (D) *class (as); ascribe* *(to); add (to)* A h w	atmen	2
zurecht|biegen *bend into shape* A h st [o, o]	kriechen	19
sich zurecht|finden (in + D) *find one's* *way around (in)* h st [a, u]	binden	4
zurecht|kommen mit + D *get on with;* *cope with* s st [am, o]	kommen	17
zurecht|legen (D) *lay out ready (for* *sb); get . . . ready* A h w	machen	21
zurecht|rücken *straighten* A h w	machen	21
zurecht|schneiden *trim; cut to shape* A h st [itt, itt]	*streiten	37
zurecht|setzen *adjust* A h w	heizen	14
zurecht|stellen *put in place* A h w	machen	21
zurecht|weisen *reprimand* A h st [ie, ie]	*schreiben	28

zu|reiten *break in;* (**auf** + D) *ride (towards)* A h (**sein** *when intrans.*) st [itt, itt]	streiten	37
zu|richten *injure* A h w	reden	24
zu|riegeln *bolt* A h w	angeln	1
zurück|be'gleiten *accompany back* A h w	reden	24
zurück|be'halten *retain; be left with* A h st [ä, ie, a]	*schlafen	27
zurück|be'kommen *get back* A h st [am, o]	kommen	17
sich zurück|be'sinnen auf + A *think back to* h s [a, o]	sprechen	33
zurück|beugen *bend back* A h w	machen	21
zurück|bleiben *stay behind; remain* s st [ie, ie]	schreiben	28
zurück|blenden (**in** + A/**auf** + A) *flash back (to)* h w	reden	24
zurück|blicken *look round;* (**auf** + A) *look back (at/on)* h w	machen	21
zurück|bringen *bring back* A h m [ach, ach]	*brennen	5
zurück|denken (**an** + A) *think back (to)* h m [ach, ach]	*brennen	5
zurück|drängen *force back* A h w	machen	21
zurück|drehen *turn back/down* A h w	machen	21
zurück|dürfen *be allowed back* h m [a, u, u]	dürfen	7
zurück|eilen *hurry back* s w	machen	21
zurück|er'obern *regain; recapture* A h w	angeln	1
zurück|er'statten (D) *refund (to sb)* A h w	reden	24
zurück|er'warten *expect back* A h w	reden	24
zurück|fahren *go back(wards); drive back; cut back* s st [ä, u, a]	tragen	38
zurück|fallen (**in** + A) *fall back (into)* s st [ä, ie, a]	schlafen	27

zurück|fallen an + A *revert to* s st [ä, ie, a]	schlafen	27
zurück|fallen auf + A *drop to; recoil on* s st [ä, ie, a]	schlafen	27
zurück|finden *find one's way back* h st [a, u]	binden	4
zurück|fliegen *fly back* A h (**sein** when intrans.) st [o, o]	kriechen	19
zurück|fordern *demand back* A h w	angeln	1
zurück|führen *take back; lead back;* (**auf** + A) *trace back (to)* A h w	machen	21
zurück|geben (D) *give back (to sb); take back; reply* A h st [i, a, e]	geben	9
zurück|gehen (**auf** + A) *go back (to); go down* s st [ing, ang]	*hängen	12
zurück|ge'winnen *win back; recover* A h st [a, o]	*sprechen	33
zurück|greifen auf + A *fall back on* h st [iff, iff]	greifen	11
zurück|haben *get back* A h m [at, att, a]	*brennen	5
zurück|halten *stop;* (**von** + D) *hold back (from)* A h st [ä, ie, a]	*schlafen	27
zurück|kämmen *comb back* A h w	machen	21
zurück|kaufen *buy back* A h w	machen	21
zurück|kehren (D) *return (to sb)* s w	machen	21
zurück|klappen *fold back* A h w	machen	21
zurück|kommen (**auf** + A) *come back (to)* s st [am, o]	kommen	17
zurück|können *be able to return* h m [a, o, o]	können	18
zurück|lassen *leave; let return* A h st [ä, ie, a]	*schlafen	27
zurück|laufen *run back* s st [äu, ie, au]	laufen	20
zurück|legen *put back; cover;* (**für** + A) *put aside (for)* A h w	machen	21
sich zurück|lehnen *lean back* h w	machen	21

zurück|liegen *lie in the past;* (**mit**
  + D) *be behind (by)* h st [a, e]   sehen   29
sich zurück|melden (**bei** + D) *report*
  back (to) h w   reden   24
zurück|müssen *have to return* h m
  [u, u, u]   müssen   23
zurück|nehmen *take back; withdraw*
  A h st [imm, a, omm]   *sprechen   33
zurück|prallen von + D *bounce back*
  (from); ricochet (from); recoil s
  w   machen   21
zurück|reichen *hand back;* (**bis in**
  + A) *go back (to)* A h w   machen   21
zurück|rollen *roll back(wards)* A h
  (**sein** *when intrans.*) w   machen   21
zurück|rufen *call back; recall* A h s
  [ie, u]   rufen   25
zurück|schalten *switch back; change*
  down h w   reden   24
zurück|schaudern vor + D *shrink back*
  from s w   angeln   1
zurück|schicken *send back* A h w   machen   21
zurück|schieben *push back* A h st [o,
  o]   kriechen   19
zurück|schlagen *fold/hit/beat/swing*
  back; (**auf** + A) *have repercussions*
  (on) A h (**sein** *when intrans.*) st
  [ä, u, a]   tragen   38
zurück|schneiden *cut back* A h st
  [itt, itt]   *streiten   37
zurück|schrauben *reduce; lower* A h w   machen   21
zurück|schrecken *deter;* (**vor** + D)
  shrink (from) A h (**sein** *when*
  intrans.) w (*past tense also* **schrak**
  zurück)   machen   21
sich zurück|sehnen (**nach** + D/**zu** + D)
  long to be back (in + *place/with*
  sb) h w   machen   21

zurück|setzen *put/move back; reverse;*
  neglect A h w   heizen   14
  sich zurück|setzen *back;* (**an** + A) *sit*
   down again (at) h w   heizen   14
zurück|springen *jump/spring back* s st
  [a, u]   klingen   16
zurück|stecken *put back* A h w   machen   21
zurück|stehen *stand behind; miss out;*
  (**hinter** + D) *take second place (to)*
  h st [and, and]   stehen   34
zurück|stellen *put back/aside; turn*
  down; defer; (**für** + A) *keep (for)*
  A h w   machen   21
zurück|stoßen *push away* A h st [ö,
  ie, o]   stoßen   36
zurück|stufen in + A *downgrade to* A
  h w   machen   21
zurück|treten *step back;* (**von** + D)
  resign (from) s st [itt, a, e]   *geben   9
zurück|ver'langen *demand back* A h
  w   machen   21
zurück|ver'setzen *transport back* A h
  w   heizen   14
  sich zurück|ver'setzen in + A *think*
  oneself back to h w   heizen   14
zurück|weichen vor + D *back away*
  from s st [i, i]   gleichen   10
zurück|weisen *turn back; turn down*
  A h st [ie, ie]   *schreiben   28
zurück|werfen *throw back; reflect;*
  repulse A h st [i, a, o]   sprechen   33
zurück|wirken auf + A *react upon* h w   machen   21
zurück|wollen *want to go back* h m
  [i, o, o]   *sollen   32
zurück|zahlen *pay back* A h w   machen   21
zurück|ziehen *draw/go back;*
  withdraw A h (**sein** *when intrans.*)
  st [og, og]   *kriechen   19

zurück|zucken *flinch; start back* h w — machen — 21

zu|rufen (D) *shout (to sb)* A h st
 [ie, u] — rufen — 25

zu|sagen *accept;* (D) *appeal (to sb);*
 promise (sb) A h w — machen — 21

zusammen|arbeiten (mit + D)
 co-operate (with) A h w — reden — 24

zusammen|bauen *assemble* A h w — machen — 21

zusammen|be'kommen *get together*
 A h st [am, o] — kommen — 17

zusammen|binden *tie together; tie up*
 A h st [a, u] — binden — 4

zusammen|bleiben *stay together* s st
 [ie, ie] — schreiben — 28

zusammen|brechen *collapse; break
 down* s st [i, a, o] — sprechen — 33

zusammen|bringen (mit + D) *bring
 together (with)* A h m [ach, ach] — *brennen — 5

zusammen|drängen *herd together;
 concentrate; condense* A h w — machen — 21

zusammen|drücken *compress* A h
 w — machen — 21

zusammen|fahren (mit + D) *collide
 (with); start* s st [ä, u, a] — tragen — 38

zusammen|fallen *collapse; coincide* s
 st [ä, iel, a] — *schlafen — 27

zusammen|falten *fold up* A h w — reden — 24

zusammen|fassen *put together;*
 (in + D) *summarize (in)* A h w — heizen — 14

sich zusammen|finden *get together;
 meet up* h st [a, u] — binden — 4

zusammen|fließen *join up; run
 together* s st [o, o] — schießen — 26

zusammen|fügen *fit together* A h w — machen — 21

zusammen|führen *bring together* A h
 w — machen — 21

zusammen|gehen mit + D *merge with*
 s st [ing, ang] — *hängen — 12

zusammen|ge'hören *belong together*
h w .... machine 21
zusammen|halten *hold/keep together*
A h st [ä, ie, a] .... *schlafen 27
zusammen|hängen mit + D *be the
result of* h st [i, a] .... hängen 12
zusammen|klappen *fold up* A h w ... machen 21
zusammen|kleben *stick together* A h
w .... machen 21
zusammen|kneifen *screw up* A h st
[iff, iff] .... greifen 11
zusammen|kommen (mit + D) *meet
(sb); occur together* s st [am, o] .... kommen 17
zusammen|koppeln *couple together* A
h w .... angeln 1
sich zusammen|krampfen *clench* h w ... machen 21
sich zusammen|krümmen *double up* h
w .... machen 21
zusammen|laufen *congregate; join up*
s st [äu, ie, au] .... laufen 20
zusammen|leben *live together* h w .... machen 21
zusammen|legen *put together; pool;
fold up* A h w .... machen 21
zusammen|nehmen *summon up* A h
st [imm, a, omm] .... *sprechen 33
 sich zusammen|nehmen *pull oneself
together* h st [imm, a, omm] .... *sprechen 33
zusammen|packen *pack up* A h w .... machen 21
zusammen|passen *be suited;* (mit
+ D) *go (with)* h w .... heizen 14
zusammen|prallen mit + D *collide
with* s w .... machen 21
zusammen|pressen *compress* A h w ..... heizen 14
zusammen|raffen *gather up; bundle
up* A h w .... machen 21
zusammen|rechnen *add up;* (mit + D)
add (to) A h w .... atmen 2
zusammen|rollen *roll up* A h w .... machen 21

sich zusammen|rotten *gang up* h w	reden	24
zusammen|rücken *move closer together* A h (**sein** *when intrans.*) w	machen	21
zusammen|rufen *call together* A h st [ie, u]	rufen	25
zusammen|schlagen *bang together; clap; beat up; fold up* A h st [ä, u, a]	tragen	38
zusammen|schlagen über + D *engulf* s st [ä, u, a]	tragen	38
sich zusammen|schließen *unite* h st [o, o]	schießen	26
zusammen|schmelzen *melt away;* (**auf** + A) *dwindle (to)* s st [i, o, o]	*dreschen	6
zusammen|schneiden *cut (film, tape)* A h st [itt, itt]	*streiten	37
zusammen|schrumpfen *shrivel* s w	machen	21
zusammen|schweißen *weld together* A h w	heizen	14
zusammen|setzen *assemble; put together* A h w	heizen	14
sich zusammen|setzen (**aus** + D) *be composed (of); get together* h w	heizen	14
zusammen|sinken *collapse; die down* s st [a, u]	klingen	16
sich [D] **zusammen|sparen** *save up for* A h w	machen	21
zusammen|spielen *work together* h w	machen	21
zusammen|stecken *fit together* A h w	machen	21
zusammen|stehen *stand together;* (**mit** + D) *stand (with)* h st [and, and]	stehen	34
zusammen|stellen *put together; compile* A h w	machen	21
zusammen|stimmen *match;* (**mit** + D) *go/agree (with)* h w	machen	21

zusammen|stoßen mit + D *collide with* s st [ö, ie, o]	stoßen	36
zusammen|strömen *join up; congregate* s w	machen	21
zusammen|stürzen *collapse* s w	heizen	14
zusammen|suchen *collect bit by bit* A h w	machen	21
zusammen|tragen *collect* A h st [ä, u, a]	tragen	38
zusammen|treffen *coincide;* (**mit** + D) *meet (sb)* s st [i, af, o]	*sprechen	33
zusammen|treiben *herd together* A h st [ie, ie]	schreiben	28
zusammen|treten (**zu** + D) *meet (for)* s st [itt, a, e]	*geben	9
zusammen|wachsen *grow together; merge* s st [ä, u, a]	*tragen	38
zusammen|wirken *combine* h w	machen	21
zusammen|zählen *add up* A h w	machen	21
zusammen|ziehen *draw together; mass; add up* A h st [og, og]	*kriechen	19
zusammen|ziehen mit + D *move in with* s st [og, og]	*kriechen	19
zusammen|zucken *start; jump* s w	machen	21
zu|schicken (D) *send (to sb)* A h w	machen	21
zu|schieben *push shut;* (D) *put (on to)* A h st [o, o]	kriechen	19
zu|schießen (**zu** + D) *contribute (towards); pass* A h st [o, o]	schießen	26
zu|schlagen *bang to; add on; strike out;* (D) *award (to)* A h (**sein** when intrans.) st [ä, u, a]	tragen	38
zu|schließen *lock (up)* A h st [o, o]	schließen	26
zu|schneien *snow in* s w	machen	21
zu|schnüren *tie (up)* A h w	machen	21
zu|schrauben *screw on* A h w	machen	21
zu|schreiben (D) *attribute (to); transfer (to)* A h st [ie, ie]	schreiben	28

zu|schütten *fill in; pour on* A h w	reden	24
zu|sehen (D) *watch (sb); make sure* h st [ie, a, e]	sehen	29
zu|setzen (D/**zu** + D) *add (to); pay out* A h w	heizen	14
zu|sichern (D) *assure (sb) of* A h w	angeln	1
zu|spielen (D) *leak (to); pass (to)* A h w	machen	21
zu|spitzen *aggravate; make pointed* A h w	heizen	14
zu|sprechen (D) *give (sb) words of; award (to sb); ascribe (to sb)* A h st [i, a, o]	sprechen	33
zu|stecken (D) *slip . . . (to sb); pin up* A h w	machen	21
zu|stehen *be within (sb's) rights* (**es steht mir zu** *I'm entitled to it*) h st [and, and]	stehen	34
zu|steigen *get on* s st [ie, ie]	schreiben	28
zu|stellen (D) *deliver (to); send (to)* A h w	machen	21
zu|steuern auf + A *head for; drive towards* A h (**sein** *when intrans.*) w	angeln	1
zu|stimmen (D) *agree (with/to)* h w	machen	21
zu|stopfen *plug (up); darn* A h w	machen	21
zu|stoßen *push shut; stab; strike* A h st [ö, ie, o]	stoßen	36
zu|stoßen (D) *happen (to)* s st [ö, ie, o]	stoßen	36
zu|streben (D/**auf** + A) *strive (for); make (for)* s w	machen	21
zu|stürmen auf + A *charge towards* s w	machen	21
zu|teilen (D) *allot (to)* A h w	machen	21
zu|trauen (D) *believe (sb) capable of* A h w	machen	21

zu|treffen *be justified;* (**auf** + A/**für** + A) *apply (to)* h st [i, af, o] — *sprechen 33

zu|treiben (D/**auf** + A) *drift (towards)* s st [ie, ie] — schreiben 28

zu|trinken (D) *drink (to)* h st [a, u] — klingen 16

zuvor|kommen (D) *anticipate (sth/sb)* s st [am, o] — kommen 17

zu|wachsen *become overgrown* s st [ä, u, a] — *tragen 38

zu|wandern *immigrate* s w — angeln 1

zu|weisen (D) *allocate to* A h st [ie, ie] — *schreiben 28

zu|wenden (D) *turn (towards); donate (to)* A h w/m [a, a] — reden/senden 24/31

sich zu|wenden (D) *turn (to); devote oneself (to)* h w/m [a, a] — reden/senden 24/31

zu|werfen (D) *throw (to sb); slam* A h st [i, a, o] — sprechen 33

zuwider|handeln (D) *infringe; defy* h w — angeln 1

zuwider|laufen (D) *run counter to* s st [äu, ie, au] — laufen 20

zu|winken (D) *wave to* h w — machen 21

zu|zahlen *pay extra* A h w — machen 21

zu|ziehen *draw; do up; call in; move here* A h (**sein** when intrans.) st [og, og] — *kriechen 19

sich [D] **zu|ziehen** *incur; contract; tighten* A h st [og, og] — *kriechen 19

zwängen *squeeze; cram* A h w — machen 21

zweckent'fremden *misuse* A h w — reden 24

zweifeln (**an** + D) *doubt (sb/sth)* h w — angeln 1

zwingen (**zu** + D) *force (into)* A h st [a, u] — klingen 16

zwinkern *blink* h w — angeln 1

zwirbeln *twirl* A h w — angeln 1

zwischen|landen in + D *stopover in* s w — reden 24

zwitschern *chirp* h w — angeln 1

VERB PATTERNS

1 angeln, *to fish*

Pattern for weak verbs with infinitive ending **-n** rather than **-en**.

past infinitive	geangelt haben
present participle	angelnd
past participle	geangelt
imperative	ang(e)le!/angel!
	angeln wir!
	angelt!
	angeln Sie!

present
ich ang(e)le
du angelst
er angelt
wir angeln
ihr angelt
sie angeln

perfect
ich habe geangelt
du hast geangelt
er hat geangelt
wir haben geangelt
ihr habt geangelt
sie haben geangelt

past (imperfect)
ich angelte
du angeltest
er angelte
wir angelten
ihr angeltet
sie angelten

future
ich werde angeln
du wirst angeln
er wird angeln
wir werden angeln
ihr werdet angeln
sie werden angeln

pluperfect
ich hatte geangelt
du hattest geangelt
er hatte geangelt
wir hatten geangelt
ihr hattet geangelt
sie hatten geangelt

conditional
ich würde angeln
du würdest angeln
er würde angeln
wir würden angeln
ihr würdet angeln
sie würden angeln

future perfect
ich werde geangelt haben
du wirst geangelt haben
er wird geangelt haben
wir werden geangelt haben
ihr werdet geangelt haben
sie werden geangelt haben

conditional perfect
ich würde geangelt haben
du würdest geangelt haben
er würde geangelt haben
wir würden geangelt haben
ihr würdet geangelt haben
sie würden geangelt haben

present subjunctive
ich ang(e)le
du angelst
er ang(e)le
wir angeln
ihr angelt
sie angeln

perfect subjunctive
ich habe geangelt
du habest geangelt
er habe geangelt
wir haben geangelt
ihr habet geangelt
sie haben geangelt

past (imperfect) subjunctive
ich angelte
du angeltest
er angelte
wir angelten
ihr angeltet
sie angelten

pluperfect subjunctive
ich hätte geangelt
du hättest geangelt
er hätte geangelt
wir hätten geangelt
ihr hättet geangelt
sie hätten geangelt

● The bracketed **e** is frequently dropped with verbs
ending **-eln**; with verbs ending **-ern** this is less
common.

2 **atmen,** *to breathe*

Pattern for weak verbs with stem ending in a consonant
followed by **m** or **n**.

past infinitive	geatmet haben
present participle	atmend
past participle	geatmet
imperative	atme!
	atmen wir!
	atmet!
	atmen Sie!

present
ich atme
du atmest
er atmet
wir atmen
ihr atmet
sie atmen

perfect
ich habe geatmet
du hast geatmet
er hat geatmet
wir haben geatmet
ihr habt geatmet
sie haben geatmet

past (imperfect)
ich atmete
du atmetest
er atmete
wir atmeten
ihr atmetet
sie atmeten

future
ich werde atmen
du wirst atmen
er wird atmen
wir werden atmen
ihr werdet atmen
sie werden atmen

pluperfect
ich hatte geatmet
du hattest geatmet
er hatte geatmet
wir hatten geatmet
ihr hattet geatmet
sie hatten geatmet

conditional
ich würde atmen
du würdest atmen
er würde atmen
wir würden atmen
ihr würdet atmen
sie würden atmen

future perfect
  ich werde geatmet haben
  du wirst geatmet haben
  er wird geatmet haben
  wir werden geatmet haben
  ihr werdet geatmet haben
  sie werden geatmet haben

present subjunctive
  ich atme
  du atmest
  er atme
  wir atmen
  ihr atmet
  sie atmen

past (imperfect) subjunctive
  ich atmete
  du atmetest
  er atmete
  wir atmeten
  ihr atmetet
  sie atmeten

conditional perfect
  ich würde geatmet haben
  du würdest geatmet haben
  er würde geatmet haben
  wir würden geatmet haben
  ihr würdet geatmet haben
  sie würden geatmet haben

perfect subjunctive
  ich habe geatmet
  du habest geatmet
  er habe geatmet
  wir haben geatmet
  ihr habet geatmet
  sie haben geatmet

pluperfect subjunctive
  ich hätte geatmet
  du hättest geatmet
  er hätte geatmet
  wir hätten geatmet
  ihr hättet geatmet
  sie hätten geatmet

3 beißen, *to bite*

Pattern for verbs with past tense in **i**, past participle in **i**, and stem ending **-ß**.

past infinitive	gebissen haben
present participle	beißend
past participle	gebissen
imperative	beiß(e)!
	beißen wir!
	beißt!
	beißen Sie!

present
ich beiße
du beißt
er beißt
wir beißen
ihr beißt
sie beißen

perfect
ich habe gebissen
du hast gebissen
er hat gebissen
wir haben gebissen
ihr habt gebissen
sie haben gebissen

past (imperfect)
ich biß
du bissest
er biß
wir bissen
ihr bißt
sie bissen

future
ich werde beißen
du wirst beißen
er wird beißen
wir werden beißen
ihr werdet beißen
sie werden beißen

pluperfect
ich hatte gebissen
du hattest gebissen
er hatte gebissen
wir hatten gebissen
ihr hattet gebissen
sie hatten gebissen

conditional
ich würde beißen
du würdest beißen
er würde beißen
wir würden beißen
ihr würdet beißen
sie würden beißen

future perfect
  ich werde gebissen haben
  du wirst gebissen haben
  er wird gebissen haben
  wir werden gebissen haben
  ihr werdet gebissen haben
  sie werden gebissen haben

present subjunctive
  ich beiße
  du beißest
  er beiße
  wir beißen
  ihr beißet
  sie beißen

past (imperfect) subjunctive
  ich bisse
  du bissest
  er bisse
  wir bissen
  ihr bisset
  sie bissen

conditional perfect
  ich würde gebissen haben
  du würdest gebissen haben
  er würde gebissen haben
  wir würden gebissen haben
  ihr würdet gebissen haben
  sie würden gebissen haben

perfect subjunctive
  ich habe gebissen
  du habest gebissen
  er habe gebissen
  wir haben gebissen
  ihr habet gebissen
  sie haben gebissen

pluperfect subjunctive
  ich hätte gebissen
  du hättest gebissen
  er hätte gebissen
  wir hätten gebissen
  ihr hättet gebissen
  sie hätten gebissen

4 binden, *to tie*

Pattern for verbs with past tense in **a**, past participle in **u**, and stem ending **-d** or **-t**.

past infinitive	gebunden haben
present participle	bindend
past participle	gebunden
imperative	bind(e)!
	binden wir!
	bindet!
	binden Sie!

present
ich binde
du bindest
er bindet
wir binden
ihr bindet
sie binden

perfect
ich habe gebunden
du hast gebunden
er hat gebunden
wir haben gebunden
ihr habt gebunden
sie haben gebunden

past (imperfect)
ich band
du bandst
er band
wir banden
ihr bandet
sie banden

future
ich werde binden
du wirst binden
er wird binden
wir werden binden
ihr werdet binden
sie werden binden

pluperfect
ich hatte gebunden
du hattest gebunden
er hatte gebunden
wir hatten gebunden
ihr hattet gebunden
sie hatten gebunden

conditional
ich würde binden
du würdest binden
er würde binden
wir würden binden
ihr würdet binden
sie würden binden

future perfect
ich werde gebunden haben
du wirst gebunden haben
er wird gebunden haben
wir werden gebunden haben
ihr werdet gebunden haben
sie werden gebunden haben

conditional perfect
ich würde gebunden haben
du würdest gebunden haben
er würde gebunden haben
wir würden gebunden haben
ihr würdet gebunden haben
sie würden gebunden haben

present subjunctive
ich binde
du bindest
er binde
wir binden
ihr bindet
sie binden

perfect subjunctive
ich habe gebunden
du habest gebunden
er habe gebunden
wir haben gebunden
ihr habet gebunden
sie haben gebunden

past (imperfect) subjunctive
ich bände
du bändest
er bände
wir bänden
ihr bändet
sie bänden

pluperfect subjunctive
ich hätte gebunden
du hättest gebunden
er hätte gebunden
wir hätten gebunden
ihr hättet gebunden
sie hätten gebunden

● The following verb and its compounds are similarly
conjugated, but with some changes:

schinden, *to maltreat*
Past tense **ich schund,** etc., past subjunctive **ich
schünde,** etc. These tenses are very rarely used.

5 **brennen,** *to burn*

Pattern for mixed verbs with past tense in **a** and past participle in **a**.

past infinitive	gebrannt haben
present participle	brennend
past participle	gebrannt
imperative	brenn(e)!
	brennen wir!
	brennt!
	brennen Sie!

present
ich brenne
du brennst
er brennt
wir brennen
ihr brennt
sie brennen

perfect
ich habe gebrannt
du hast gebrannt
er hat gebrannt
wir haben gebrannt
ihr habt gebrannt
sie haben gebrannt

past (imperfect)
ich brannte
du branntest
er brannte
wir brannten
ihr branntet
sie brannten

future
ich werde brennen
du wirst brennen
er wird brennen
wir werden brennen
ihr werdet brennen
sie werden brennen

pluperfect
ich hatte gebrannt
du hattest gebrannt
er hatte gebrannt
wir hatten gebrannt
ihr hattet gebrannt
sie hatten gebrannt

conditional
ich würde brennen
du würdest brennen
er würde brennen
wir würden brennen
ihr würdet brennen
sie würden brennen

future perfect
  ich werde gebrannt haben
  du wirst gebrannt haben
  er wird gebrannt haben
  wir werden gebrannt haben
  ihr werdet gebrannt haben
  sie werden gebrannt haben

conditional perfect
  ich würde gebrannt haben
  du würdest gebrannt haben
  er würde gebrannt haben
  wir würden gebrannt haben
  ihr würdet gebrannt haben
  sie würden gebrannt haben

present subjunctive
  ich brenne
  du brennest
  er brenne
  wir brennen
  ihr brennet
  sie brennen

perfect subjunctive
  ich habe gebrannt
  du habest gebrannt
  er habe gebrannt
  wir haben gebrannt
  ihr habet gebrannt
  sie haben gebrannt

past (imperfect) subjunctive
  ich brennte
  du brenntest
  er brennte
  wir brennten
  ihr brenntet
  sie brennten

pluperfect subjunctive
  ich hätte gebrannt
  du hättest gebrannt
  er hätte gebrannt
  wir hätten gebrannt
  ihr hättet gebrannt
  sie hätten gebrannt

● The following verbs and their compounds are
  similarly conjugated, but with some changes:
bringen, *to bring*
  Past tense: **ich brachte,** etc. Past participle: **gebracht.**
  Past subjunctive: **ich brächte,** etc.
denken, *to think*
  Past tense: **ich dachte,** etc. Past participle: **gedacht.**
  Past subjunctive: **ich dächte,** etc.
haben, *to have*
  Present tense: **du hast, er hat.** Past tense: **ich hatte,**
  etc. Past subjunctive: **ich hätte,** etc.

6 **dreschen,** *to thresh*

Pattern for verbs with present tense **du** and **er** forms in **i,** past tense in **o,** and past participle in **o.**

past infinitive	gedroschen haben
present participle	dreschend
past participle	gedroschen
imperative	drisch!
	dreschen wir!
	drescht!
	dreschen Sie!

present
ich dresche
du drischst
er drischt
wir dreschen
ihr drescht
sie dreschen

perfect
ich habe gedroschen
du hast gedroschen
er hat gedroschen
wir haben gedroschen
ihr habt gedroschen
sie haben gedroschen

past (imperfect)
ich drosch
du droschst
er drosch
wir droschen
ihr droscht
sie droschen

future
ich werde dreschen
du wirst dreschen
er wird dreschen
wir werden dreschen
ihr werdet dreschen
sie werden dreschen

pluperfect
ich hatte gedroschen
du hattest gedroschen
er hatte gedroschen
wir hatten gedroschen
ihr hattet gedroschen
sie hatten gedroschen

conditional
ich würde dreschen
du würdest dreschen
er würde dreschen
wir würden dreschen
ihr würdet dreschen
sie würden dreschen

future perfect
ich werde gedroschen haben
du wirst gedroschen haben
er wird gedroschen haben
wir werden gedroschen haben
ihr werdet gedroschen haben
sie werden gedroschen haben

conditional perfect
ich würde gedroschen haben
du würdest gedroschen haben
er würde gedroschen haben
wir würden gedroschen haben
ihr würdet gedroschen haben
sie würden gedroschen haben

present subjunctive
ich dresche
du dreschest
er dresche
wir dreschen
ihr dreschet
sie dreschen

perfect subjunctive
ich habe gedroschen
du habest gedroschen
er habe gedroschen
wir haben gedroschen
ihr habet gedroschen
sie haben gedroschen

past (imperfect) subjunctive
ich drösche
du dröschest
er drösche
wir dröschen
ihr dröschet
sie dröschen

pluperfect subjunctive
ich hätte gedroschen
du hättest gedroschen
er hätte gedroschen
wir hätten gedroschen
ihr hättet gedroschen
sie hätten gedroschen

● The following verbs and their compounds are similarly conjugated, but with some changes:

fechten, to fence
Present tense: **er ficht, ihr fechtet.** Imperative: **fechtet!** Past tense: **ihr fochtet.**

flechten, *to weave*
Present tense: **er flicht, ihr flechtet.** Imperative: **flechtet!** Past tense: **ihr flochtet.**

melken, *to milk*
Has alternative present-tense forms, **du melkst, er melkt,** and alternative **du** form of the imperative, **melk(e)!**

schmelzen, *to melt*
Present tense: **du schmilzt.** Past tense: **du schmolzest.**

7 **dürfen,** *to be allowed to*

past infinitive	gedurft haben
present participle	dürfend
past participle	gedurft

present
ich darf
du darfst
er darf
wir dürfen
ihr dürft
sie dürfen

perfect
ich habe gedurft
du hast gedurft
er hat gedurft
wir haben gedurft
ihr habt gedurft
sie haben gedurft

past (imperfect)
ich durfte
du durftest
er durfte
wir durften
ihr durftet
sie durften

future
ich werde dürfen
du wirst dürfen
er wird dürfen
wir werden dürfen
ihr werdet dürfen
sie werden dürfen

pluperfect
ich hatte gedurft
du hattest gedurft
er hatte gedurft
wir hatten gedurft
ihr hattet gedurft
sie hatten gedurft

conditional
ich würde dürfen
du würdest dürfen
er würde dürfen
wir würden dürfen
ihr würdet dürfen
sie würden dürfen

future perfect
ich werde gedurft haben
du wirst gedurft haben
er wird gedurft haben
wir werden gedurft haben
ihr werdet gedurft haben
sie werden gedurft haben

conditional perfect
ich würde gedurft haben
du würdest gedurft haben
er würde gedurft haben
wir würden gedurft haben
ihr würdet gedurft haben
sie würden gedurft haben

present subjunctive
ich dürfe
du dürfest
er dürfe
wir dürfen
ihr dürfet
sie dürfen

perfect subjunctive
ich habe gedurft
du habest gedurft
er habe gedurft
wir haben gedurft
ihr habet gedurft
sie haben gedurft

past (imperfect) subjunctive
ich dürfte
du dürftest
er dürfte
wir dürften
ihr dürftet
sie dürften

pluperfect subjunctive
ich hätte gedurft
du hättest gedurft
er hätte gedurft
wir hätten gedurft
ihr hättet gedurft
sie hätten gedurft

● **Dürfen** has no imperative. Compound tenses of **dürfen** have the past participle form **dürfen** instead of **gedurft** when used with a dependent infinitive: **ich hätte gehen dürfen,** *I ought to have been allowed to go.*

8 fressen, *to eat (of animals)*

Pattern for verbs with **du** and **er** forms of present tense in **i**, past tense in **a**, past participle in **e**, and stem ending in an **s** sound.

past infinitive	gefressen haben
present participle	fressend
past participle	gefressen
imperative	friß!
	fressen wir!
	freßt!
	fressen Sie!

present
 ich fresse
 du frißt
 er frißt
 wir fressen
 ihr freßt
 sie fressen

perfect
 ich habe gefressen
 du hast gefressen
 er hat gefressen
 wir haben gefressen
 ihr habt gefressen
 sie haben gefressen

past (imperfect)
 ich fraß
 du fraßest
 er fraß
 wir fraßen
 ihr fraßt
 sie fraßen

future
 ich werde fressen
 du wirst fressen
 er wird fressen
 wir werden fressen
 ihr werdet fressen
 sie werden fressen

pluperfect
 ich hatte gefressen
 du hattest gefressen
 er hatte gefressen
 wir hatten gefressen
 ihr hattet gefressen
 sie hatten gefressen

conditional
 ich würde fressen
 du würdest fressen
 er würde fressen
 wir würden fressen
 ihr würdet fressen
 sie würden fressen

future perfect
ich werde gefressen haben
du wirst gefressen haben
er wird gefressen haben
wir werden gefressen haben
ihr werdet gefressen haben
sie werden gefressen haben

conditional perfect
ich würde gefressen haben
du würdest gefressen haben
er würde gefressen haben
wir würden gefressen haben
ihr würdet gefressen haben
sie würden gefressen haben

present subjunctive
ich fresse
du fressest
er fresse
wir fressen
ihr fresset
sie fressen

perfect subjunctive
ich habe gefressen
du habest gefressen
er habe gefressen
wir haben gefressen
ihr habet gefressen
sie haben gefressen

past (imperfect) subjunctive
ich fräße
du fräßest
er fräße
wir fräßen
ihr fräßet
sie fräßen

pluperfect subjunctive
ich hätte gefressen
du hättest gefressen
er hätte gefressen
wir hätten gefressen
ihr hättet gefressen
sie hätten gefressen

● The following verbs and their compounds are similarly conjugated, but with some changes:

essen, *to eat*
Past participle: **gegessen**

genesen, *to recover*
Present tense has no vowel change: **du genest, er genest**

sitzen, *to sit*
The **tz** changes to **ß** throughout the past tense (**ich saß,** etc.) and past subjunctive (**ich säße,** etc.) and to **ss** in the past participle (**gesessen**).

9 geben, *to give*

Pattern for verbs with **du** and **er** forms of present tense in **i**, past tense in **a**, and past participle in **e**.

past infinitive	gegeben haben
present participle	gebend
past participle	gegeben
imperative	gib!
	geben wir!
	gebt!
	geben Sie!

present
ich gebe
du gibst
er gibt
wir geben
ihr gebt
sie geben

perfect
ich habe gegeben
du hast gegeben
er hat gegeben
wir haben gegeben
ihr habt gegeben
sie haben gegeben

past (imperfect)
ich gab
du gabst
er gab
wir gaben
ihr gabt
sie gaben

future
ich werde geben
du wirst geben
er wird geben
wir werden geben
ihr werdet geben
sie werden geben

pluperfect
ich hatte gegeben
du hattest gegeben
er hatte gegeben
wir hatten gegeben
ihr hattet gegeben
sie hatten gegeben

conditional
ich würde geben
du würdest geben
er würde geben
wir würden geben
ihr würdet geben
sie würden geben

future perfect
ich werde gegeben haben
du wirst gegeben haben
er wird gegeben haben
wir werden gegeben haben
ihr werdet gegeben haben
sie werden gegeben haben

conditional perfect
ich würde gegeben haben
du würdest gegeben haben
er würde gegeben haben
wir würden gegeben haben
ihr würdet gegeben haben
sie würden gegeben haben

present subjunctive
ich gebe
du gebest
er gebe
wir geben
ihr gebet
sie geben

perfect subjunctive
ich habe gegeben
du habest gegeben
er habe gegeben
wir haben gegeben
ihr habet gegeben
sie haben gegeben

past (imperfect) subjunctive
ich gäbe
du gäbest
er gäbe
wir gäben
ihr gäbet
sie gäben

pluperfect subjunctive
ich hätte gegeben
du hättest gegeben
er hätte gegeben
wir hätten gegeben
ihr hättet gegeben
sie hätten gegeben

● The following verbs and their compounds are similarly conjugated, but with some changes:

bitten, *to ask*
Has one t in past tense (**ich bat**, etc), past participle (**gebeten**), and past subjunctive (**ich bäte**, etc.). Present tense: **du bittest, er bittet, ihr bittet**. Imperative: **bittet!** Past tense: **ihr batet**.

treten, *to step*
Present tense: **du trittst, er tritt, ihr tretet**. Imperative: **tritt!, tretet!** Past tense: **ihr tratet**.

10 gleichen, *to resemble*

Pattern for verbs with past tense in **i**, past participle in **i**.

past infinitive	geglichen haben
present participle	gleichend
past participle	geglichen
imperative	gleich(e)!
	gleichen wir!
	gleicht!
	gleichen Sie!

present
  ich gleiche
  du gleichst
  er gleicht
  wir gleichen
  ihr gleicht
  sie gleichen

perfect
  ich habe geglichen
  du hast geglichen
  er hat geglichen
  wir haben geglichen
  ihr habt geglichen
  sie haben geglichen

past (imperfect)
  ich glich
  du glichst
  er glich
  wir glichen
  ihr glicht
  sie glichen

future
  ich werde gleichen
  du wirst gleichen
  er wird gleichen
  wir werden gleichen
  ihr werdet gleichen
  sie werden gleichen

pluperfect
  ich hatte geglichen
  du hattest geglichen
  er hatte geglichen
  wir hatten geglichen
  ihr hattet geglichen
  sie hatten geglichen

conditional
  ich würde gleichen
  du würdest gleichen
  er würde gleichen
  wir würden gleichen
  ihr würdet gleichen
  sie würden gleichen

future perfect
  ich werde geglichen haben
  du wirst geglichen haben
  er wird geglichen haben
  wir werden geglichen haben
  ihr werdet geglichen haben
  sie werden geglichen haben

conditional perfect
  ich würde geglichen haben
  du würdest geglichen haben
  er würde geglichen haben
  wir würden geglichen haben
  ihr würdet geglichen haben
  sie würden geglichen haben

present subjunctive
  ich gleiche
  du gleichest
  er gleiche
  wir gleichen
  ihr gleichet
  sie gleichen

perfect subjunctive
  ich habe geglichen
  du habest geglichen
  er habe geglichen
  wir haben geglichen
  ihr habet geglichen
  sie haben geglichen

past (imperfect) subjunctive
  ich gliche
  du glichest
  er gliche
  wir glichen
  ihr glichet
  sie glichen

pluperfect subjunctive
  ich hätte geglichen
  du hättest geglichen
  er hätte geglichen
  wir hätten geglichen
  ihr hättet geglichen
  sie hätten geglichen

11 greifen, *to grasp*

Pattern for verbs with past tense in **i**, past participle in **i**, and doubled consonant.

past infinitive	gegriffen haben
present participle	greifend
past participle	gegriffen
imperative	greif(e)!
	greifen wir!
	greift!
	greifen Sie!

present
ich greife
du greifst
er greift
wir greifen
ihr greift
sie greifen

perfect
ich habe gegriffen
du hast gegriffen
er hat gegriffen
wir haben gegriffen
ihr habt gegriffen
sie haben gegriffen

past (imperfect)
ich griff
du griffst
er griff
wir griffen
ihr grifft
sie griffen

future
ich werde greifen
du wirst greifen
er wird greifen
wir werden greifen
ihr werdet greifen
sie werden greifen

pluperfect
ich hatte gegriffen
du hattest gegriffen
er hatte gegriffen
wir hatten gegriffen
ihr hattet gegriffen
sie hatten gegriffen

conditional
ich würde greifen
du würdest greifen
er würde greifen
wir würden greifen
ihr würdet greifen
sie würden greifen

future perfect
ich werde gegriffen haben
du wirst gegriffen haben
er wird gegriffen haben
wir werden gegriffen haben
ihr werdet gegriffen haben
sie werden gegriffen haben

present subjunctive
ich greife
du greifest
er greife
wir greifen
ihr greifet
sie greifen

past (imperfect) subjunctive
ich griffe
du griffest
er griffe
wir griffen
ihr griffet
sie griffen

conditional perfect
ich würde gegriffen haben
du würdest gegriffen haben
er würde gegriffen haben
wir würden gegriffen haben
ihr würdet gegriffen haben
sie würden gegriffen haben

perfect subjunctive
ich habe gegriffen
du habest gegriffen
er habe gegriffen
wir haben gegriffen
ihr habet gegriffen
sie haben gegriffen

pluperfect subjunctive
ich hätte gegriffen
du hättest gegriffen
er hätte gegriffen
wir hätten gegriffen
ihr hättet gegriffen
sie hätten gegriffen

12 hängen, *to hang*

Pattern for verbs with past tense in **i** and past participle in **a**.

past infinitive	gehangen haben
present participle	hängend
past participle	gehangen
imperative	häng(e)!
	hängen wir!
	hängt!
	hängen Sie!

present
ich hänge
du hängst
er hängt
wir hängen
ihr hängt
sie hängen

perfect
ich habe gehangen
du hast gehangen
er hat gehangen
wir haben gehangen
ihr habt gehangen
sie haben gehangen

past (imperfect)
ich hing
du hingst
er hing
wir hingen
ihr hingt
sie hingen

future
ich werde hängen
du wirst hängen
er wird hängen
wir werden hängen
ihr werdet hängen
sie werden hängen

pluperfect
ich hatte gehangen
du hattest gehangen
er hatte gehangen
wir hatten gehangen
ihr hattet gehangen
sie hatten gehangen

conditional
ich würde hängen
du würdest hängen
er würde hängen
wir würden hängen
ihr würdet hängen
sie würden hängen

future perfect
ich werde gehangen haben
du wirst gehangen haben
er wird gehangen haben
wir werden gehangen haben
ihr werdet gehangen haben
sie werden gehangen haben

conditional perfect
ich würde gehangen haben
du würdest gehangen haben
er würde gehangen haben
wir würden gehangen haben
ihr würdet gehangen haben
sie würden gehangen haben

present subjunctive
ich hänge
du hängest
er hänge
wir hängen
ihr hänget
sie hängen

perfect subjunctive
ich habe gehangen
du habest gehangen
er habe gehangen
wir haben gehangen
ihr habet gehangen
sie haben gehangen

past (imperfect) subjunctive
ich hinge
du hingest
er hinge
wir hingen
ihr hinget
sie hingen

pluperfect subjunctive
ich hätte gehangen
du hättest gehangen
er hätte gehangen
wir hätten gehangen
ihr hättet gehangen
sie hätten gehangen

● The following verbs and their compounds are
  similarly conjugated, but with some changes:
fangen, *to catch*
  Present tense: (**ich fange**), **du fängst, er fängt, (wir
  fangen,** etc.).
gehen, *to go*
  Changes **h** to **ng** in past tense (**ich ging,** etc.), past
  participle (**gegangen**), and past subjunctive (**ich ginge,**
  etc.).

13 heißen, *to be called*

past infinitive	geheißen haben
present participle	heißend
past participle	geheißen
imperative	heiß(e)!
	heißen wir!
	heißt!
	heißen Sie!

present
ich heiße
du heißt
er heißt
wir heißen
ihr heißt
sie heißen

perfect
ich habe geheißen
du hast geheißen
er hat geheißen
wir haben geheißen
ihr habt geheißen
sie haben geheißen

past (imperfect)
ich hieß
du hießest
er hieß
wir hießen
ihr hießt
sie hießen

future
ich werde heißen
du wirst heißen
er wird heißen
wir werden heißen
ihr werdet heißen
sie werden heißen

pluperfect
ich hatte geheißen
du hattest geheißen
er hatte geheißen
wir hatten geheißen
ihr hattet geheißen
sie hatten geheißen

conditional
ich würde heißen
du würdest heißen
er würde heißen
wir würden heißen
ihr würdet heißen
sie würden heißen

future perfect
ich werde geheißen haben
du wirst geheißen haben
er wird geheißen haben
wir werden geheißen haben
ihr werdet geheißen haben
sie werden geheißen haben

present subjunctive
ich heiße
du heißest
er heiße
wir heißen
ihr heißet
sie heißen

past (imperfect) subjunctive
ich hieße
du hießest
er hieße
wir hießen
ihr hießet
sie hießen

conditional perfect
ich würde geheißen haben
du würdest geheißen haben
er würde geheißen haben
wir würden geheißen haben
ihr würdet geheißen haben
sie würden geheißen haben

perfect subjunctive
ich habe geheißen
du habest geheißen
er habe geheißen
wir haben geheißen
ihr habet geheißen
sie haben geheißen

pluperfect subjunctive
ich hätte geheißen
du hättest geheißen
er hätte geheißen
wir hätten geheißen
ihr hättet geheißen
sie hätten geheißen

14 heizen, *to heat*

Pattern for weak verbs with stem ending -z, -s, -ß, -x.
The irregularity is in the **du** form of the present tense
only.

past infinitive	geheizt haben
present participle	heizend
past participle	geheizt
imperative	heiz(e)!
	heizen wir!
	heizt!
	heizen Sie!

present	*perfect*
ich heize	ich habe geheizt
du heizt	du hast geheizt
er heizt	er hat geheizt
wir heizen	wir haben geheizt
ihr heizt	ihr habt geheizt
sie heizen	sie haben geheizt

past (imperfect)	*future*
ich heizte	ich werde heizen
du heiztest	du wirst heizen
er heizte	er wird heizen
wir heizten	wir werden heizen
ihr heiztet	ihr werdet heizen
sie heizten	sie werden heizen

pluperfect	*conditional*
ich hatte geheizt	ich würde heizen
du hattest geheizt	du würdest heizen
er hatte geheizt	er würde heizen
wir hatten geheizt	wir würden heizen
ihr hattet geheizt	ihr würdet heizen
sie hatten geheizt	sie würden heizen

future perfect
ich werde geheizt haben
du wirst geheizt haben
er wird geheizt haben
wir werden geheizt haben
ihr werdet geheizt haben
sie werden geheizt haben

conditional perfect
ich würde geheizt haben
du würdest geheizt haben
er würde geheizt haben
wir würden geheizt haben
ihr würdet geheizt haben
sie würden geheizt haben

present subjunctive
ich heize
du heizest
er heize
wir heizen
ihr heizet
sie heizen

perfect subjunctive
ich habe geheizt
du habest geheizt
er habe geheizt
wir haben geheizt
ihr habet geheizt
sie haben geheizt

past (imperfect) subjunctive
ich heizte
du heiztest
er heizte
wir heizten
ihr heiztet
sie heizten

pluperfect subjunctive
ich hätte geheizt
du hättest geheizt
er hätte geheizt
wir hätten geheizt
ihr hättet geheizt
sie hätten geheizt

● The following verb and its compounds are similarly
   conjugated, but with a change:
salzen, *to salt*
   Past participle: **gesalzen.**

15 informieren, *to inform*

Pattern for weak verbs ending **-ieren** and **-eien**. The irregularity is in the past participle only.

past infinitive	informiert haben
present participle	informierend
past participle	informiert
imperative	informier(e)!
	informieren wir!
	informiert!
	informieren Sie!

present	*perfect*
ich informiere	ich habe informiert
du informierst	du hast informiert
er informiert	er hat informiert
wir informieren	wir haben informiert
ihr informiert	ihr habt informiert
sie informieren	sie haben informiert

past (imperfect)	*future*
ich informierte	ich werde informieren
du informiertest	du wirst informieren
er informierte	er wird informieren
wir informierten	wir werden informieren
ihr informiertet	ihr werdet informieren
sie informierten	sie werden informieren

pluperfect	*conditional*
ich hatte informiert	ich würde informieren
du hattest informiert	du würdest informieren
er hatte informiert	er würde informieren
wir hatten informiert	wir würden informieren
ihr hattet informiert	ihr würdet informieren
sie hatten informiert	sie würden informieren

future perfect
  ich werde informiert haben
  du wirst informiert haben
  er wird informiert haben
  wir werden informiert haben
  ihr werdet informiert haben
  sie werden informiert haben

conditional perfect
  ich würde informiert haben
  du würdest informiert haben
  er würde informiert haben
  wir würden informiert haben
  ihr würdet informiert haben
  sie würden informiert haben

present subjunctive
  ich informiere
  du informierest
  er informiere
  wir informieren
  ihr informieret
  sie informieren

perfect subjunctive
  ich habe informiert
  du habest informiert
  er habe informiert
  wir haben informiert
  ihr habet informiert
  sie haben informiert

past (imperfect) subjunctive
  ich informierte
  du informiertest
  er informierte
  wir informierten
  ihr informiertet
  sie informierten

pluperfect subjunctive
  ich hätte informiert
  du hättest informiert
  er hätte informiert
  wir hätten informiert
  ihr hättet informiert
  sie hätten informiert

● The very few verbs (such as **zieren**) with a single-syllable stem ending **-ieren** or **-eien** follow the regular weak pattern of **machen**, 21.

16 **klingen,** *to sound*

Pattern for verbs with past tense in **a** and past participle in **u**.

past infinitive	geklungen haben
present participle	klingend
past participle	geklungen
imperative	kling(e)!
	klingen wir!
	klingt!
	klingen Sie!

present
 ich klinge
 du klingst
 er klingt
 wir klingen
 ihr klingt
 sie klingen

perfect
 ich habe geklungen
 du hast geklungen
 er hat geklungen
 wir haben geklungen
 ihr habt geklungen
 sie haben geklungen

past (imperfect)
 ich klang
 du klangst
 er klang
 wir klangen
 ihr klangt
 sie klangen

future
 ich werde klingen
 du wirst klingen
 er wird klingen
 wir werden klingen
 ihr werdet klingen
 sie werden klingen

pluperfect
 ich hatte geklungen
 du hattest geklungen
 er hatte geklungen
 wir hatten geklungen
 ihr hattet geklungen
 sie hatten geklungen

conditional
 ich würde klingen
 du würdest klingen
 er würde klingen
 wir würden klingen
 ihr würdet klingen
 sie würden klingen

future perfect
ich werde geklungen haben
du wirst geklungen haben
er wird geklungen haben
wir werden geklungen haben
ihr werdet geklungen haben
sie werden geklungen haben

present subjunctive
ich klinge
du klingest
er klinge
wir klingen
ihr klinget
sie klingen

past (imperfect) subjunctive
ich klänge
du klängest
er klänge
wir klängen
ihr klänget
sie klängen

conditional perfect
ich würde geklungen haben
du würdest geklungen haben
er würde geklungen haben
wir würden geklungen haben
ihr würdet geklungen haben
sie würden geklungen haben

perfect subjunctive
ich habe geklungen
du habest geklungen
er habe geklungen
wir haben geklungen
ihr habet geklungen
sie haben geklungen

pluperfect subjunctive
ich hätte geklungen
du hättest geklungen
er hätte geklungen
wir hätten geklungen
ihr hättet geklungen
sie hätten geklungen

17 **kommen,** *to come*

past infinitive	gekommen sein
present participle	kommend
past participle	gekommen
imperative	komm(e)!
	kommen wir!
	kommt!
	kommen Sie!

present
ich komme
du kommst
er kommt
wir kommen
ihr kommt
sie kommen

perfect
ich bin gekommen
du bist gekommen
er ist gekommen
wir sind gekommen
ihr seid gekommen
sie sind gekommen

past (imperfect)
ich kam
du kamst
er kam
wir kamen
ihr kamt
sie kamen

future
ich werde kommen
du wirst kommen
er wird kommen
wir werden kommen
ihr werdet kommen
sie werden kommen

pluperfect
ich war gekommen
du warst gekommen
er war gekommen
wir waren gekommen
ihr wart gekommen
sie waren gekommen

conditional
ich würde kommen
du würdest kommen
er würde kommen
wir würden kommen
ihr würdet kommen
sie würden kommen

future perfect
 ich werde gekommen sein
 du wirst gekommen sein
 er wird gekommen sein
 wir werden gekommen sein
 ihr werdet gekommen sein
 sie werden gekommen sein

present subjunctive
 ich komme
 du kommest
 er komme
 wir kommen
 ihr kommet
 sie kommen

past (imperfect) subjunctive
 ich käme
 du kämest
 er käme
 wir kämen
 ihr kämet
 sie kämen

conditional perfect
 ich würde gekommen sein
 du würdest gekommen sein
 er würde gekommen sein
 wir würden gekommen sein
 ihr würdet gekommen sein
 sie würden gekommen sein

perfect subjunctive
 ich sei gekommen
 du sei(e)st gekommen
 er sei gekommen
 wir seien gekommen
 ihr seiet gekommen
 sie seien gekommen

pluperfect subjunctive
 ich wäre gekommen
 du wär(e)st gekommen
 er wäre gekommen
 wir wären gekommen
 ihr wär(e)t gekommen
 sie wären gekommen

18 **können,** *to be able to; can*

past infinitive	gekonnt haben
present participle	könnend
past participle	gekonnt

present
ich kann
du kannst
er kann
wir können
ihr könnt
sie können

perfect
ich habe gekonnt
du hast gekonnt
er hat gekonnt
wir haben gekonnt
ihr habt gekonnt
sie haben gekonnt

past (imperfect)
ich konnte
du konntest
er konnte
wir konnten
ihr konntet
sie konnten

future
ich werde können
du wirst können
er wird können
wir werden können
ihr werdet können
sie werden können

pluperfect
ich hatte gekonnt
du hattest gekonnt
er hatte gekonnt
wir hatten gekonnt
ihr hattet gekonnt
sie hatten gekonnt

conditional
ich würde können
du würdest können
er würde können
wir würden können
ihr würdet können
sie würden können

future perfect
ich werde gekonnt haben
du wirst gekonnt haben
er wird gekonnt haben
wir werden gekonnt haben
ihr werdet gekonnt haben
sie werden gekonnt haben

conditional perfect
ich würde gekonnt haben
du würdest gekonnt haben
er würde gekonnt haben
wir würden gekonnt haben
ihr würdet gekonnt haben
sie würden gekonnt haben

present subjunctive
ich könne
du könnest
er könne
wir können
ihr könnet
sie können

perfect subjunctive
ich habe gekonnt
du habest gekonnt
er habe gekonnt
wir haben gekonnt
ihr habet gekonnt
sie haben gekonnt

past (imperfect) subjunctive
ich könnte
du könntest
er könnte
wir könnten
ihr könntet
sie könnten

pluperfect subjunctive
ich hätte gekonnt
du hättest gekonnt
er hätte gekonnt
wir hätten gekonnt
ihr hättet gekonnt
sie hätten gekonnt

● **Können** has no imperative. Compound tenses of **können** have the past participle form **können** instead of **gekonnt** when used with a dependent infinitive: **ich hätte gehen können**, *I could have gone.*

19 **kriechen,** *to crawl*

Pattern for verbs with past tense in **o**, past participle in **o**. The pattern verb takes **sein**; many verbs that follow this pattern take **haben**.

past infinitive	gekrochen sein	*imperative*	kriech(e)!
			kriechen wir!
present participle	kriechend		kriecht!
past participle	gekrochen		kriechen Sie!

present
ich krieche
du kriechst
er kriecht
wir kriechen
ihr kriecht
sie kriechen

perfect
ich bin gekrochen
du bist gekrochen
er ist gekrochen
wir sind gekrochen
ihr seid gekrochen
sie sind gekrochen

past (imperfect)
ich kroch
du krochst
er kroch
wir krochen
ihr krocht
sie krochen

future
ich werde kriechen
du wirst kriechen
er wird kriechen
wir werden kriechen
ihr werdet kriechen
sie werden kriechen

pluperfect
ich war gekrochen
du warst gekrochen
er war gekrochen
wir waren gekrochen
ihr wart gekrochen
sie waren gekrochen

conditional
ich würde kriechen
du würdest kriechen
er würde kriechen
wir würden kriechen
ihr würdet kriechen
sie würden kriechen

future perfect
ich werde gekrochen sein
du wirst gekrochen sein
er wird gekrochen sein
wir werden gekrochen sein
ihr werdet gekrochen sein
sie werden gekrochen sein

conditional perfect
ich würde gekrochen sein
du würdest gekrochen sein
er würde gekrochen sein
wir würden gekrochen sein
ihr würdet gekrochen sein
sie würden gekrochen sein

present subjunctive
ich krieche
du kriechest
er krieche
wir kriechen
ihr kriechet
sie kriechen

perfect subjunctive
ich sei gekrochen
du sei(e)st gekrochen
er sei gekrochen
wir seien gekrochen
ihr seiet gekrochen
sie seien gekrochen

past (imperfect) subjunctive
ich kröche
du kröchest
er kröche
wir kröchen
ihr kröchet
sie kröchen

pluperfect subjunctive
ich wäre gekrochen
du wär(e)st gekrochen
er wäre gekrochen
wir wären gekrochen
ihr wär(e)t gekrochen
sie wären gekrochen

● The following verbs and their compounds are similarly conjugated, but with some changes:

bieten, *to offer*
Present tense: **du bietest, er bietet, ihr bietet.** Imperative: **bietet!** Past tense: **ihr botet.**

saufen, *to drink (of animals; or excessively)*
Present tense: **du säufst, er säuft.** Past tense: **ich soff,** etc. Past subjunctive: **ich söffe,** etc. Past participle: **gesoffen.**

schwören, *to swear*
Past subjunctive: **ich schwüre,** etc.

sieden, *to boil*
Present tense: **du siedest, er siedet, ihr siedet.** Imperative: **siedet!** Past tense: **ich sott,** etc. **Ihr** form of past tense: **ihr sottet.** Past subjunctive: **ich sötte,** etc. Past participle: **gesotten. Sieden** is, however, mostly weak in modern German (see **reden,** 24).

triefen, *to drip*
Past tense: **ich troff,** etc. Past subjunctive: **ich tröffe,** etc. Past participle: **getroffen. Triefen** may also be weak (see **machen,** 21).

ziehen, *to pull*
Past tense: **ich zog,** etc. Past subjunctive: **ich zöge,** etc. Past participle: **gezogen.**

20 laufen, *to run*

The pattern verb takes **sein**; some verbs that follow this pattern take **haben**.

past infinitive	gelaufen sein
present participle	laufend
past participle	gelaufen
imperative	lauf(e)!
	laufen wir!
	lauft!
	laufen Sie!

present	*perfect*
ich laufe	ich bin gelaufen
du läufst	du bist gelaufen
er läuft	er ist gelaufen
wir laufen	wir sind gelaufen
ihr lauft	ihr seid gelaufen
sie laufen	sie sind gelaufen

past (imperfect)	*future*
ich lief	ich werde laufen
du liefst	du wirst laufen
er lief	er wird laufen
wir liefen	wir werden laufen
ihr lieft	ihr werdet laufen
sie liefen	sie werden laufen

pluperfect	*conditional*
ich war gelaufen	ich würde laufen
du warst gelaufen	du würdest laufen
er war gelaufen	er würde laufen
wir waren gelaufen	wir würden laufen
ihr wart gelaufen	ihr würdet laufen
sie waren gelaufen	sie würden laufen

future perfect
  ich werde gelaufen sein
  du wirst gelaufen sein
  er wird gelaufen sein
  wir werden gelaufen sein
  ihr werdet gelaufen sein
  sie werden gelaufen sein

conditional perfect
  ich würde gelaufen sein
  du würdest gelaufen sein
  er würde gelaufen sein
  wir würden gelaufen sein
  ihr würdet gelaufen sein
  sie würden gelaufen sein

present subjunctive
  ich laufe
  du laufest
  er laufe
  wir laufen
  ihr laufet
  sie laufen

perfect subjunctive
  ich sei gelaufen
  du sei(e)st gelaufen
  er sei gelaufen
  wir seien gelaufen
  ihr seiet gelaufen
  sie seien gelaufen

past (imperfect) subjunctive
  ich liefe
  du liefest
  er liefe
  wir liefen
  ihr liefet
  sie liefen

pluperfect subjunctive
  ich wäre gelaufen
  du wär(e)st gelaufen
  er wäre gelaufen
  wir wären gelaufen
  ihr wär(e)t gelaufen
  sie wären gelaufen

● The following verb and its compounds are similarly
  conjugated, but with some changes:
hauen, *to punch*
  Present tense: **du haust, er haut**. Past tense: **ich hieb,**
  etc. Past subjunctive: **ich hiebe**, etc. **Hauen** is also very
  frequently weak.

21 machen, *to make*
Pattern for regular weak verbs.

past infinitive	gemacht haben
present participle	machend
past participle	gemacht
imperative	mach(e)!
	machen wir!
	macht!
	machen Sie!

present
  ich mache
  du machst
  er macht
  wir machen
  ihr macht
  sie machen

perfect
  ich habe gemacht
  du hast gemacht
  er hat gemacht
  wir haben gemacht
  ihr habt gemacht
  sie haben gemacht

past (imperfect)
  ich machte
  du machtest
  er machte
  wir machten
  ihr machtet
  sie machten

future
  ich werde machen
  du wirst machen
  er wird machen
  wir werden machen
  ihr werdet machen
  sie werden machen

pluperfect
  ich hatte gemacht
  du hattest gemacht
  er hatte gemacht
  wir hatten gemacht
  ihr hattet gemacht
  sie hatten gemacht

conditional
  ich würde machen
  du würdest machen
  er würde machen
  wir würden machen
  ihr würdet machen
  sie würden machen

future perfect
ich werde gemacht haben
du wirst gemacht haben
er wird gemacht haben
wir werden gemacht haben
ihr werdet gemacht haben
sie werden gemacht haben

present subjunctive
ich mache
du machest
er mache
wir machen
ihr machet
sie machen

past (imperfect) subjunctive
ich machte
du machtest
er machte
wir machten
ihr machtet
sie machten

conditional perfect
ich würde gemacht haben
du würdest gemacht haben
er würde gemacht haben
wir würden gemacht haben
ihr würdet gemacht haben
sie würden gemacht haben

perfect subjunctive
ich habe gemacht
du habest gemacht
er habe gemacht
wir haben gemacht
ihr habet gemacht
sie haben gemacht

pluperfect subjunctive
ich hätte gemacht
du hättest gemacht
er hätte gemacht
wir hätten gemacht
ihr hättet gemacht
sie hätten gemacht

● The following verbs and their compounds are
  similarly conjugated, but with some changes:
knien, *to kneel*
  Spelled with a single **e** throughout, so the present is
  ich knie, du kniest, er kniet, wir knien, etc. In speech,
  however, an extra **e** is often heard ('**knie-en**').
mahlen, *to grind*
  Past participle: **gemahlen.**

22 **mögen,** *to like; may*

past infinitive	gemocht haben
present participle	mögend
past participle	gemocht

present
ich mag
du magst
er mag
wir mögen
ihr mögt
sie mögen

perfect
ich habe gemocht
du hast gemocht
er hat gemocht
wir haben gemocht
ihr habt gemocht
sie haben gemocht

past (imperfect)
ich mochte
du mochtest
er mochte
wir mochten
ihr mochtet
sie mochten

future
ich werde mögen
du wirst mögen
er wird mögen
wir werden mögen
ihr werdet mögen
sie werden mögen

pluperfect
ich hatte gemocht
du hattest gemocht
er hatte gemocht
wir hatten gemocht
ihr hattet gemocht
sie hatten gemocht

conditional
ich würde mögen
du würdest mögen
er würde mögen
wir würden mögen
ihr würdet mögen
sie würden mögen

future perfect
ich werde gemocht haben
du wirst gemocht haben
er wird gemocht haben
wir werden gemocht haben
ihr werdet gemocht haben
sie werden gemocht haben

conditional perfect
ich würde gemocht haben
du würdest gemocht haben
er würde gemocht haben
wir würden gemocht haben
ihr würdet gemocht haben
sie würden gemocht haben

present subjunctive
ich möge
du mögest
er möge
wir mögen
ihr möget
sie mögen

perfect subjunctive
ich habe gemocht
du habest gemocht
er habe gemocht
wir haben gemocht
ihr habet gemocht
sie haben gemocht

past (imperfect) subjunctive
ich möchte
du möchtest
er möchte
wir möchten
ihr möchtet
sie möchten

pluperfect subjunctive
ich hätte gemocht
du hättest gemocht
er hätte gemocht
wir hätten gemocht
ihr hättet gemocht
sie hätten gemocht

● **Mögen** has no imperative. Compound tenses of
mögen have the past participle form **mögen** instead of
gemocht when used with a dependent infinitive: **ich
hätte gehen mögen,** *I should have liked to go.*

23 **müssen,** *to have to; must*

past infinitive	gemußt haben
present participle	müssend
past participle	gemußt

present	*perfect*
ich muß	ich habe gemußt
du mußt	du hast gemußt
er muß	er hat gemußt
wir müssen	wir haben gemußt
ihr müßt	ihr habt gemußt
sie müssen	sie haben gemußt

past (imperfect)	*future*
ich mußte	ich werde müssen
du mußtest	du wirst müssen
er mußte	er wird müssen
wir mußten	wir werden müssen
ihr mußtet	ihr werdet müssen
sie mußten	sie werden müssen

pluperfect	*conditional*
ich hatte gemußt	ich würde müssen
du hattest gemußt	du würdest müssen
er hatte gemußt	er würde müssen
wir hatten gemußt	wir würden müssen
ihr hattet gemußt	ihr würdet müssen
sie hatten gemußt	sie würden müssen

future perfect
ich werde gemußt haben
du wirst gemußt haben
er wird gemußt haben
wir werden gemußt haben
ihr werdet gemußt haben
sie werden gemußt haben

conditional perfect
ich würde gemußt haben
du würdest gemußt haben
er würde gemußt haben
wir würden gemußt haben
ihr würdet gemußt haben
sie würden gemußt haben

present subjunctive
ich müsse
du müssest
er müsse
wir müssen
ihr müsset
sie müssen

perfect subjunctive
ich habe gemußt
du habest gemußt
er habe gemußt
wir haben gemußt
ihr habet gemußt
sie haben gemußt

past (imperfect) subjunctive
ich müßte
du müßtest
er müßte
wir müßten
ihr müßtet
sie müßten

pluperfect subjunctive
ich hätte gemußt
du hättest gemußt
er hätte gemußt
wir hätten gemußt
ihr hättet gemußt
sie hätten gemußt

● **Müssen** has no imperative. Compound tenses of
müssen have the past participle form **müssen** instead
of **gemußt** when used with a dependent infinitive: **ich
hätte gehen müssen,** *I would have had to go.*

24 **reden,** *to talk*

Pattern for weak verbs with stem ending **-d** or **-t.**

past infinitive	geredet haben
present participle	redend
past participle	geredet
imperative	red(e)!
	reden wir!
	redet!
	reden Sie!

present
ich rede
du redest
er redet
wir reden
ihr redet
sie reden

perfect
ich habe geredet
du hast geredet
er hat geredet
wir haben geredet
ihr habt geredet
sie haben geredet

past (imperfect)
ich redete
du redetest
er redete
wir redeten
ihr redetet
sie redeten

future
ich werde reden
du wirst reden
er wird reden
wir werden reden
ihr werdet reden
sie werden reden

pluperfect
ich hatte geredet
du hattest geredet
er hatte geredet
wir hatten geredet
ihr hattet geredet
sie hatten geredet

conditional
ich würde reden
du würdest reden
er würde reden
wir würden reden
ihr würdet reden
sie würden reden

future perfect
ich werde geredet haben
du wirst geredet haben
er wird geredet haben
wir werden geredet haben
ihr werdet geredet haben
sie werden geredet haben

conditional perfect
ich würde geredet haben
du würdest geredet haben
er würde geredet haben
wir würden geredet haben
ihr würdet geredet haben
sie würden geredet haben

present subjunctive
ich rede
du redest
er rede
wir reden
ihr redet
sie reden

perfect subjunctive
ich habe geredet
du habest geredet
er habe geredet
wir haben geredet
ihr habet geredet
sie haben geredet

past (imperfect) subjunctive
ich redete
du redetest
er redete
wir redeten
ihr redetet
sie redeten

pluperfect subjunctive
ich hätte geredet
du hättest geredet
er hätte geredet
wir hätten geredet
ihr hättet geredet
sie hätten geredet

● The following verbs and their compounds are similarly conjugated, but with some changes:

schinden, *to maltreat*
Past participle: **geschunden.**

spalten, *to split*
Past participle: **gespalten**; sometimes weak: **gespaltet**.

25 **rufen,** *to call*

past infinitive	gerufen haben
present participle	rufend
past participle	gerufen
imperative	ruf(e)!
	rufen wir!
	ruft!
	rufen Sie!

present
ich rufe
du rufst
er ruft
wir rufen
ihr ruft
sie rufen

perfect
ich habe gerufen
du hast gerufen
er hat gerufen
wir haben gerufen
ihr habt gerufen
sie haben gerufen

past (imperfect)
ich rief
du riefst
er rief
wir riefen
ihr rieft
sie riefen

future
ich werde rufen
du wirst rufen
er wird rufen
wir werden rufen
ihr werdet rufen
sie werden rufen

pluperfect
ich hatte gerufen
du hattest gerufen
er hatte gerufen
wir hatten gerufen
ihr hattet gerufen
sie hatten gerufen

conditional
ich würde rufen
du würdest rufen
er würde rufen
wir würden rufen
ihr würdet rufen
sie würden rufen

future perfect
 ich werde gerufen haben
 du wirst gerufen haben
 er wird gerufen haben
 wir werden gerufen haben
 ihr werdet gerufen haben
 sie werden gerufen haben

present subjunctive
 ich rufe
 du rufest
 er rufe
 wir rufen
 ihr rufet
 sie rufen

past (imperfect) subjunctive
 ich riefe
 du riefest
 er riefe
 wir riefen
 ihr riefet
 sie riefen

conditional perfect
 ich würde gerufen haben
 du würdest gerufen haben
 er würde gerufen haben
 wir würden gerufen haben
 ihr würdet gerufen haben
 sie würden gerufen haben

perfect subjunctive
 ich habe gerufen
 du habest gerufen
 er habe gerufen
 wir haben gerufen
 ihr habet gerufen
 sie haben gerufen

pluperfect subjunctive
 ich hätte gerufen
 du hättest gerufen
 er hätte gerufen
 wir hätten gerufen
 ihr hättet gerufen
 sie hätten gerufen

26 schießen, *to shoot*

Pattern for verbs with past tense in **o**, past participle in **o**, and stem ending **-ß**.

past infinitive	geschossen haben
present participle	schießend
past participle	geschossen
imperative	schieß(e)!
	schießen wir!
	schießt!
	schießen Sie!

present
ich schieße
du schießt
er schießt
wir schießen
ihr schießt
sie schießen

perfect
ich habe geschossen
du hast geschossen
er hat geschossen
wir haben geschossen
ihr habt geschossen
sie haben geschossen

past (imperfect)
ich schoß
du schossest
er schoß
wir schossen
ihr schoßt
sie schossen

future
ich werde schießen
du wirst schießen
er wird schießen
wir werden schießen
ihr werdet schießen
sie werden schießen

pluperfect
ich hatte geschossen
du hattest geschossen
er hatte geschossen
wir hatten geschossen
ihr hattet geschossen
sie hatten geschossen

conditional
ich würde schießen
du würdest schießen
er würde schießen
wir würden schießen
ihr würdet schießen
sie würden schießen

future perfect
ich werde geschossen haben
du wirst geschossen haben
er wird geschossen haben
wir werden geschossen haben
ihr werdet geschossen haben
sie werden geschossen haben

conditional perfect
ich würde geschossen haben
du würdest geschossen haben
er würde geschossen haben
wir würden geschossen haben
ihr würdet geschossen haben
sie würden geschossen haben

present subjunctive
ich schieße
du schießest
er schieße
wir schießen
ihr schießet
sie schießen

perfect subjunctive
ich habe geschossen
du habest geschossen
er habe geschossen
wir haben geschossen
ihr habet geschossen
sie haben geschossen

past (imperfect) subjunctive
ich schösse
du schössest
er schösse
wir schössen
ihr schösset
sie schössen

pluperfect subjunctive
ich hätte geschossen
du hättest geschossen
er hätte geschossen
wir hätten geschossen
ihr hättet geschossen
sie hätten geschossen

27 schlafen, *to sleep*

Pattern for verbs with **du** and **er** forms of present tense in **ä**, past tense in **ie**, and past participle in **a**.

past infinitive	geschlafen haben	*imperative*	schlaf(e)! schlafen wir!
present participle	schlafend		schlaft!
past participle	geschlafen		schlafen Sie!

present
ich schlafe
du schläfst
er schläft
wir schlafen
ihr schlaft
sie schlafen

perfect
ich habe geschlafen
du hast geschlafen
er hat geschlafen
wir haben geschlafen
ihr habt geschlafen
sie haben geschlafen

past (imperfect)
ich schlief
du schliefst
er schlief
wir schliefen
ihr schlieft
sie schliefen

future
ich werde schlafen
du wirst schlafen
er wird schlafen
wir werden schlafen
ihr werdet schlafen
sie werden schlafen

pluperfect
ich hatte geschlafen
du hattest geschlafen
er hatte geschlafen
wir hatten geschlafen
ihr hattet geschlafen
sie hatten geschlafen

conditional
ich würde schlafen
du würdest schlafen
er würde schlafen
wir würden schlafen
ihr würdet schlafen
sie würden schlafen

future perfect
ich werde geschlafen haben
du wirst geschlafen haben
er wird geschlafen haben

conditional perfect
ich würde geschlafen haben
du würdest geschlafen haben
er würde geschlafen haben

wir werden geschlafen haben
ihr werdet geschlafen haben
sie werden geschlafen haben

wir würden geschlafen haben
ihr würdet geschlafen haben
sie würden geschlafen haben

present subjunctive
ich schlafe
du schlafest
er schlafe
wir schlafen
ihr schlafet
sie schlafen

perfect subjunctive
ich habe geschlafen
du habest geschlafen
er habe geschlafen
wir haben geschlafen
ihr habet geschlafen
sie haben geschlafen

past (imperfect) subjunctive
ich schliefe
du schliefest
er schliefe
wir schliefen
ihr schliefet
sie schliefen

pluperfect subjunctive
ich hätte geschlafen
du hättest geschlafen
er hätte geschlafen
wir hätten geschlafen
ihr hättet geschlafen
sie hätten geschlafen

● The following verbs and their compounds are similarly conjugated, but with some changes:

blasen, *to blow*
Present tense: **du bläst.** Past tense: **du bliesest.**

braten, *to fry*
Present tense: **er brät, ihr bratet.** Imperative: **bratet!**
Past tense: **ihr brietet.**

fallen, *to fall*
Has one l in past tense (**ich fiel,** etc.) and past subjunctive (**ich fiele,** etc.).

halten, *to stop*
Present tense: **er hält, ihr haltet.** Imperative: **haltet!**
Past tense: **ihr hieltet.**

lassen, *to let*
Present tense: **du läßt.** Past tense: **du ließest.**

raten, *to advise*
Present tense: **er rät, ihr ratet.** Imperative: **ratet!** Past tense: **ihr rietet.**

28 schreiben, *to write*

Pattern for verbs with past tense in **ie**, past participle in **ie**.

past infinitive	geschrieben haben	*imperative*	schreib(e)!
present participle	schreibend		schreiben wir!
past participle	geschrieben		schreibt!
			schreiben Sie!

present
ich schreibe
du schreibst
er schreibt
wir schreiben
ihr schreibt
sie schreiben

perfect
ich habe geschrieben
du hast geschrieben
er hat geschrieben
wir haben geschrieben
ihr habt geschrieben
sie haben geschrieben

past (imperfect)
ich schrieb
du schriebst
er schrieb
wir schrieben
ihr schriebt
sie schrieben

future
ich werde schreiben
du wirst schreiben
er wird schreiben
wir werden schreiben
ihr werdet schreiben
sie werden schreiben

pluperfect
ich hatte geschrieben
du hattest geschrieben
er hatte geschrieben
wir hatten geschrieben
ihr hattet geschrieben
sie hatten geschrieben

conditional
ich würde schreiben
du würdest schreiben
er würde schreiben
wir würden schreiben
ihr würdet schreiben
sie würden schreiben

future perfect
ich werde geschrieben haben
du wirst geschrieben haben
er wird geschrieben haben

conditional perfect
ich würde geschrieben haben
du würdest geschrieben haben
er würde geschrieben haben

wir werden geschrieben haben	wir würden geschrieben haben
ihr werdet geschrieben haben	ihr würdet geschrieben haben
sie werden geschrieben haben	sie würden geschrieben haben

present subjunctive	*perfect subjunctive*
ich schreibe	ich habe geschrieben
du schreibest	du habest geschrieben
er schreibe	er habe geschrieben
wir schreiben	wir haben geschrieben
ihr schreibet	ihr habet geschrieben
sie schreiben	sie haben geschrieben

past (imperfect) subjunctive	*pluperfect subjunctive*
ich schriebe	ich hätte geschrieben
du schriebest	du hättest geschrieben
er schriebe	er hätte geschrieben
wir schrieben	wir hätten geschrieben
ihr schriebet	ihr hättet geschrieben
sie schrieben	sie hätten geschrieben

● The following verbs and their compounds are similarly conjugated, but with some changes:

meiden, *to avoid*
Present tense: **du meidest, er meidet, ihr meidet.** Imperative: **meidet!** Past tense: **ihr miedet.**

preisen, *to praise*
Present tense: **du preist.** Past tense: **du priesest.**

scheiden, *to separate*
Present tense: **du scheidest, er scheidet, ihr scheidet.** Imperative: **scheidet!** Past tense: **ihr schiedet.**

schreien, *to yell*
Sometimes loses the last **e** of its past participle: **geschrie(e)n.**

speien, *to spit*
Sometimes loses the last **e** of its past participle: **gespie(e)n.**

weisen, *to send*
Present tense: **du weist.** Past tense: **du wiesest.**

29 **sehen,** *to see*

Pattern for verbs with **du** and **er** forms of present tense in **ie**, past tense in **a**, and past participle in **e**.

past infinitive	gesehen haben
present participle	sehend
past participle	gesehen
imperative	sieh!
	sehen wir!
	seht!
	sehen Sie!

present	*perfect*
ich sehe	ich habe gesehen
du siehst	du hast gesehen
er sieht	er hat gesehen
wir sehen	wir haben gesehen
ihr seht	ihr habt gesehen
sie sehen	sie haben gesehen

past (imperfect)	*future*
ich sah	ich werde sehen
du sahst	du wirst sehen
er sah	er wird sehen
wir sahen	wir werden sehen
ihr saht	ihr werdet sehen
sie sahen	sie werden sehen

pluperfect	*conditional*
ich hatte gesehen	ich würde sehen
du hattest gesehen	du würdest sehen
er hatte gesehen	er würde sehen
wir hatten gesehen	wir würden sehen
ihr hattet gesehen	ihr würdet sehen
sie hatten gesehen	sie würden sehen

future perfect
ich werde gesehen haben
du wirst gesehen haben
er wird gesehen haben
wir werden gesehen haben
ihr werdet gesehen haben
sie werden gesehen haben

conditional perfect
ich würde gesehen haben
du würdest gesehen haben
er würde gesehen haben
wir würden gesehen haben
ihr würdet gesehen haben
sie würden gesehen haben

present subjunctive
ich sehe
du sehest
er sehe
wir sehen
ihr sehet
sie sehen

perfect subjunctive
ich habe gesehen
du habest gesehen
er habe gesehen
wir haben gesehen
ihr habet gesehen
sie haben gesehen

past (imperfect) subjunctive
ich sähe
du sähest
er sähe
wir sähen
ihr sähet
sie sähen

pluperfect subjunctive
ich hätte gesehen
du hättest gesehen
er hätte gesehen
wir hätten gesehen
ihr hättet gesehen
sie hätten gesehen

- In giving references the imperative form **siehe** is used: **siehe Seite 17**, *see page 17.*

- The following verb and its compounds are similarly conjugated, but with some changes:

lesen, *to read*
  Present tense: **du liest**. Past tense: **du lasest**.

30   sein, *to be*

past infinitive	gewesen sein
past participle	gewesen
imperative	sei!
	seien wir!
	seid!
	seien Sie!

present
ich bin
du bist
er ist
wir sind
ihr seid
sie sind

perfect
ich bin gewesen
du bist gewesen
er ist gewesen
wir sind gewesen
ihr seid gewesen
sie sind gewesen

past (imperfect)
ich war
du warst
er war
wir waren
ihr wart
sie waren

future
ich werde sein
du wirst sein
er wird sein
wir werden sein
ihr werdet sein
sie werden sein

pluperfect
ich war gewesen
du warst gewesen
er war gewesen
wir waren gewesen
ihr wart gewesen
sie waren gewesen

conditional
ich würde sein
du würdest sein
er würde sein
wir würden sein
ihr würdet sein
sie würden sein

future perfect
ich werde gewesen sein
du wirst gewesen sein
er wird gewesen sein
wir werden gewesen sein
ihr werdet gewesen sein
sie werden gewesen sein

conditional perfect
ich würde gewesen sein
du würdest gewesen sein
er würde gewesen sein
wir würden gewesen sein
ihr würdet gewesen sein
sie würden gewesen sein

present subjunctive
ich sei
du sei(e)st
er sei
wir seien
ihr seiet
sie seien

perfect subjunctive
ich sei gewesen
du sei(e)st gewesen
er sei gewesen
wir seien gewesen
ihr seiet gewesen
sie seien gewesen

past (imperfect) subjunctive
ich wäre
du wär(e)st
er wäre
wir wären
ihr wär(e)t
sie wären

pluperfect subjunctive
ich wäre gewesen
du wär(e)st gewesen
er wäre gewesen
wir wären gewesen
ihr wär(e)t gewesen
sie wären gewesen

● The present participle **seiend** exists but is virtually never used.

31 senden, *to send*

past infinitive	gesandt haben
present participle	sendend
past participle	gesandt
imperative	send(e)!
	senden wir!
	sendet!
	senden Sie!

present
ich sende
du sendest
er sendet
wir senden
ihr sendet
sie senden

perfect
ich habe gesandt
du hast gesandt
er hat gesandt
wir haben gesandt
ihr habt gesandt
sie haben gesandt

past (imperfect)
ich sandte
du sandtest
er sandte
wir sandten
ihr sandtet
sie sandten

future
ich werde senden
du wirst senden
er wird senden
wir werden senden
ihr werdet senden
sie werden senden

pluperfect
ich hatte gesandt
du hattest gesandt
er hatte gesandt
wir hatten gesandt
ihr hattet gesandt
sie hatten gesandt

conditional
ich würde senden
du würdest senden
er würde senden
wir würden senden
ihr würdet senden
sie würden senden

future perfect
ich werde gesandt haben
du wirst gesandt haben
er wird gesandt haben
wir werden gesandt haben
ihr werdet gesandt haben
sie werden gesandt haben

conditional perfect
ich würde gesandt haben
du würdest gesandt haben
er würde gesandt haben
wir würden gesandt haben
ihr würdet gesandt haben
sie würden gesandt haben

present subjunctive
ich sende
du sendest
er sende
wir senden
ihr sendet
sie senden

perfect subjunctive
ich habe gesandt
du habest gesandt
er habe gesandt
wir haben gesandt
ihr habet gesandt
sie haben gesandt

past (imperfect) subjunctive
ich sendete
du sendetest
er sendete
wir sendeten
ihr sendetet
sie sendeten

pluperfect subjunctive
ich hätte gesandt
du hättest gesandt
er hätte gesandt
wir hätten gesandt
ihr hättet gesandt
sie hätten gesandt

● **Senden** meaning *to send* is sometimes weak; it is always weak meaning *to broadcast* (see **reden**, 24).

32 **sollen,** *to be to; to be supposed to*

past infinitive	gesollt haben
present participle	sollend
past participle	gesollt

present
 ich soll
 du sollst
 er soll
 wir sollen
 ihr sollt
 sie sollen

perfect
 ich habe gesollt
 du hast gesollt
 er hat gesollt
 wir haben gesollt
 ihr habt gesollt
 sie haben gesollt

past (imperfect)
 ich sollte
 du solltest
 er sollte
 wir sollten
 ihr solltet
 sie sollten

future
 ich werde sollen
 du wirst sollen
 er wird sollen
 wir werden sollen
 ihr werdet sollen
 sie werden sollen

pluperfect
 ich hatte gesollt
 du hattest gesollt
 er hatte gesollt
 wir hatten gesollt
 ihr hattet gesollt
 sie hatten gesollt

conditional
 ich würde sollen
 du würdest sollen
 er würde sollen
 wir würden sollen
 ihr würdet sollen
 sie würden sollen

future perfect
ich werde gesollt haben
du wirst gesollt haben
er wird gesollt haben
wir werden gesollt haben
ihr werdet gesollt haben
sie werden gesollt haben

present subjunctive
ich solle
du sollest
er solle
wir sollen
ihr sollet
sie sollen

past (imperfect) subjunctive
ich sollte
du solltest
er sollte
wir sollten
ihr solltet
sie sollten

conditional perfect
ich würde gesollt haben
du würdest gesollt haben
er würde gesollt haben
wir würden gesollt haben
ihr würdet gesollt haben
sie würden gesollt haben

perfect subjunctive
ich habe gesollt
du habest gesollt
er habe gesollt
wir haben gesollt
ihr habet gesollt
sie haben gesollt

pluperfect subjunctive
ich hätte gesollt
du hättest gesollt
er hätte gesollt
wir hätten gesollt
ihr hättet gesollt
sie hätten gesollt

● **Sollen** has no imperative.

● The following verb and its compounds are similarly conjugated, but with some changes:
wollen, *to want*
Present tense: **ich will, du willst, er will. Wollen** has no imperative.

● Compound tenses of **sollen** and **wollen** have the past participle forms **sollen** and **wollen** instead of **gesollt** and **gewollt** when used with a dependent infinitive: **ich hätte gehen sollen,** *I ought to have gone.*

33 sprechen, *to speak*

Pattern for verbs with **du** and **er** forms of present tense in **i**, past tense in **a**, and past participle in **o**.

past infinitive	gesprochen haben
present participle	sprechend
past participle	gesprochen
imperative	sprich!
	sprechen wir!
	sprecht!
	sprechen Sie!

present
ich spreche
du sprichst
er spricht
wir sprechen
ihr sprecht
sie sprechen

perfect
ich habe gesprochen
du hast gesprochen
er hat gesprochen
wir haben gesprochen
ihr habt gesprochen
sie haben gesprochen

past (imperfect)
ich sprach
du sprachst
er sprach
wir sprachen
ihr spracht
sie sprachen

future
ich werde sprechen
du wirst sprechen
er wird sprechen
wir werden sprechen
ihr werdet sprechen
sie werden sprechen

pluperfect
ich hatte gesprochen
du hattest gesprochen
er hatte gesprochen
wir hatten gesprochen
ihr hattet gesprochen
sie hatten gesprochen

conditional
ich würde sprechen
du würdest sprechen
er würde sprechen
wir würden sprechen
ihr würdet sprechen
sie würden sprechen

future perfect
ich werde gesprochen haben
du wirst gesprochen haben
er wird gesprochen haben
wir werden gesprochen haben
ihr werdet gesprochen haben
sie werden gesprochen haben

conditional perfect
ich würde gesprochen haben
du würdest gesprochen haben
er würde gesprochen haben
wir würden gesprochen haben
ihr würdet gesprochen haben
sie würden gesprochen haben

present subjunctive
ich spreche
du sprechest
er spreche
wir sprechen
ihr sprechet
sie sprechen

perfect subjunctive
ich habe gesprochen
du habest gesprochen
er habe gesprochen
wir haben gesprochen
ihr habet gesprochen
sie haben gesprochen

past (imperfect) subjunctive
ich spräche
du sprächest
er spräche
wir sprächen
ihr sprächet
sie sprächen

pluperfect subjunctive
ich hätte gesprochen
du hättest gesprochen
er hätte gesprochen
wir hätten gesprochen
ihr hättet gesprochen
sie hätten gesprochen

● The verbs listed overleaf and their compounds are similarly conjugated but with some changes.

33 sprechen, *to speak*

(*continued*)

● The following verbs and their compounds are similarly conjugated, but with some changes:

bersten, *to burst*
  Present tense: **du birst, er birst, ihr berstet.** Imperative: **berstet!** Past tense: **du barstest, ihr barstet.**

gelten, *to be valid*
  Present tense: **er gilt, ihr geltet.** Imperative: **geltet!** Past tense: **ihr galtet.**

nehmen, *to take*
  Present tense: **du nimmst, er nimmt.** Imperative, **du** form: **nimm!** Past participle: **genommen.**

schelten, *to scold*
  Present tense: **er schilt, ihr scheltet.** Imperative: **scheltet!** Past subjunctive: **ich schölte,** etc.

schrecken, *to start*
  When strong has **k** instead of **ck** in past tense (**ich schrak,** etc.) and past subjunctive (**ich schräke,** etc.). In modern German **schrecken** and most of its compounds are usually weak.

schwimmen, *to swim*
  Past subjunctive: **ich schwömme,** etc., or, more rarely, **ich schwämme,** etc.

spinnen, *to spin*
  Past subjunctive: **ich spönne,** etc., or **ich spänne,** etc.

treffen, *to meet*
  Only one **f** in past tense (**ich traf,** etc.) and past subjunctive (**ich träfe,** etc.)

● Many verbs in this group have irregular past subjunctives (usually avoided, especially in speech).

Helfen, *to help,* **sterben,** *to die,* **verderben,** *to spoil,* **werben,** *to advertise,* **werfen,** *to throw* form their past subjunctive in **ü: ich hülfe, ich stürbe, ich verdürbe, ich würbe, ich würfe,** etc. For **helfen** the form **ich hälfe** also exists but is very rare.

As well as a regularly formed past subjunctive, **beginnen,** *to begin,* **gelten,** *to be valid,* **gewinnen,** *to win,* **rinnen,** *to run* have an alternative, less frequent form in **ö: ich begönne, ich gölte, ich gewönne, ich rönne,** etc.

34 stehen, *to stand*

past infinitive	gestanden haben
present participle	stehend
past participle	gestanden
imperative	steh(e)!
	stehen wir!
	steht!
	stehen Sie!

present
 ich stehe
 du stehst
 er steht
 wir stehen
 ihr steht
 sie stehen

perfect
 ich habe gestanden
 du hast gestanden
 er hat gestanden
 wir haben gestanden
 ihr habt gestanden
 sie haben gestanden

past (imperfect)
 ich stand
 du standst
 er stand
 wir standen
 ihr standet
 sie standen

future
 ich werde stehen
 du wirst stehen
 er wird stehen
 wir werden stehen
 ihr werdet stehen
 sie werden stehen

pluperfect
 ich hatte gestanden
 du hattest gestanden
 er hatte gestanden
 wir hatten gestanden
 ihr hattet gestanden
 sie hatten gestanden

conditional
 ich würde stehen
 du würdest stehen
 er würde stehen
 wir würden stehen
 ihr würdet stehen
 sie würden stehen

future perfect
  ich werde gestanden haben
  du wirst gestanden haben
  er wird gestanden haben
  wir werden gestanden haben
  ihr werdet gestanden haben
  sie werden gestanden haben

conditional perfect
  ich würde gestanden haben
  du würdest gestanden haben
  er würde gestanden haben
  wir würden gestanden haben
  ihr würdet gestanden haben
  sie würden gestanden haben

present subjunctive
  ich stehe
  du stehest
  er stehe
  wir stehen
  ihr stehet
  sie stehen

perfect subjunctive
  ich habe gestanden
  du habest gestanden
  er habe gestanden
  wir haben gestanden
  ihr habet gestanden
  sie haben gestanden

past (imperfect) subjunctive
  ich stünde
  du stündest
  er stünde
  wir stünden
  ihr stündet
  sie stünden

pluperfect subjunctive
  ich hätte gestanden
  du hättest gestanden
  er hätte gestanden
  wir hätten gestanden
  ihr hättet gestanden
  sie hätten gestanden

● The past subjunctive **ich stände**, etc. is also found.
● In S. Germany **stehen** is often conjugated with **sein**.

35 stehlen, *to steal*

Pattern for verbs with **du** and **er** forms of present tense in **ie**, past tense in **a,** and past participle in **o**.

past infinitive	gestohlen haben
present participle	stehlend
past participle	gestohlen
imperative	stiehl!
	stehlen wir!
	stehlt!
	stehlen Sie!

present
ich stehle
du stiehlst
er stiehlt
wir stehlen
ihr stehlt
sie stehlen

perfect
ich habe gestohlen
du hast gestohlen
er hat gestohlen
wir haben gestohlen
ihr habt gestohlen
sie haben gestohlen

past (imperfect)
ich stahl
du stahlst
er stahl
wir stahlen
ihr stahlt
sie stahlen

future
ich werde stehlen
du wirst stehlen
er wird stehlen
wir werden stehlen
ihr werdet stehlen
sie werden stehlen

pluperfect
ich hatte gestohlen
du hattest gestohlen
er hatte gestohlen
wir hatten gestohlen
ihr hattet gestohlen
sie hatten gestohlen

conditional
ich würde stehlen
du würdest stehlen
er würde stehlen
wir würden stehlen
ihr würdet stehlen
sie würden stehlen

future perfect
ich werde gestohlen haben
du wirst gestohlen haben
er wird gestohlen haben
wir werden gestohlen haben
ihr werdet gestohlen haben
sie werden gestohlen haben

conditional perfect
ich würde gestohlen haben
du würdest gestohlen haben
er würde gestohlen haben
wir würden gestohlen haben
ihr würdet gestohlen haben
sie würden gestohlen haben

present subjunctive
ich stehle
du stehlest
er stehle
wir stehlen
ihr stehlet
sie stehlen

perfect subjunctive
ich habe gestohlen
du habest gestohlen
er habe gestohlen
wir haben gestohlen
ihr habet gestohlen
sie haben gestohlen

past (imperfect) subjunctive
ich stähle
du stählest
er stähle
wir stählen
ihr stählet
sie stählen

pluperfect subjunctive
ich hätte gestohlen
du hättest gestohlen
er hätte gestohlen
wir hätten gestohlen
ihr hättet gestohlen
sie hätten gestohlen

● The past subjunctive form **ich stöhle**, etc. also exists.
● The following verbs and their compounds are similarly conjugated, but with some changes:
befehlen, *to command*
Past subjunctive: **ich beföhle**, etc. **Befähle**, etc. also exists but is uncommon.
empfehlen, *to recommend*
Past subjunctive: **ich empföhle**, etc. **Empfähle**, etc. also exists but is uncommon.
gebären, *to bear*
Present tense and imperative are regular: **du gebärst, sie gebärt; gebär(e)!** In older German **gebierst, gebiert,** and **gebier!** are found.

36 stoßen, *to push*

past infinitive	gestoßen haben
present participle	stoßend
past participle	gestoßen
imperative	stoß(e)!
	stoßen wir!
	stoßt!
	stoßen Sie!

present
ich stoße
du stößt
er stößt
wir stoßen
ihr stoßt
sie stoßen

perfect
ich habe gestoßen
du hast gestoßen
er hat gestoßen
wir haben gestoßen
ihr habt gestoßen
sie haben gestoßen

past (imperfect)
ich stieß
du stießest
er stieß
wir stießen
ihr stießt
sie stießen

future
ich werde stoßen
du wirst stoßen
er wird stoßen
wir werden stoßen
ihr werdet stoßen
sie werden stoßen

pluperfect
ich hatte gestoßen
du hattest gestoßen
er hatte gestoßen
wir hatten gestoßen
ihr hattet gestoßen
sie hatten gestoßen

conditional
ich würde stoßen
du würdest stoßen
er würde stoßen
wir würden stoßen
ihr würdet stoßen
sie würden stoßen

future perfect
ich werde gestoßen haben
du wirst gestoßen haben
er wird gestoßen haben
wir werden gestoßen haben
ihr werdet gestoßen haben
sie werden gestoßen haben

present subjunctive
ich stoße
du stoßest
er stoße
wir stoßen
ihr stoßet
sie stoßen

past (imperfect) subjunctive
ich stieße
du stießest
er stieße
wir stießen
ihr stießet
sie stießen

conditional perfect
ich würde gestoßen haben
du würdest gestoßen haben
er würde gestoßen haben
wir würden gestoßen haben
ihr würdet gestoßen haben
sie würden gestoßen haben

perfect subjunctive
ich habe gestoßen
du habest gestoßen
er habe gestoßen
wir haben gestoßen
ihr habet gestoßen
sie haben gestoßen

pluperfect subjunctive
ich hätte gestoßen
du hättest gestoßen
er hätte gestoßen
wir hätten gestoßen
ihr hättet gestoßen
sie hätten gestoßen

37 streiten, *to quarrel*

Pattern for verbs with stem ending **-d** or **-t**, having past tense and past participle in **i** + double consonant.

past infinitive	gestritten haben
present participle	streitend
past participle	gestritten
imperative	streit(e)!
	streiten wir!
	streitet!
	streiten Sie!

present
ich streite
du streitest
er streitet
wir streiten
ihr streitet
sie streiten

perfect
ich habe gestritten
du hast gestritten
er hat gestritten
wir haben gestritten
ihr habt gestritten
sie haben gestritten

past (imperfect)
ich stritt
du strittst
er stritt
wir stritten
ihr strittet
sie stritten

future
ich werde streiten
du wirst streiten
er wird streiten
wir werden streiten
ihr werdet streiten
sie werden streiten

pluperfect
ich hatte gestritten
du hattest gestritten
er hatte gestritten
wir hatten gestritten
ihr hattet gestritten
sie hatten gestritten

conditional
ich würde streiten
du würdest streiten
er würde streiten
wir würden streiten
ihr würdet streiten
sie würden streiten

future perfect
 ich werde gestritten haben
 du wirst gestritten haben
 er wird gestritten haben
 wir werden gestritten haben
 ihr werdet gestritten haben
 sie werden gestritten haben

conditional perfect
 ich würde gestritten haben
 du würdest gestritten haben
 er würde gestritten haben
 wir würden gestritten haben
 ihr würdet gestritten haben
 sie würden gestritten haben

present subjunctive
 ich streite
 du streitest
 er streite
 wir streiten
 ihr streitet
 sie streiten

perfect subjunctive
 ich habe gestritten
 du habest gestritten
 er habe gestritten
 wir haben gestritten
 ihr habet gestritten
 sie haben gestritten

past (imperfect) subjunctive
 ich stritte
 du strittest
 er stritte
 wir stritten
 ihr strittet
 sie stritten

pluperfect subjunctive
 ich hätte gestritten
 du hättest gestritten
 er hätte gestritten
 wir hätten gestritten
 ihr hättet gestritten
 sie hätten gestritten

● The following verbs and their compounds are similarly conjugated, but with some changes:

leiden, *to suffer*
 Past tense: **ich litt**, etc. Past subjunctive: **ich litte**, etc. Past participle: **gelitten**.

schneiden, *to cut*
 Past tense: **ich schnitt,** etc. Past subjunctive: **ich schnitte**, etc. Past participle: **geschnitten**.

38 tragen, *to wear; to carry*

Pattern for verbs with **du** and **er** forms of present tense in **ä**, past tense in **u**, and past participle in **a**.

past infinitive	getragen haben	*imperative*	trag(e)!
			tragen wir!
present participle	tragend		tragt!
past participle	getragen		tragen Sie!

present
ich trage
du trägst
er trägt
wir tragen
ihr tragt
sie tragen

perfect
ich habe getragen
du hast getragen
er hat getragen
wir haben getragen
ihr habt getragen
sie haben getragen

past (imperfect)
ich trug
du trugst
er trug
wir trugen
ihr trugt
sie trugen

future
ich werde tragen
du wirst tragen
er wird tragen
wir werden tragen
ihr werdet tragen
sie werden tragen

pluperfect
ich hatte getragen
du hattest getragen
er hatte getragen
wir hatten getragen
ihr hattet getragen
sie hatten getragen

conditional
ich würde tragen
du würdest tragen
er würde tragen
wir würden tragen
ihr würdet tragen
sie würden tragen

future perfect
ich werde getragen haben
du wirst getragen haben
er wird getragen haben

conditional perfect
ich würde getragen haben
du würdest getragen haben
er würde getragen haben

wir werden getragen haben	wir würden getragen haben
ihr werdet getragen haben	ihr würdet getragen haben
sie werden getragen haben	sie würden getragen haben

present subjunctive	*perfect subjunctive*
ich trage	ich habe getragen
du tragest	du habest getragen
er trage	er habe getragen
wir tragen	wir haben getragen
ihr traget	ihr habet getragen
sie tragen	sie haben getragen

past (imperfect) subjunctive	*pluperfect subjunctive*
ich trüge	ich hätte getragen
du trügest	du hättest getragen
er trüge	er hätte getragen
wir trügen	wir hätten getragen
ihr trüget	ihr hättet getragen
sie trügen	sie hätten getragen

● The following verbs and their compounds are
similarly conjugated, but with some changes:

backen, *to bake*
Formerly strong, now usually weak. Present tense: **du
bäckst** or **du backst, er bäckt** or **er backt**. Past tense
and past subjunctive: **ich backte**, etc. The strong
forms of past tense and past subjunctive **ich buk** and
ich büke, etc., still exist but are rarely used. Past
participle still strong: **gebacken.**

laden, *to load*
Present tense: **ihr ladet.** Imperative: **ladet!** Past tense:
ihr ludet.

schaffen, *to create*
Present tense: **du schaffst, er schafft.** Loses an **f** in
past tense (**ich schuf**, etc.) and past subjunctive (**ich
schüfe**, etc.). Meaning *to manage,* **schaffen** is weak.

wachsen, *to grow*
Present tense: **du wächst.** Past tense: **du wuchsest.**

39 **tun,** *to do*

past infinitive	getan haben
present participle	tuend
past participle	getan
imperative	tu(e)!
	tun wir!
	tut!
	tun Sie!

present	*perfect*
ich tue	ich habe getan
du tust	du hast getan
er tut	er hat getan
wir tun	wir haben getan
ihr tut	ihr habt getan
sie tun	sie haben getan

past (imperfect)	*future*
ich tat	ich werde tun
du tatst	du wirst tun
er tat	er wird tun
wir taten	wir werden tun
ihr tatet	ihr werdet tun
sie taten	sie werden tun

pluperfect	*conditional*
ich hatte getan	ich würde tun
du hattest getan	du würdest tun
er hatte getan	er würde tun
wir hatten getan	wir würden tun
ihr hattet getan	ihr würdet tun
sie hatten getan	sie würden tun

future perfect
  ich werde getan haben
  du wirst getan haben
  er wird getan haben
  wir werden getan haben
  ihr werdet getan haben
  sie werden getan haben

present subjunctive
  ich tue
  du tuest
  er tue
  wir tuen
  ihr tuet
  sie tuen

past (imperfect) subjunctive
  ich täte
  du tätest
  er täte
  wir täten
  ihr tätet
  sie täten

conditional perfect
  ich würde getan haben
  du würdest getan haben
  er würde getan haben
  wir würden getan haben
  ihr würdet getan haben
  sie würden getan haben

perfect subjunctive
  ich habe getan
  du habest getan
  er habe getan
  wir haben getan
  ihr habet getan
  sie haben getan

pluperfect subjunctive
  ich hätte getan
  du hättest getan
  er hätte getan
  wir hätten getan
  ihr hättet getan
  sie hätten getan

40 **werden,** *to become*

past infinitive	geworden sein
present participle	werdend
past participle	geworden
imperative	werde!
	werden wir!
	werdet!
	werden Sie!

present
ich werde
du wirst
er wird
wir werden
ihr werdet
sie werden

perfect
ich bin geworden
du bist geworden
er ist geworden
wir sind geworden
ihr seid geworden
sie sind geworden

past (imperfect)
ich wurde
du wurdest
er wurde
wir wurden
ihr wurdet
sie wurden

future
ich werde werden
du wirst werden
er wird werden
wir werden werden
ihr werdet werden
sie werden werden

pluperfect
ich war geworden
du warst geworden
er war geworden
wir waren geworden
ihr wart geworden
sie waren geworden

conditional
ich würde werden
du würdest werden
er würde werden
wir würden werden
ihr würdet werden
sie würden werden

future perfect
ich werde geworden sein
du wirst geworden sein
er wird geworden sein
wir werden geworden sein
ihr werdet geworden sein
sie werden geworden sein

conditional perfect
ich würde geworden sein
du würdest geworden sein
er würde geworden sein
wir würden geworden sein
ihr würdet geworden sein
sie würden geworden sein

present subjunctive
ich werde
du werdest
er werde
wir werden
ihr werdet
sie werden

perfect subjunctive
ich sei geworden
du sei(e)st geworden
er sei geworden
wir seien geworden
ihr seiet geworden
sie seien geworden

past (imperfect) subjunctive
ich würde
du würdest
er würde
wir würden
ihr würdet
sie würden

pluperfect subjunctive
ich wäre geworden
du wär(e)st geworden
er wäre geworden
wir wären geworden
ihr wär(e)t geworden
sie wären geworden

● As an auxiliary verb used in forming the tenses of the passive, **werden** has the past participle **worden**.

● **Werden** also has an obsolete and poetic strong past tense: **ich ward**, etc.

41 **wissen,** *to know*

past infinitive	gewußt haben
present participle	wissend
past participle	gewußt
imperative	wisse!
	wissen wir!
	wißt!/wisset!
	wissen Sie!

present
ich weiß
du weißt
er weiß
wir wissen
ihr wißt
sie wissen

perfect
ich habe gewußt
du hast gewußt
er hat gewußt
wir haben gewußt
ihr habt gewußt
sie haben gewußt

past (imperfect)
ich wußte
du wußtest
er wußte
wir wußten
ihr wußtet
sie wußten

future
ich werde wissen
du wirst wissen
er wird wissen
wir werden wissen
ihr werdet wissen
sie werden wissen

pluperfect
ich hatte gewußt
du hattest gewußt
er hatte gewußt
wir hatten gewußt
ihr hattet gewußt
sie hatten gewußt

conditional
ich würde wissen
du würdest wissen
er würde wissen
wir würden wissen
ihr würdet wissen
sie würden wissen

future perfect
ich werde gewußt haben
du wirst gewußt haben
er wird gewußt haben
wir werden gewußt haben
ihr werdet gewußt haben
sie werden gewußt haben

present subjunctive
ich wisse
du wissest
er wisse
wir wissen
ihr wisset
sie wissen

past (imperfect) subjunctive
ich wüßte
du wüßtest
er wüßte
wir wüßten
ihr wüßtet
sie wüßten

conditional perfect
ich würde gewußt haben
du würdest gewußt haben
er würde gewußt haben
wir würden gewußt haben
ihr würdet gewußt haben
sie würden gewußt haben

perfect subjunctive
ich habe gewußt
du habest gewußt
er habe gewußt
wir haben gewußt
ihr habet gewußt
sie haben gewußt

pluperfect subjunctive
ich hätte gewußt
du hättest gewußt
er hätte gewußt
wir hätten gewußt
ihr hättet gewußt
sie hätten gewußt

IDENTIFICATION LIST

for irregular parts of strong and mixed verbs

aß, äße → essen
band, bände → binden
barg, bärge → bergen
barst, bärste → bersten
bat, bäte → bitten
befahl, befähle → befehlen
befiehlt → befehlen
beföhle, befohlen →
  befehlen
begann, begänne →
  beginnen
begönne → beginnen
betrog, betröge, betrogen
  → betrügen
bewog, bewöge, bewogen
  → bewegen
bin, bist → sein
birgt → bergen
birst → bersten
biß → beißen
bläst → blasen
blieb, bliebe → bleiben
blies, bliese → blasen
bog, böge → biegen
bot, böte → bieten
brach, bräche → brechen
brachte, brächte →
  bringen
brannte → brennen
brät → braten
bricht → brechen
briet, briete → braten
dachte, dächte → denken

darf → dürfen
drang, dränge → dringen
drischt → dreschen
drosch, drösche →
  dreschen
durfte → dürfen
empfahl, empfähle →
  empfehlen
empfiehlt → empfehlen
empföhle, empfohlen →
  empfehlen
erlischt → erlöschen
erlosch, erloschen →
  erlöschen
erscholl, erschölle,
  erschollen → erschallen
fährt → fahren
fällt → fallen
fand, fände → finden
fängt → fangen
ficht → fechten
fing, finge → fangen
fiel, fiele → fallen
flicht → flechten
flocht, flöchte → flechten
flog, flöge → fliegen
floh, flöhe → fliehen
floß, flösse → fließen
focht, föchte → fechten
fraß, fräße → fressen
frißt → fressen
fror, fröre → frieren
fuhr, führe → fahren

gab, gäbe → geben

galt, gälte → gelten

gebar, gebäre → gebären

gebeten → bitten

gebissen → beißen

geblieben → bleiben

gebogen → biegen

geboren → gebären

geborgen → bergen

geborsten → bersten

geboten → bieten

gebracht → bringen

gebrannt → brennen

gebrochen → brechen

gebunden → binden

gedacht → denken

gedieh, gediehen → gedeihen

gedroschen → dreschen

gedrungen → dringen

gedurft → dürfen

geflochten → flechten

geflogen → fliegen

geflohen → fliehen

gefochten → fechten

gefroren → frieren

gefunden → finden

gegangen → gehen

gegessen → essen

geglichen → gleichen

geglitten → gleiten

geglommen → glimmen

gegolten → gelten

gegoren → gären

gegossen → gießen

gegriffen → greifen

gehangen → hängen

gehoben → heben

geholfen → helfen

gekannt → kennen

geklommen → klimmen

geklungen → klingen

gekniffen → kneifen

gekonnt → können

gekrochen → kriechen

gelang, gelänge → gelingen

gelegen → liegen

geliehen → leihen

gelitten → leiden

gelogen → lügen

gelungen → gelingen

gemocht → mögen

gemolken → melken

gemußt → müssen

genannt → nennen

genas, genäse → genesen

genommen → nehmen

genoß, genösse, genossen → genießen

gepfiffen → pfeifen

gepriesen → preisen

gequollen → quellen

gerannt → rennen

gerieben → reiben

gerissen → reißen

geritten → reiten

gerochen → riechen

geronnen → rinnen

gerungen → ringen

gesandt → senden

geschah, geschähe → geschehen

geschieden → scheiden

geschieht → geschehen

geschienen → scheinen

geschissen → scheißen

geschlichen → schleichen

geschliffen → schleifen

geschlissen → schleißen

geschlossen → schließen

geschlungen → schlingen

geschmissen → schmeißen

geschmolzen → schmelzen

geschnitten → schneiden

geschoben → schieben

gescholten → schelten

geschoren → scheren

geschossen → schießen

geschrieben → schreiben

geschrie(e)n → schreien

geschritten → schreiten

geschrocken → schrecken

geschunden → schinden

geschwiegen → schweigen

geschwollen → schwellen

geschwommen → schwimmen

geschworen → schwören

geschwunden → schwinden

geschwungen → schwingen

gesessen → sitzen

gesoffen → saufen

gesotten → sieden

gesogen → saugen

gesonnen → sinnen

gespie(e)n → speien

gesplissen → spleißen

gesponnen → spinnen

gesprochen → sprechen

gesprossen → sprießen

gesprungen → springen

gestanden → stehen

gestiegen → steigen

gestochen → stechen

gestohlen → stehlen

gestoben → stieben

gestorben → sterben

gestrichen → streichen

gestritten → streiten

gestunken → stinken

gesungen → singen

gesunken → sinken

getan → tun

getrieben → treiben

getroffen → treffen *and* triefen

getrogen → trügen

getrunken → trinken

gewandt → wenden

gewann, gewänne → gewinnen

gewesen → sein

gewichen → weichen

gewiesen → weisen

gewoben → weben

gewogen → wägen *and* wiegen

gewönne, gewonnen → gewinnen

geworben → werben

geworden → werden

geworfen → werfen

gewrungen → wringen

gewunden → winden

gewußt → wissen

gezogen → ziehen

gezwungen → zwingen

gibt → geben

gilt → gelten

ging, ginge → gehen
glich, gliche → gleichen
glitt, glitte → gleiten
glomm, glömme →
   glimmen
gölte → gelten
gor, göre → gären
goß, gösse → gießen
gräbt → graben
griff, griffe → greifen
grub, grübe → graben
half, hälfe → helfen
hält → halten
hat, hatte, hätte → haben
hieb, hiebe → hauen
hielt, hielte → halten
hieß, hieße → heißen
hilft → helfen
hing, hinge → hängen
hob, höbe → heben
hülfe → helfen
ißt → essen
ist → sein
kam, käme → kommen
kann → können
kannte → kennen
klang, klänge → klingen
klomm, klömme →
   klimmen
kniff, kniffe → kneifen
konnte → können
kroch, kröche → kriechen
lädt → laden
lag, läge → liegen
las, läse → lesen
läßt → lassen
läuft → laufen
lief, liefe → laufen

lieh, liehe → leihen
ließ, ließe → lassen
liest → lesen
litt, litte → leiden
log, löge → lügen
lud, lüde → laden
mag → mögen
maß, mäße → messen
mied, miede → meiden
milkt → melken
mißlang, mißlänge →
   mißlingen
mißlungen → mißlingen
mißt → messen
mochte, möchte → mögen
molk, mölke → melken
muß, mußte → müssen
nahm, nähme → nehmen
nannte → nennen
nimmt → nehmen
pfiff, pfiffe → pfeifen
pries, priese → preisen
quillt → quellen
quoll, quölle → quellen
rang, ränge → ringen
rann, ränne → rinnen
rannte → rennen
rät → raten
rieb, riebe → reiben
rief, riefe → rufen
riet, riete → raten
riß, risse → reißen
ritt, ritte → reiten
roch, röche → riechen
rönne → rinnen
sah, sähe → sehen
sandte → senden
sang, sänge → singen

sank, sänke → sinken
sann, sänne → sinnen
saß, säße → sitzen
säuft → saufen
schalt → schelten
schied, schiede → scheiden
schien, schiene → scheinen
schilt → schelten
schiß → scheißen
schläft → schlafen
schlägt → schlagen
schlang, schlänge → schlingen
schlich, schliche → schleichen
schlief, schliefe → schlafen
schliff, schliffe → schleifen
schliß, schlisse → schleißen
schloß, schlösse → schließen
schlug, schlüge → schlagen
schmilzt → schmelzen
schmiß, schmisse → schmeißen
schmolz, schmölze → schmelzen
schnitt, schnitte → schneiden
schob, schöbe → schieben
scholl, schölle → schallen
schölte → schelten
schor, schöre → scheren
schoß, schöße → schießen
schrak, schräke → schrecken

schrickt → schrecken
schrie → schreien
schrieb, schriebe → schreiben
schritt, schritte → schreiten
schuf, schüfe → schaffen
schund, schünde → schinden
schwamm, schwämme → schwimmen
schwand, schwände → schwinden
schwang, schwänge → schwingen
schwieg, schwiege → schweigen
schwillt → schwellen
schwoll, schwölle → schwellen
schwömme → schwimmen
schwor → schwören
schwüre → schwören
sei, seid, seien → sein
sieht → sehen
sind → sein
soff, söffe → saufen
sog, söge → saugen
soll → sollen
sott, sötte → sieden
spann, spänne → spinnen
spie → speien
spliß, splisse → spleißen
spönne → spinnen
sprach, spräche → sprechen
sprang, spränge → springen

sproß, sprösse → sprießen
stach, stäche → stechen
stahl, stähle → stehlen
stand, stände → stehen
stank, stänke → stinken
starb → sterben
sticht → stechen
stieg, stiege → steigen
stiehlt → stehlen
stieß, stieße → stoßen
stirbt → sterben
stob, stöbe → stieben
stöhle → stehlen
stößt → stoßen
strich, striche → streichen
stritt, stritte → streiten
stünde → stehen
stürbe → sterben
tat, täte → tun
traf, träfe → treffen
trägt → tragen
trank, tränke → trinken
trat, träte → treten
trieb, triebe → treiben
trifft → treffen
tritt → treten
troff, tröffe → triefen
trog, tröge → trugen
trug, trüge → tragen
tut → tun
verdarb → verderben
verdirbt → verderben
verdorben → verderben
verdroß, verdrösse,
  verdrossen → verdrießen
verdürbe → verderben
vergaß, vergäße →
  vergessen

vergißt → vergessen
verlischt → verlöschen
verlosch, verlösche →
  verlöschen
verlor, verlöre, verloren →
  verlieren
verzieh, verziehe,
  verziehen → verzeihen
wächst → wachsen
wand, wände → winden
wandte → wenden
war, wäre → sein
warb → werben
ward → werden
warf → werfen
wäscht → waschen
weiß → wissen
wich, wiche → weichen
wies, wiese → weisen
will → wollen
wirbt → werben
wird → werden
wirft → werfen
wob, wöbe → weben
wog, wöge → wägen *and*
  wiegen
worden → werden
wrange, wränge →
  wringen
wuchs, wüchse → wachsen
würbe → werben
wurde, würde → werden
würfe → werfen
wusch, wüsche → waschen
wußte, wüßte → wissen
zog, zöge → ziehen
zwang, zwänge →
  zwingen

Also available

The Oxford Paperback German Dictionary
German Grammar
German Verbs

The Oxford Paperback French Dictionary
French Grammar
French Verbs
10,000 French Words

The Oxford Paperback Italian Dictionary
The Oxford Paperback Spanish Dictionary